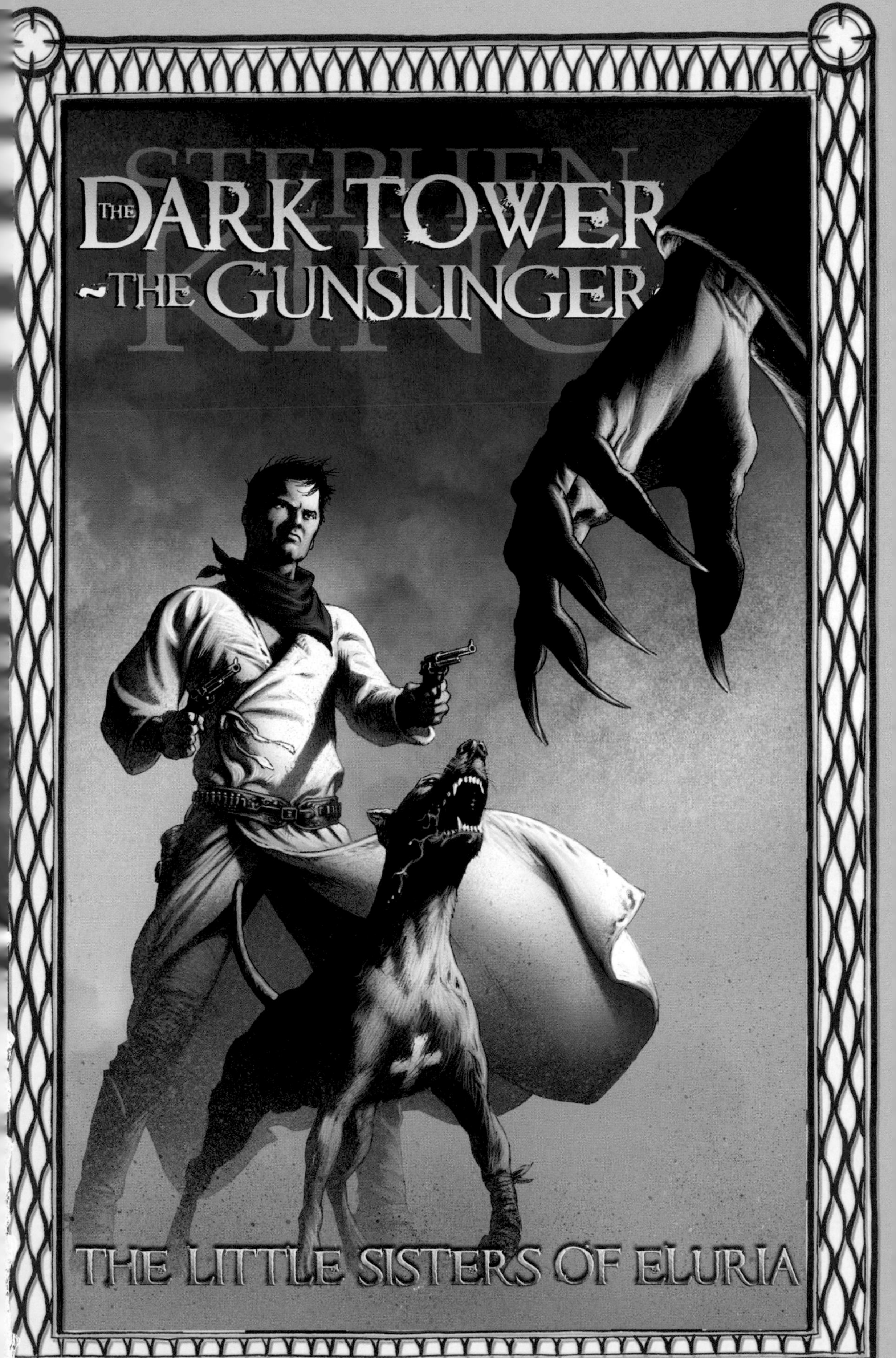
STEPHEN KING
THE DARK TOWER
THE GUNSLINGER
THE LITTLE SISTERS OF ELURIA

# THE DARK TOWER
## ~THE GUNSLINGER~

## THE LITTLE SISTERS OF ELURIA

CREATIVE DIRECTOR AND EXECUTIVE DIRECTOR
### STEPHEN KING

PLOTTING AND CONSULTATION
### ROBIN FURTH

SCRIPT
### PETER DAVID

ART
### LUKE ROSS & RICHARD ISANOVE

LETTERING
### VC'S RUS WOOTON

PRODUCTION
### TAYLOR ESPOSITO & IRENE LEE

ASSISTANT EDITOR
### CHARLIE BECKERMAN

SENIOR EDITOR
### RALPH MACCHIO

COVER ART
### LUKE ROSS & RICHARD ISANOVE

**DARK TOWER: THE GUNSLINGER — THE LITTLE SISTERS OF ELURIA.** Contains material originally published in magazine form as DARK TOWER: THE GUNSLINGER - THE LITTLE SISTERS OF ELURIA #1-5. First printing 2011. ISBN# 978-0-7851-4931-6. Published by MARVEL WORLDWIDE, INC., a subsidiary of MARVEL ENTERTAINMENT, LLC. OFFICE OF PUBLICATION: 135 West 50th Street, New York, NY 10020. Copyright © 2010 and 2011 Stephen King. All rights reserved. $24.99 per copy in the U.S. and $27.99 in Canada (GST #R127032852); Canadian Agreement #40668537. All characters featured in this publication and the distinctive names and likenesses thereof, and all related indicia are trademarks of Stephen King. No similarity between any of the names, characters, persons, and/or institutions in this magazine with those of any living or dead person or institution is intended, and any such similarity which may exist is purely coincidental. Marvel and its logos are TM & © Marvel Characters, Inc. **Printed in the U.S.A.** ALAN FINE, EVP - Office of the President, Marvel Worldwide, Inc. and EVP & CMO Marvel Characters B.V.; DAN BUCKLEY, Publisher & President - Print, Animation & Digital Divisions; JOE QUESADA, Chief Creative Officer; JIM SOKOLOWSKI, Chief Operating Officer; DAVID BOGART, SVP of Business Affairs & Talent Management; TOM BREVOORT, SVP of Publishing; C.B. CEBULSKI, SVP of Creator & Content Development; DAVID GABRIEL, SVP of Publishing Sales & Circulation; MICHAEL PASCIULLO, SVP of Brand Planning & Communications; JIM O'KEEFE, VP of Operations & Logistics; DAN CARR, Executive Director of Publishing Technology; JUSTIN F. GABRIE, Director of Publishing & Editorial Operations; SUSAN CRESPI, Editorial Operations Manager; ALEX MORALES, Publishing Operations Manager; STAN LEE, Chairman Emeritus. For information regarding advertising in Marvel Comics or on Marvel.com, please contact John Dokes, SVP Integrate Sales & Marketing, at jdokes@marvel.com. For Marvel subscription inquiries, please call 800-217-9158. **Manufactured between 4/25/2011 and 5/23/2011 by R.R. DONNELLEY, INC., SALEM, VA, USA.**

10 9 8 7 6 5 4 3 2 1

# INTRODUCTION

Dear Fellow Constant Readers:

Welcome to Eluria! Over the past decade I have trekked with Roland through many exotic and terrifying lands. I have braved harriers, and mutants, and demons. I have stumbled across the deadly, abandoned machinery of the Great Old Ones, and I have fallen into traps left by the Man in Black. At varying times I have been awed, and amazed, and stunned into speechlessness by the wonders I have encountered along the byways I have traveled. But of all the places in Mid-World where I have set up camp and lit my fire, none have left me with such a profound sense of disquiet as Eluria.

In his brief introduction to the original novella, Stephen King tells us that *The Little Sisters of Eluria* began with a single image that came to him upon waking. That image was of a beautiful royal pavilion of billowing white silk. To Steve King, this was a familiar place, and perhaps even comforting. After all, that gorgeous summer palace belonged to Queen Laura of the Territories, and he and his good friend Peter Straub had spent much time there while co-writing the wonderful fantasy novel, *The Talisman*.

As many of you know, Queen Laura's pavilion was the summer home of her court, but it was also her sickroom. You see, the Queen of the Territories had been afflicted by a mysterious, magical illness which kept her in a coma. And though her courtyards were still filled with conniving courtiers as well as loyal subjects, her chambers had been transformed into a hospital ward. Constantly coming and going through the palace corridors—quiet as the breezes, or as distant birds—were white, nun-like nurses in clean white habits. These women—and they were all women—kept the ensorcelled Queen alive, despite her deep, trance-like state.

Queen Laura's palace was a beautiful if melancholy place, but by the time Steve King had climbed into the shower, that lovely pavilion and those white, quiet nurses had begun to transform into something much more sinister. As shower water sprayed over him, Steve saw the royal tent fall to ruins. No longer was it a palace worthy of a queen. It had become a haunted house full of whispering wraith-women who were nurses of death, not life. Were they ghosts? Were they vampires? Sai King did not yet know. But as he watched, those eerie, wraith-women strung their tent with strings of tinkling, silver bells, and waited for whatever unwary travelers were unlucky enough to fall into their trap . . .

As I wrote in the introduction to the first volume of my *Dark Tower Concordance*, Roland's story is not just an adventure tale. Our gunslinger's pilgrimage across Mid-World's ruined landscape is constantly echoing the myths and stories of our shared cultural heritage. In some of the Dark Tower novels, Roland is the king of the wasteland who must bring redemption and life to his destroyed kingdom. Yet in others, he is the everyman who must face those hardships and losses which we all encounter over the course of a life. In *The Little Sisters of Eluria*, Roland is the mortal man forced to enter the gates of the Underworld.

As anyone who has lost a dear one knows, when our dead journey to the afterworld, a small part of our spirit follows them into the dark lands. This is as true for Roland as it is for us. In his introduction, Steve King tells us that *The Little Sisters* takes place after Roland has lost his companions but before he has stumbled upon the trail of the Man in Black.

In other words, Roland travels through the Desatoya mountains while the horrors of Jericho Hill are still fresh in his mind. On that killing ground, Roland not only lost his ka-

COLLECTION EDITOR
MARK D. BEAZLEY

EDITORIAL ASSISTANTS
JOE HOCHSTEIN & JAMES EMMETT

ASSISTANT EDITORS
NELSON RIBEIRO & ALEX STARBUCK

EDITOR, SPECIAL PROJECTS
JENNIFER GRÜNWALD

SENIOR EDITOR, SPECIAL PROJECTS
JEFF YOUNGQUIST

SENIOR VICE PRESIDENT OF SALES
DAVID GABRIEL

SVP OF BRAND PLANNING & COMMUNICATIONS
MICHAEL PASCIULLO

SENIOR VICE PRESIDENT OF STRATEGIC DEVELOPMENT
RUWAN JAYATILLEKE

BOOK DESIGN
SPRING HOTELING & PATRICK McGRATH


EDITOR IN CHIEF
AXEL ALONSO

CHIEF CREATIVE OFFICER
JOE QUESADA

PUBLISHER
DAN BUCKLEY


SPECIAL THANKS TO
CHUCK VERRILL, MARSHA DEFILIPPO, BARBARA ANN McINTYRE, BRIAN
STARK, JIM NAUSEDAS, JIM McCANN, ARUNE SINGH, JEFF SUTER, JOHN
BARBER, LAUREN SANKOVITCH, MIKE HORWITZ & CHRIS ELIOPOULOS

For more information on Dark Tower comics, visit Marvel.com/darktower.
To find Marvel Comics at a local comic shop, call 1-888-COMICBOOK.

tet, but he witnessed the obliteration of a whole way of life. So violent and cruel were his enemies that Roland only survived by hiding in a pile of corpses. When he emerged, he literally rose from the dead. Hence it is not so surprising that he was destined to wander into a land of wraiths.

From the moment Roland sees Eluria's open gate strung with dead flowers, he knows that there is something profoundly wrong with this town. The silence beyond is unnerving. Even on a sweltering day during Full Earth, the streets should be full of bustle and life. The air should be filled with the sounds of horses' hooves, and wagon wheels, and merchants' huckstering voices. But in Eluria, there is only the delicate tinkling of bells, the sweet singing of insects, and a rhythmic thudding that sounds like a fist pounding upon a coffin top.

Calling "Hello, the town!" Roland leads his dying roan through the deserted streets. He finds dried blood, an abandoned pipe, a pair of shoes, but no people. That is, until he reaches the town square.

There, Roland sees the corpse of a young cowboy whose head and upper body are stewing in the thick, spoiled water of an ironwood trough. I would venture to say that this is one of the most subtle but psychologically disturbing images in the Dark Tower series, since not only does this boy remind us of Roland's young companions—all of whom are dead—but because the boy's leg is being chewed by a dog with a cross on its chest fur. Not only is man's best friend now a carrion-eater, but the symbol of the Man Jesus has become desecrated. In these terrible reversals, GOD becomes DOG, and the symbol of the Man Jesus—he who shares his body and his blood—is borne by a cur eating the corpse of an innocent boy. Even Roland, who believes that in the end all gods drink blood, finds this disturbing enough to chase the cur away with a gunshot, yet he is too superstitious to kill the animal outright, since to destroy the one creature left alive in Eluria—other than himself and the insects—seems unlucky.

The next encounter Roland has is with the terrible and toxic Green Folk, mutants that have emerged from the nearby radium mines. These creatures—as horrific as any imagined by Hieronymus Bosch in his visions of Hell—come upon Roland just as he is caught between giving the dead boy a decent burial and tending to his horse, which has collapsed and died. It actually proves to be lucky for Roland that his roan does reach the clearing at the end of the path at this moment. Otherwise he might not have had any warning about the Green Folk's advance, though in the long run this warning does him little good.

Unlike the Roland we meet in *The Gunslinger*, a man whose trigger-fingers work faster than his conscience, this younger version of our hero still has qualms about killing those armed with clubs rather than six-shooters. In order to warn the approaching mutants to back off, Roland shoots at the dirt in front of their leader's feet. When that doesn't work, he kills the toad-like monstrosity that runs for him. As it falls, Mr. Toad almost immediately begins to dissolve in the heat. This is not surprising, since these mutants are creatures of underground places and dark caverns—beings that do not belong in daylight at all.

But Roland's trials aren't over yet. As he backs around the watering trough where the dead boy lies, he is ambushed by a two-headed mutant. "BOO!" the creature cries, and then clubs Roland's shoulder, numbing his arm to the wrist. Roland's first shot goes wide, but with his second bullet he kills his attacker. This only serves to enrage the rest of the mutant pack, and they give our hero a beating unlike any other he has ever received. In fact, Roland would probably have met his death at the hands of these punishing devils had he not been saved by demons far worse than the Green Folk. But who and what these fiends are—and what they want with Roland—we do not yet know. All we can say for certain is that each has the sigul of the Dark Tower embroidered upon its breast. And in our hearts, we know that this, too, is a desecration.

Our next scene—Roland's dream sequence, which takes place in the Little Sisters' hospital tent after he has been beaten to within an inch of his life—was the most challenging section to conceptualize. I wanted to capture, in a brief series of images, Roland's delirious inner monologue: "I'm dead," Roland thinks to himself. "Dead and rising into whatever afterlife there is. That's what it must be. The singing I hear is the singing of dead souls." I wanted to encapsulate those thoughts, but I also wanted to hint at the greater themes of death and rebirth which this monologue touches upon.

Although in the original story Roland does not see himself tied to the cross above Eluria's gates as he does in our version of the tale, this visual image was my attempt to weave together the many sensations and thoughts Roland has during his delirium. How else could I bring together his visions of the Jesus-Man's heaven, of his own terrible and overwhelming sense of pain and punishment, and his fear that he has been burned to death or perhaps even been resurrected? How could I get across his emotional and physical response to the singing of those strange, otherworldly insects? And how could I reference his greater quest for the Dark Tower, and his importance as Mid-World's savior—its last and only hope?

As you can see by the beautiful pages penciled by Luke Ross, colored by Richard Isanove, and scripted by Peter David, I decided to play on Christian imagery. My reasons for doing this were many. Not only is Eluria a Christian town and thoughts of the Man-Jesus preoccupy Roland while he is there, but I also wanted to evoke a sense of martyrdom, of Roland paying for past sins—and for sins to come. If Roland is Mid-World's savior, then I thought his punishment in Eluria could be compared to a kind of crucifixion. After all, according to many Christian sources, Jesus was beaten before he was nailed to the cross, and then descended into the underworld to converse with un-saved souls before returning to the world above.

Whether Roland will redeem Eluria—or any of the beings he meets in this underworld—has yet to be seen. But of one thing we can be certain. There is much more in store for Roland—both of damnation and salvation—before his time in Eluria is over.

Thanks for listening. Until we meet again next month, long days and pleasant nights!


Robin Furth

# In a world that has moved on...

Roland Deschain is the last descendant of the line of Arthur Eld. His late father, Steven, was the king of the barony of Gilead. Seeking to emulate his father, Roland became the youngest man to ever become a gunslinger.

Roland became the last survivor of the Battle of Jericho Hill in which Gilead was lost to the forces of John Farson the Good Man, and his ka-tet slain. Since then, the young gunslinger has pursued his destiny.

His quest is to reach the mysterious Dark Tower from which Roland can set this out-of-synch world right. The key to his goal lies with the Man in Black, who Roland now doggedly tracks.

# STEPHEN KING

## THE DARK TOWER
### ~ THE GUNSLINGER ~

# THE LITTLE SISTERS
# OF ELURIA

## CHAPTER ONE

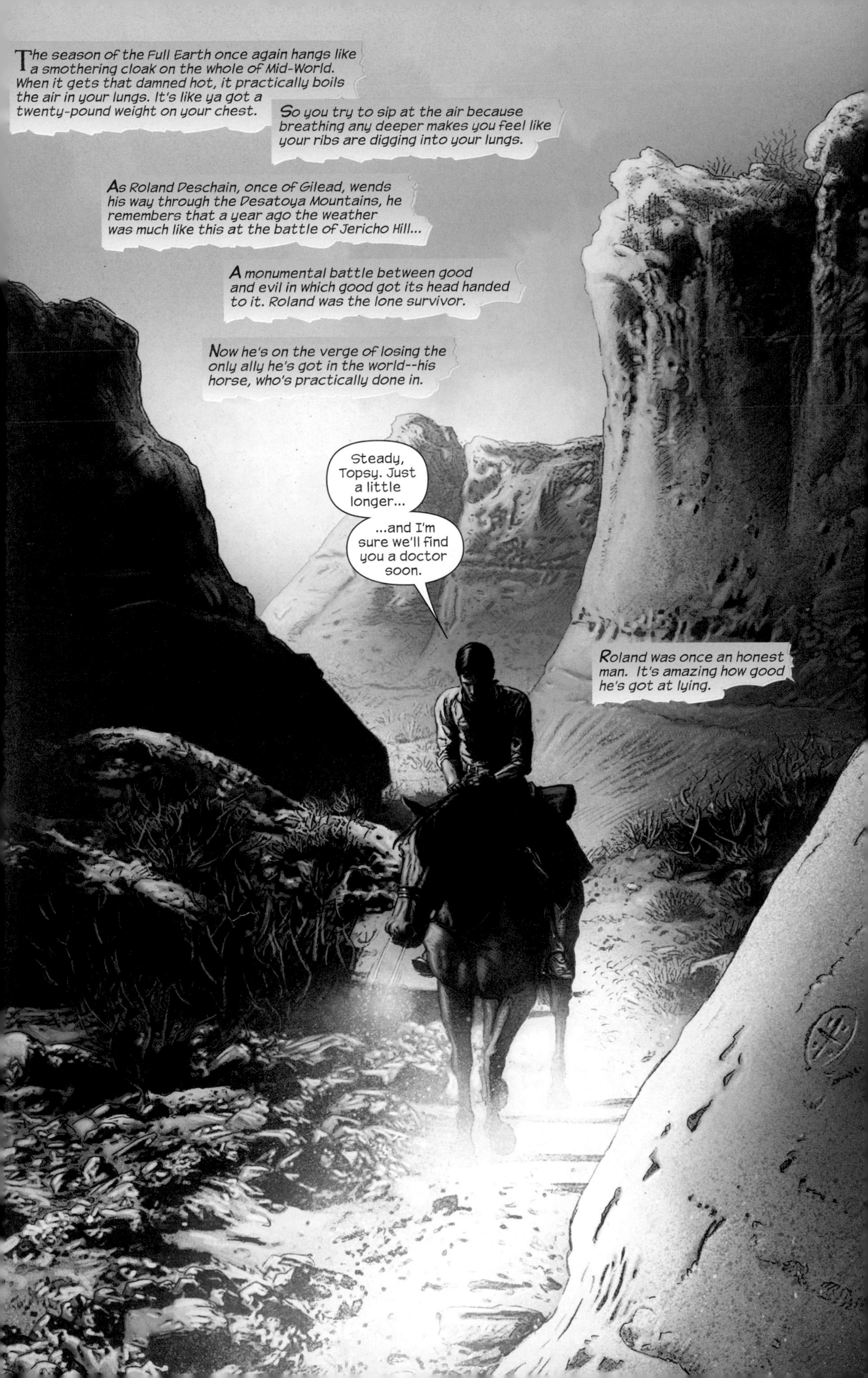

The season of the Full Earth once again hangs like a smothering cloak on the whole of Mid-World. When it gets that damned hot, it practically boils the air in your lungs. It's like ya got a twenty-pound weight on your chest.
So you try to sip at the air because breathing any deeper makes you feel like your ribs are digging into your lungs.
As Roland Deschain, once of Gilead, wends his way through the Desatoya Mountains, he remembers that a year ago the weather was much like this at the battle of Jericho Hill...
A monumental battle between good and evil in which good got its head handed to it. Roland was the lone survivor.
Now he's on the verge of losing the only ally he's got in the world--his horse, who's practically done in.
Steady, Topsy. Just a little longer...
...and I'm sure we'll find you a doctor soon.
Roland was once an honest man. It's amazing how good he's got at lying.

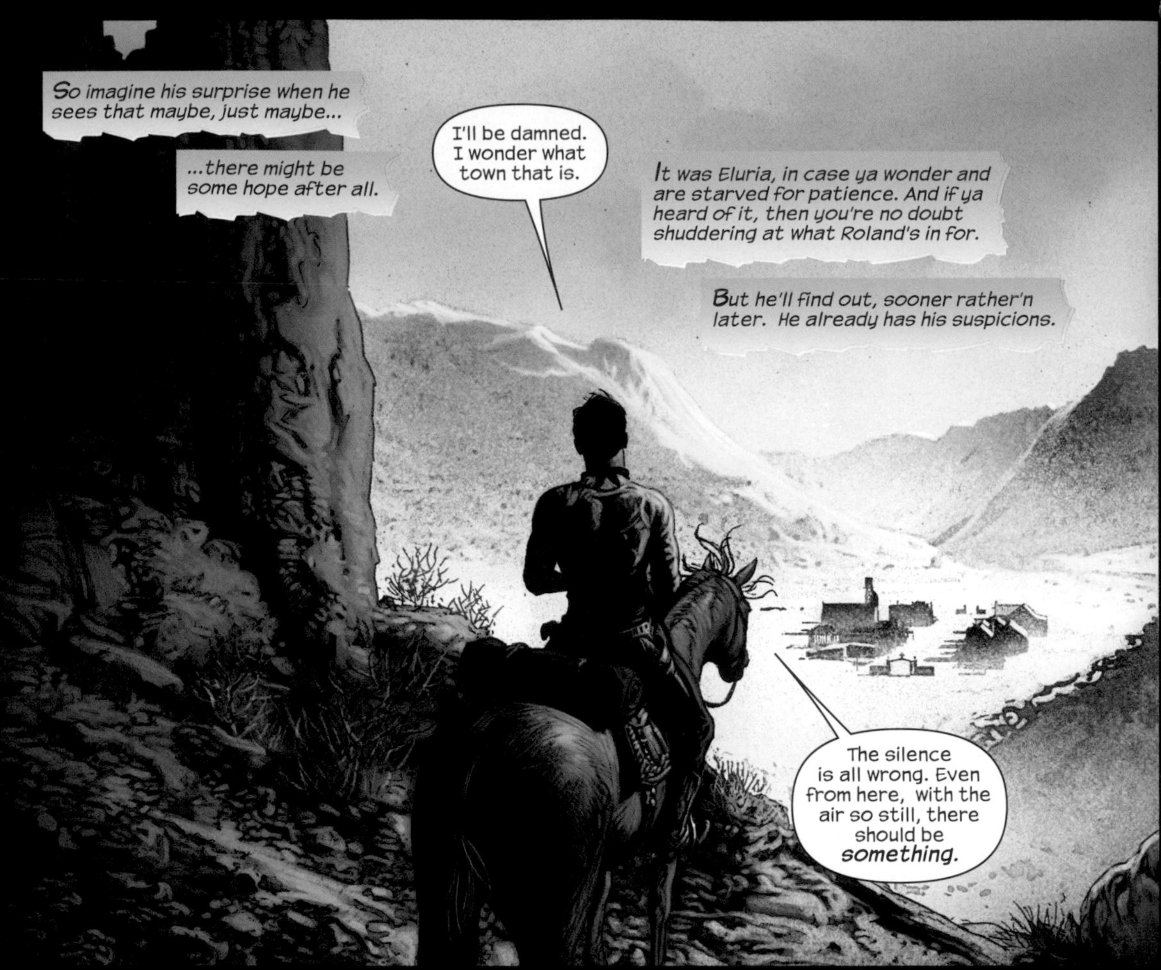
So imagine his surprise when he sees that maybe, just maybe...
...there might be some hope after all.
I'll be damned. I wonder what town that is.
It was Eluria, in case ya wonder and are starved for patience. And if ya heard of it, then you're no doubt shuddering at what Roland's in for.
But he'll find out, sooner rather'n later. He already has his suspicions.
The silence is all wrong. Even from here, with the air so still, there should be *something.*

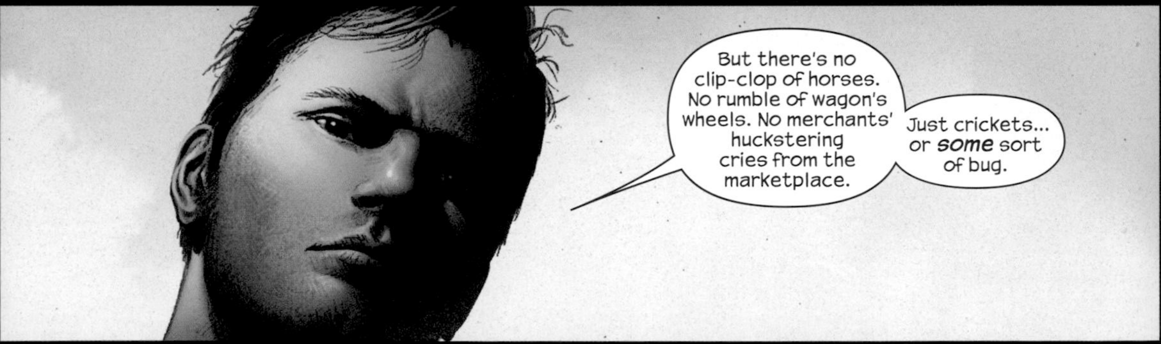
But there's no clip-clop of horses. No rumble of wagon's wheels. No merchants' huckstering cries from the marketplace.
Just crickets... or *some* sort of bug.

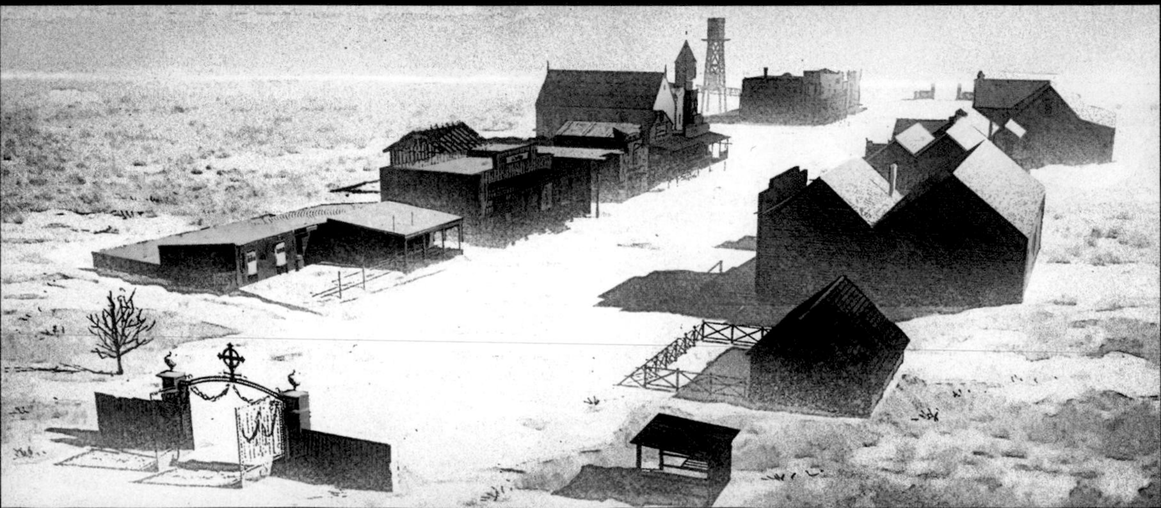

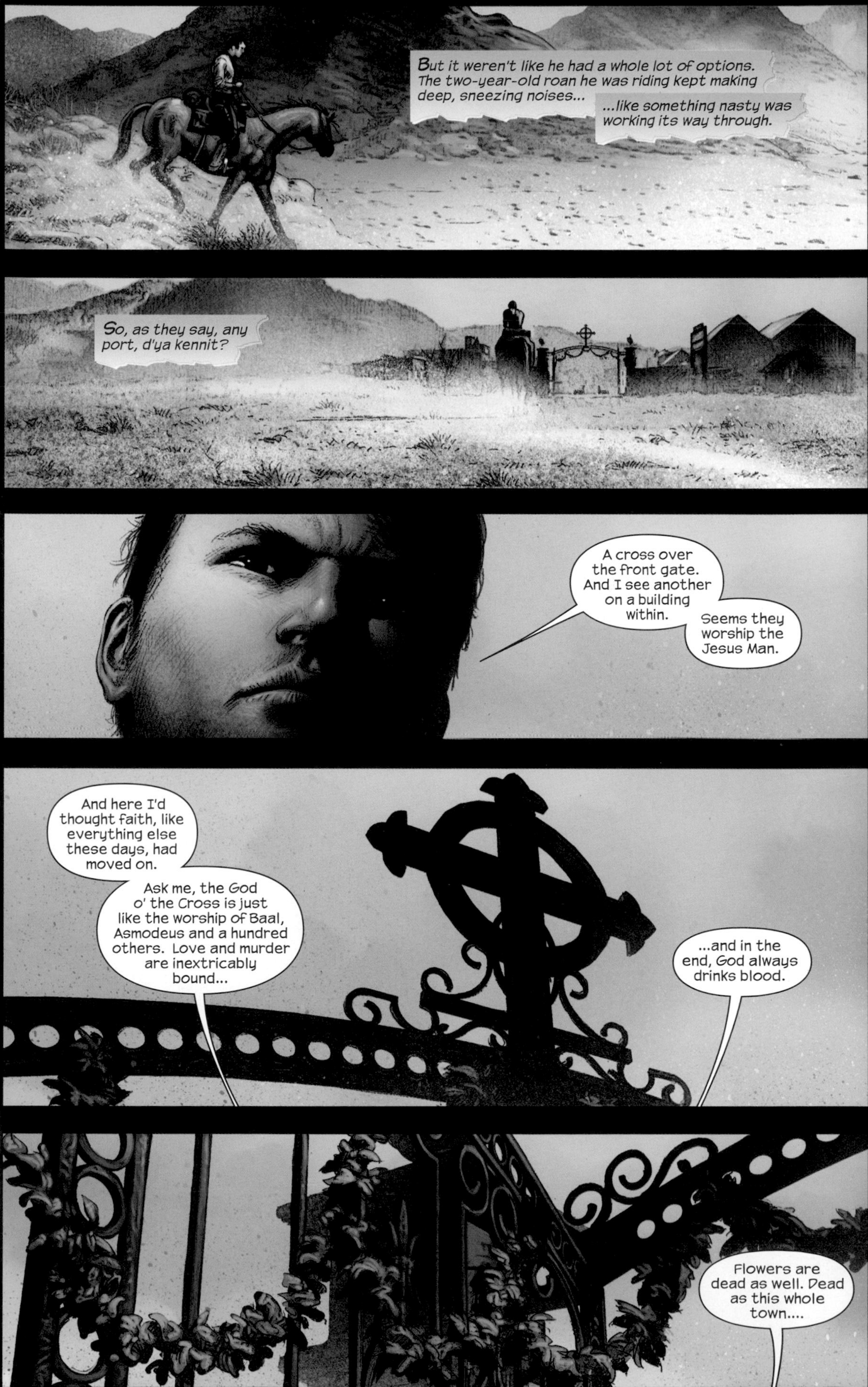
But it weren't like he had a whole lot of options. The two-year-old roan he was riding kept making deep, sneezing noises...
...like something nasty was working its way through.
So, as they say, any port, d'ya kennit?
A cross over the front gate. And I see another on a building within.
Seems they worship the Jesus Man.
And here I'd thought faith, like everything else these days, had moved on.
Ask me, the God o' the Cross is just like the worship of Baal, Asmodeus and a hundred others. Love and murder are inextricably bound...
...and in the end, God always drinks blood.
Flowers are dead as well. Dead as this whole town....

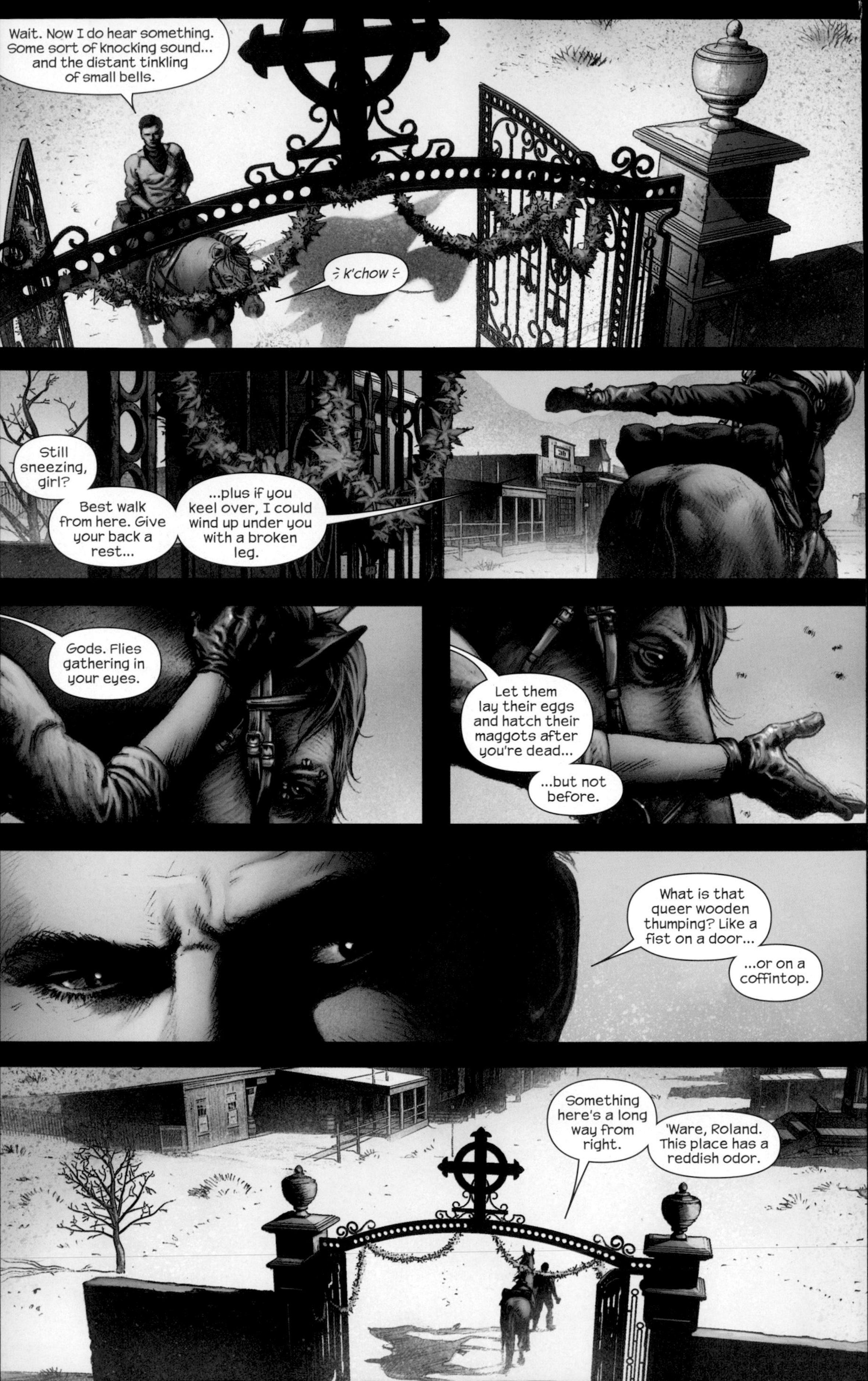
Wait. Now I do hear something. Some sort of knocking sound... and the distant tinkling of small bells.
K'CHOW
Still sneezing, girl?
Best walk from here. Give your back a rest...
...plus if you keel over, I could wind up under you with a broken leg.
Gods. Flies gathering in your eyes.
Let them lay their eggs and hatch their maggots after you're dead...
...but not before.
What is that queer wooden thumping? Like a fist on a door...
...or on a coffintop.
Something here's a long way from right.
'Ware, Roland. This place has a reddish odor.

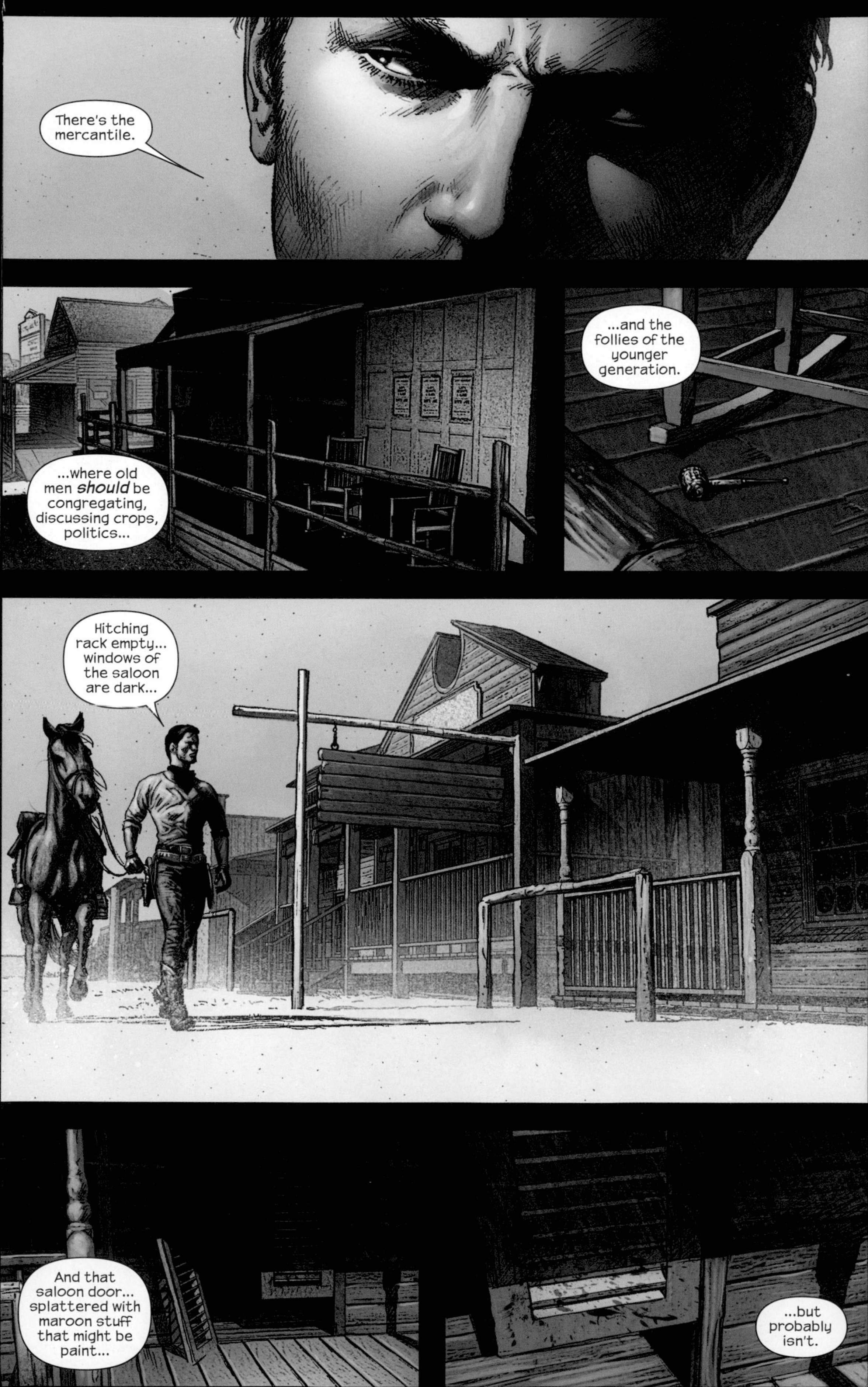
There's the mercantile.
...where old men *should* be congregating, discussing crops, politics...
...and the follies of the younger generation.
Hitching rack empty... windows of the saloon are dark...
And that saloon door... splattered with maroon stuff that might be paint...
...but probably isn't.

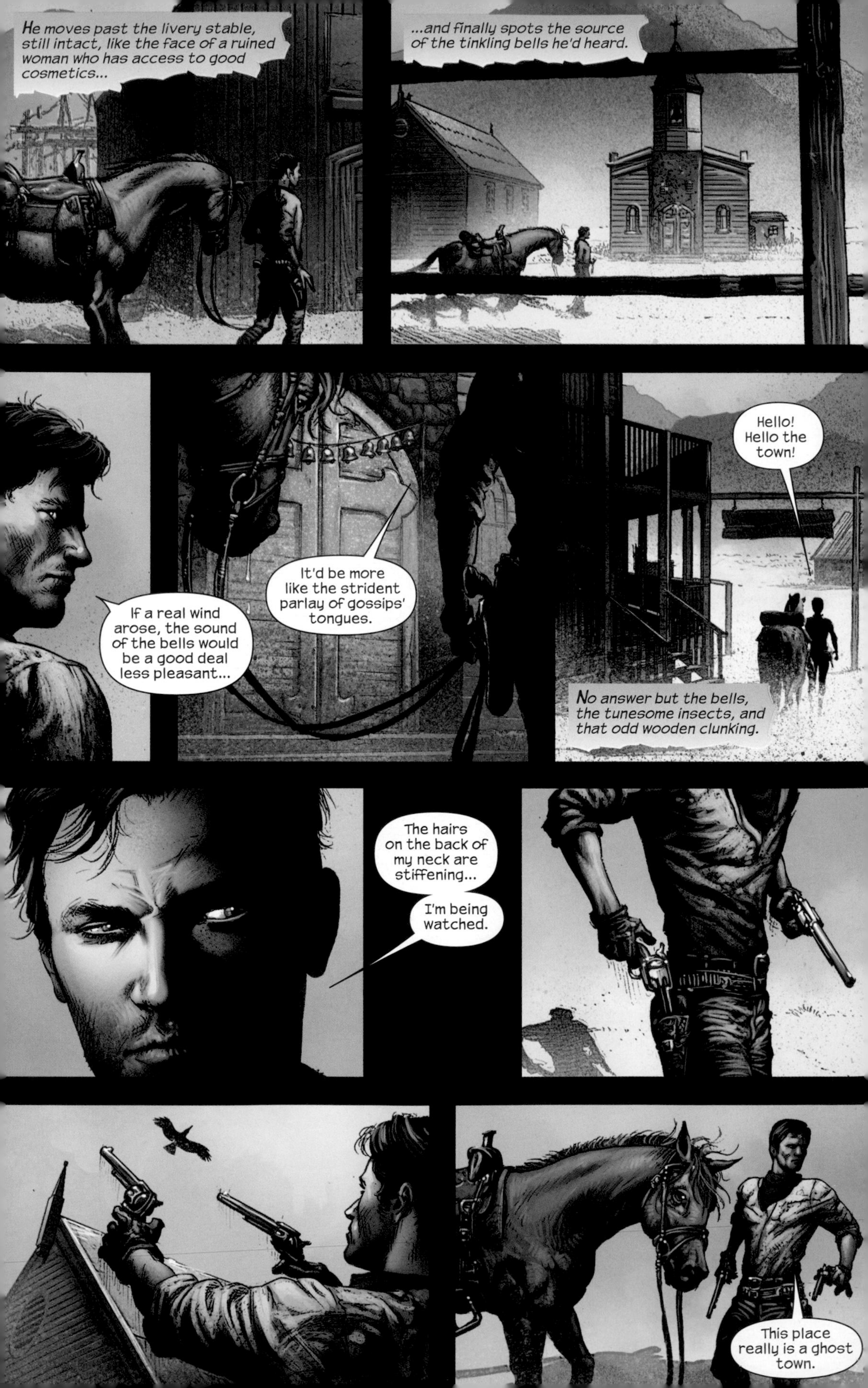
He moves past the livery stable, still intact, like the face of a ruined woman who has access to good cosmetics...
...and finally spots the source of the tinkling bells he'd heard.
If a real wind arose, the sound of the bells would be a good deal less pleasant...
It'd be more like the strident parlay of gossips' tongues.
Hello! Hello the town!
No answer but the bells, the tunesome insects, and that odd wooden clunking.
The hairs on the back of my neck are stiffening...
I'm being watched.
This place really is a ghost town.

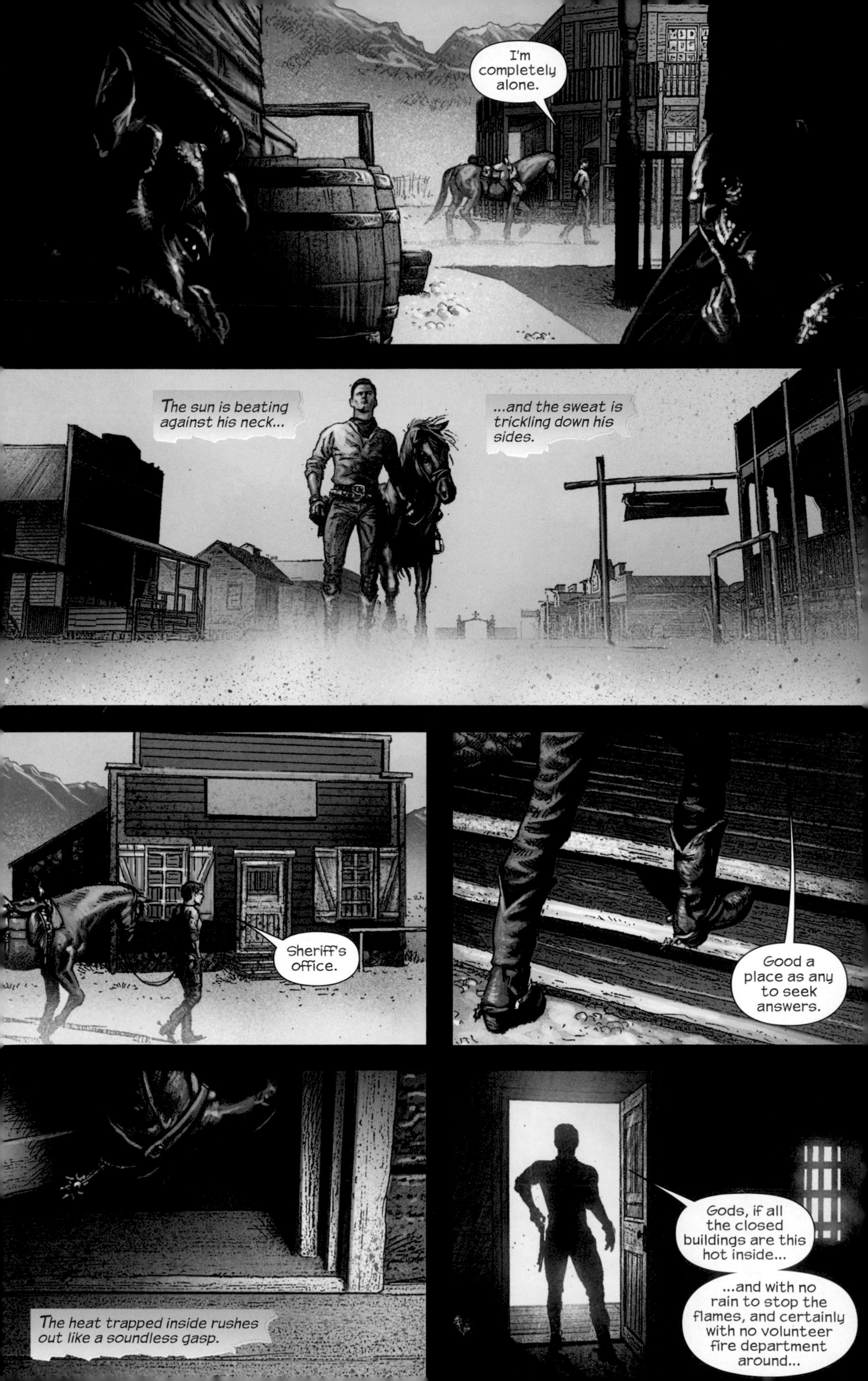
I'm completely alone.
The sun is beating against his neck...
...and the sweat is trickling down his sides.
Sheriff's office.
Good a place as any to seek answers.
The heat trapped inside rushes out like a soundless gasp.
Gods, if all the closed buildings are this hot inside...
...and with no rain to stop the flames, and certainly with no volunteer fire department around...

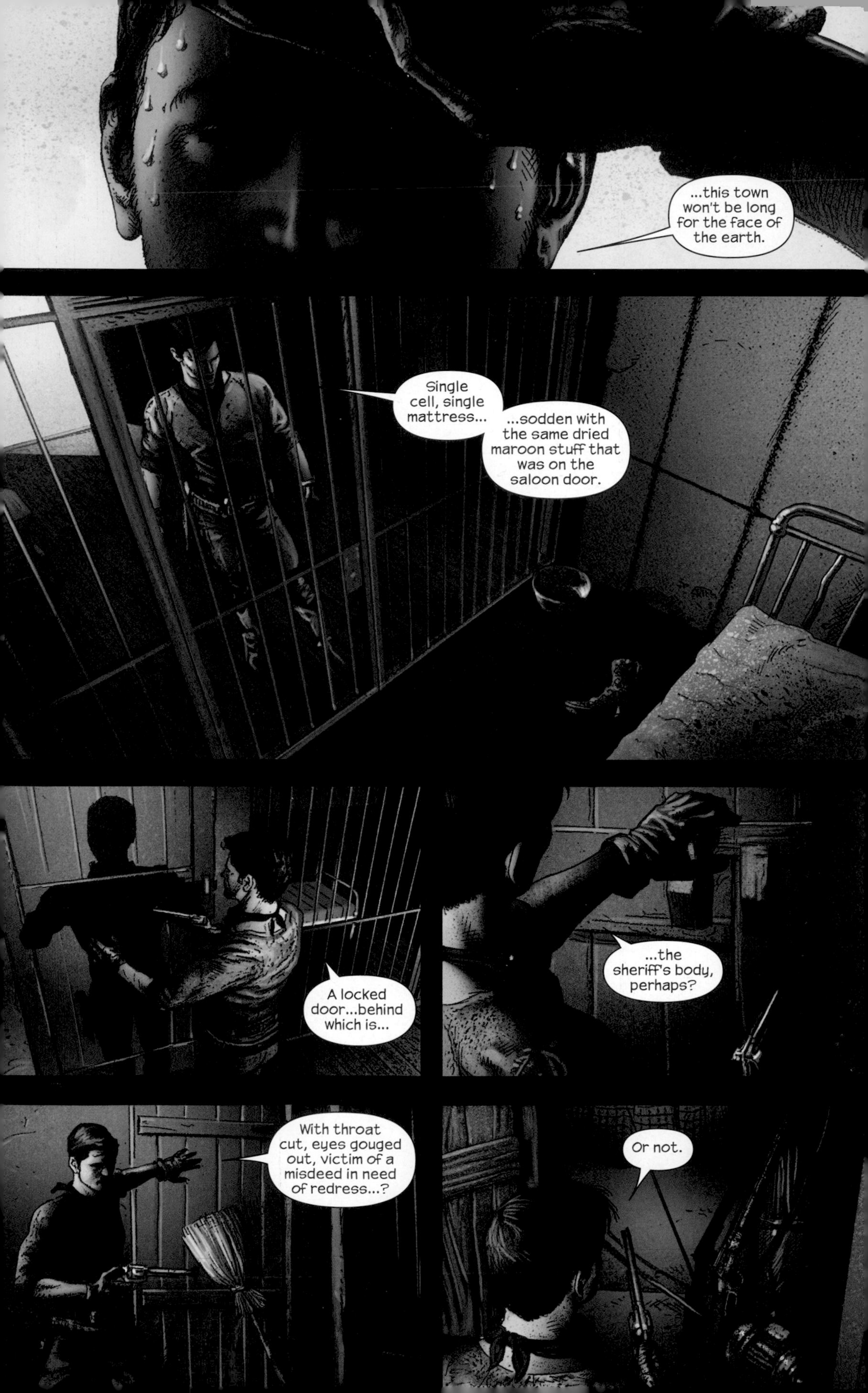
...this town won't be long for the face of the earth.
Single cell, single mattress...
...sodden with the same dried maroon stuff that was on the saloon door.
A locked door...behind which is...
...the sheriff's body, perhaps?
With throat cut, eyes gouged out, victim of a misdeed in need of redress...?
Or not.

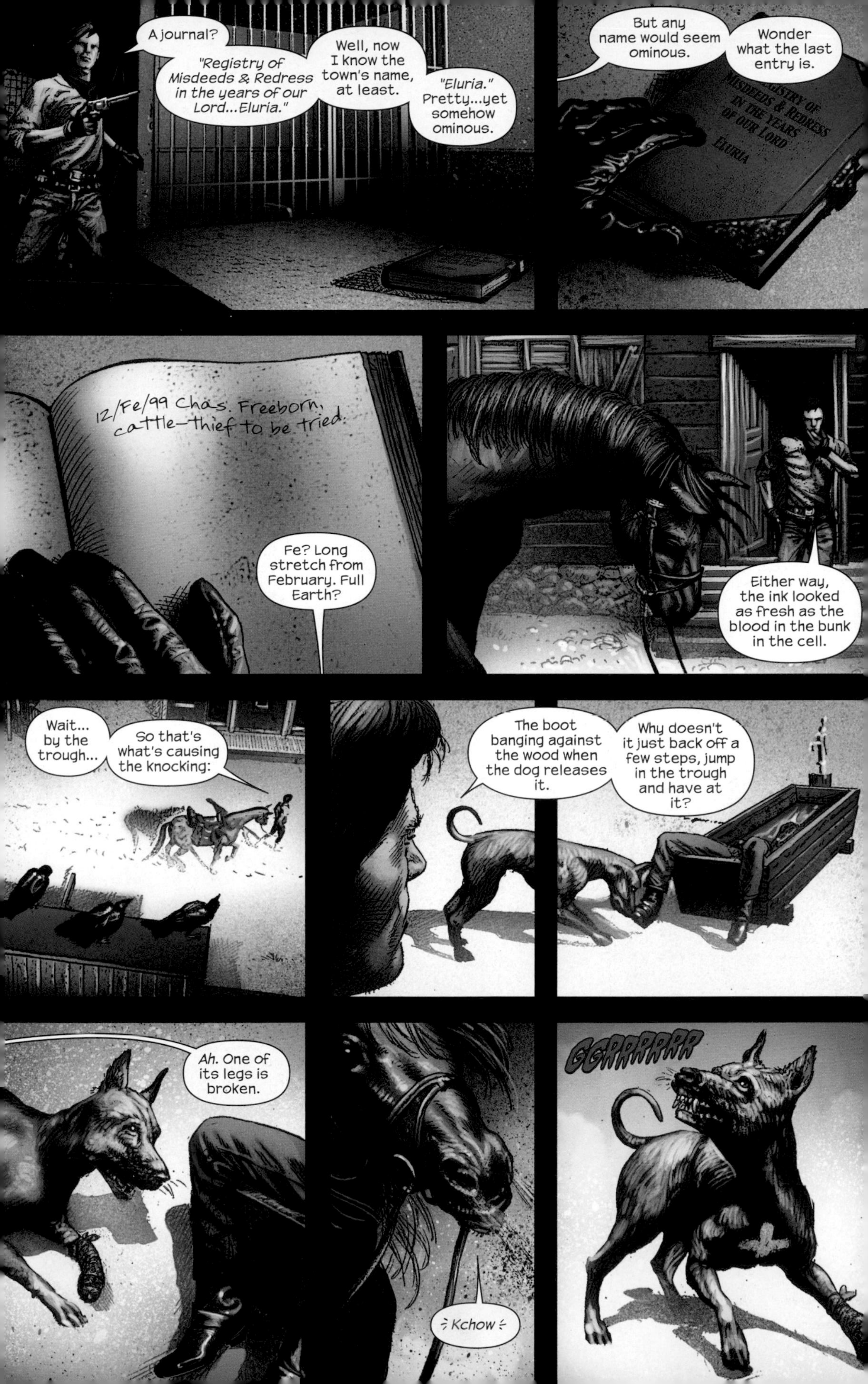
A journal?
"Registry of Misdeeds & Redress in the years of our Lord...Eluria."
Well, now I know the town's name, at least.
"Eluria." Pretty...yet somehow ominous.
But any name would seem ominous.
Wonder what the last entry is.
REGISTRY OF MISDEEDS & REDRESS IN THE YEARS OF OUR LORD ELURIA
12/Fe/99 Chas. Freeborn, cattle-thief to be tried.
Fe? Long stretch from February. Full Earth?
Either way, the ink looked as fresh as the blood in the bunk in the cell.
Wait... by the trough...
So that's what's causing the knocking:
The boot banging against the wood when the dog releases it.
Why doesn't it just back off a few steps, jump in the trough and have at it?
Ah. One of its legs is broken.
Kchow
GGRRRRRRR

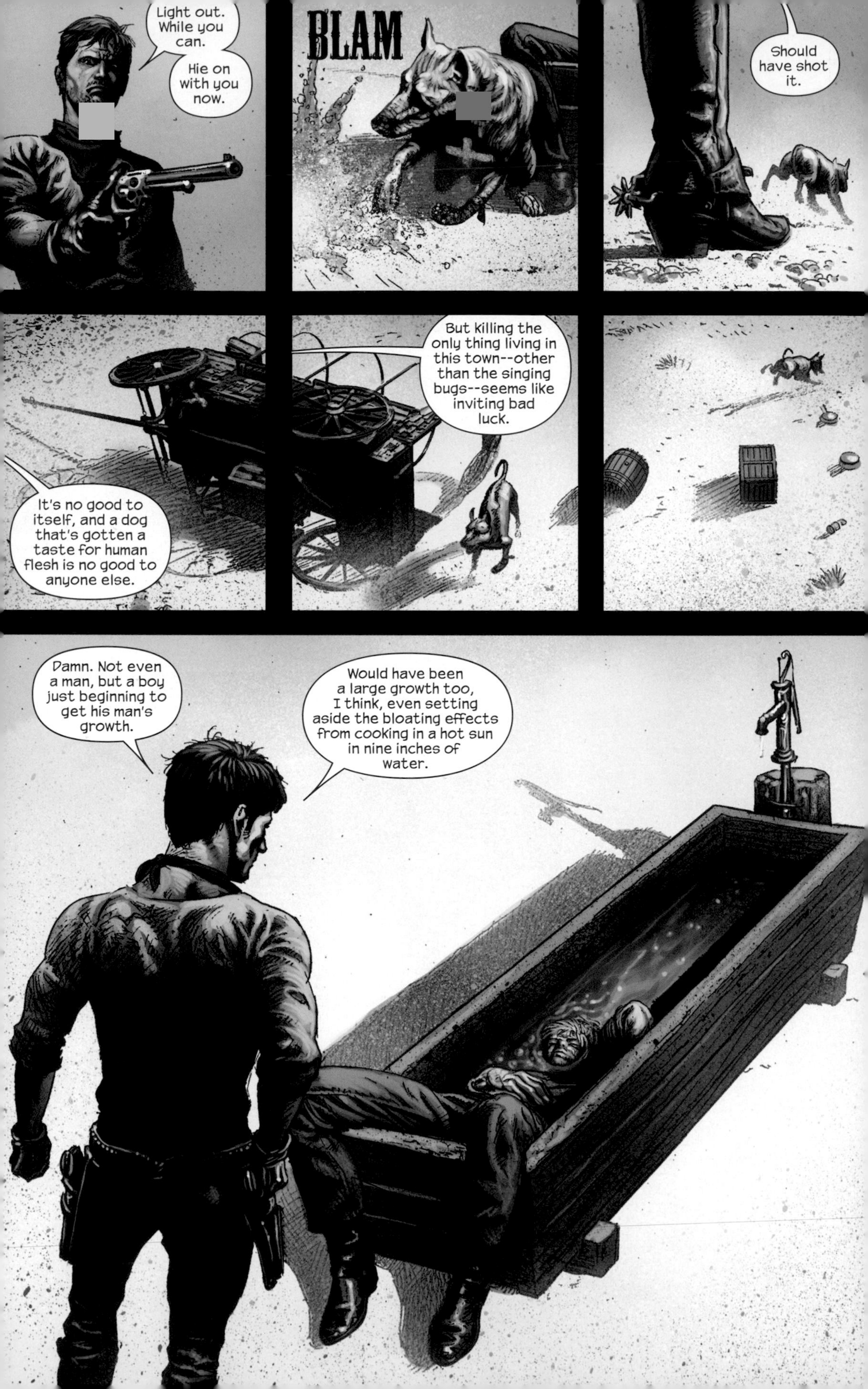
Light out. While you can.
Hie on with you now.
BLAM
Should have shot it.
It's no good to itself, and a dog that's gotten a taste for human flesh is no good to anyone else.
But killing the only thing living in this town--other than the singing bugs--seems like inviting bad luck.
Damn. Not even a man, but a boy just beginning to get his man's growth.
Would have been a large growth too, I think, even setting aside the bloating effects from cooking in a hot sun in nine inches of water.

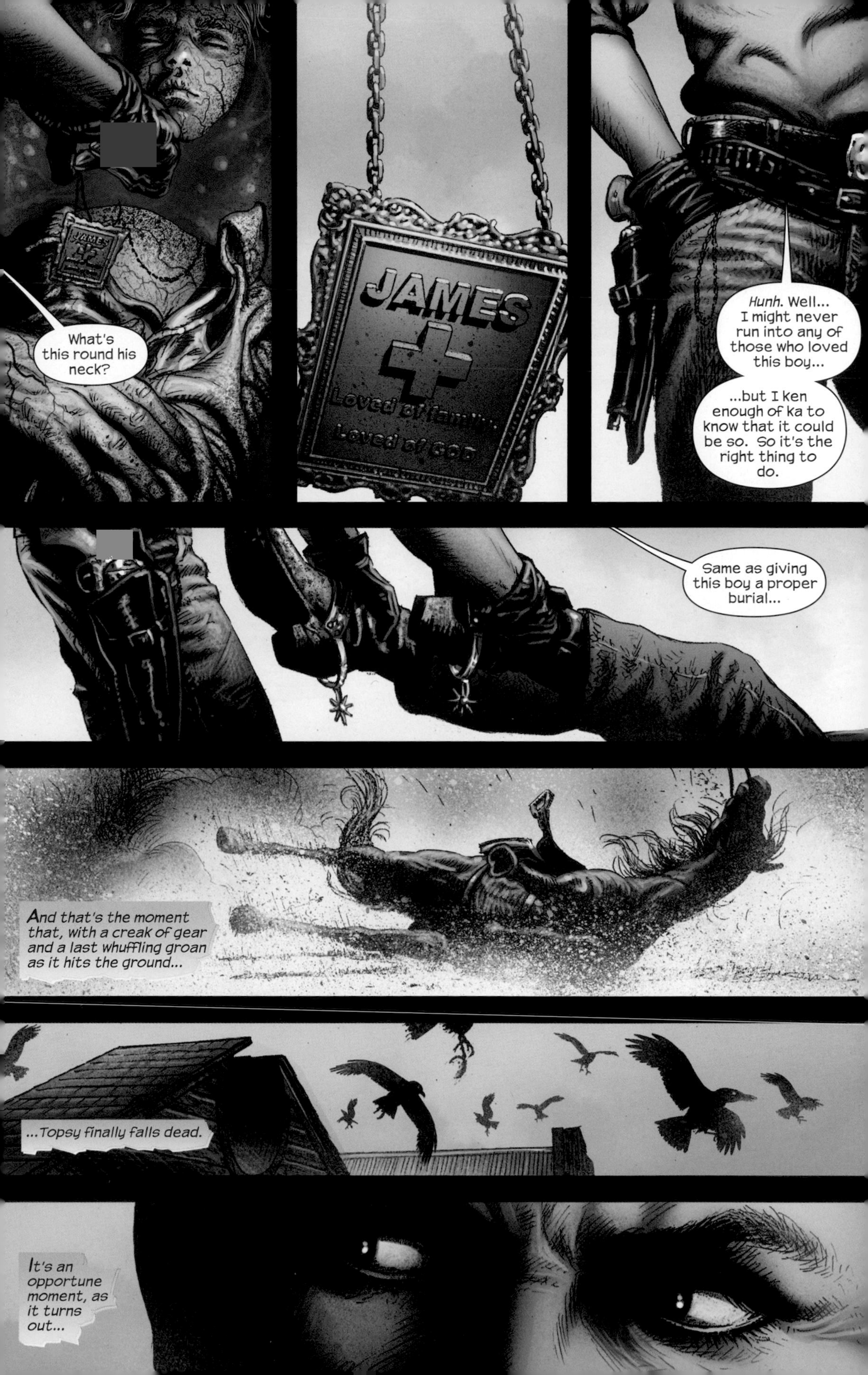
What's this round his neck?
JAMES
Loved of GOD
*Hunh.* Well... I might never run into any of those who loved this boy...
...but I ken enough of ka to know that it could be so. So it's the right thing to do.
Same as giving this boy a proper burial...
And that's the moment that, with a creak of gear and a last whuffling groan as it hits the ground...
...Topsy finally falls dead.
It's an opportune moment, as it turns out...

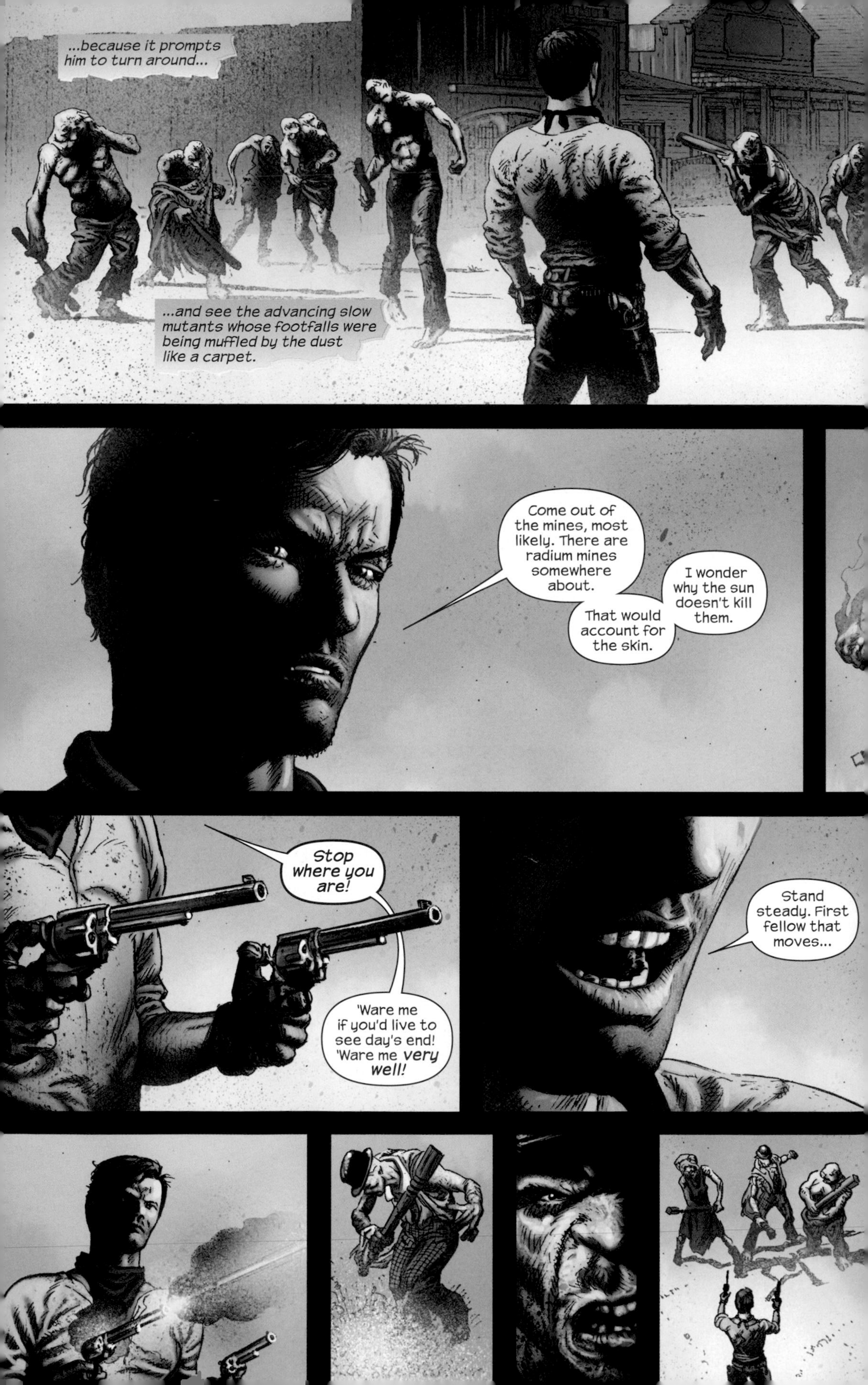
...because it prompts him to turn around...
...and see the advancing slow mutants whose footfalls were being muffled by the dust like a carpet.
Come out of the mines, most likely. There are radium mines somewhere about.
That would account for the skin.
I wonder why the sun doesn't kill them.
Stop where you are!
'Ware me if you'd live to see day's end! 'Ware me very well!
Stand steady. First fellow that moves...

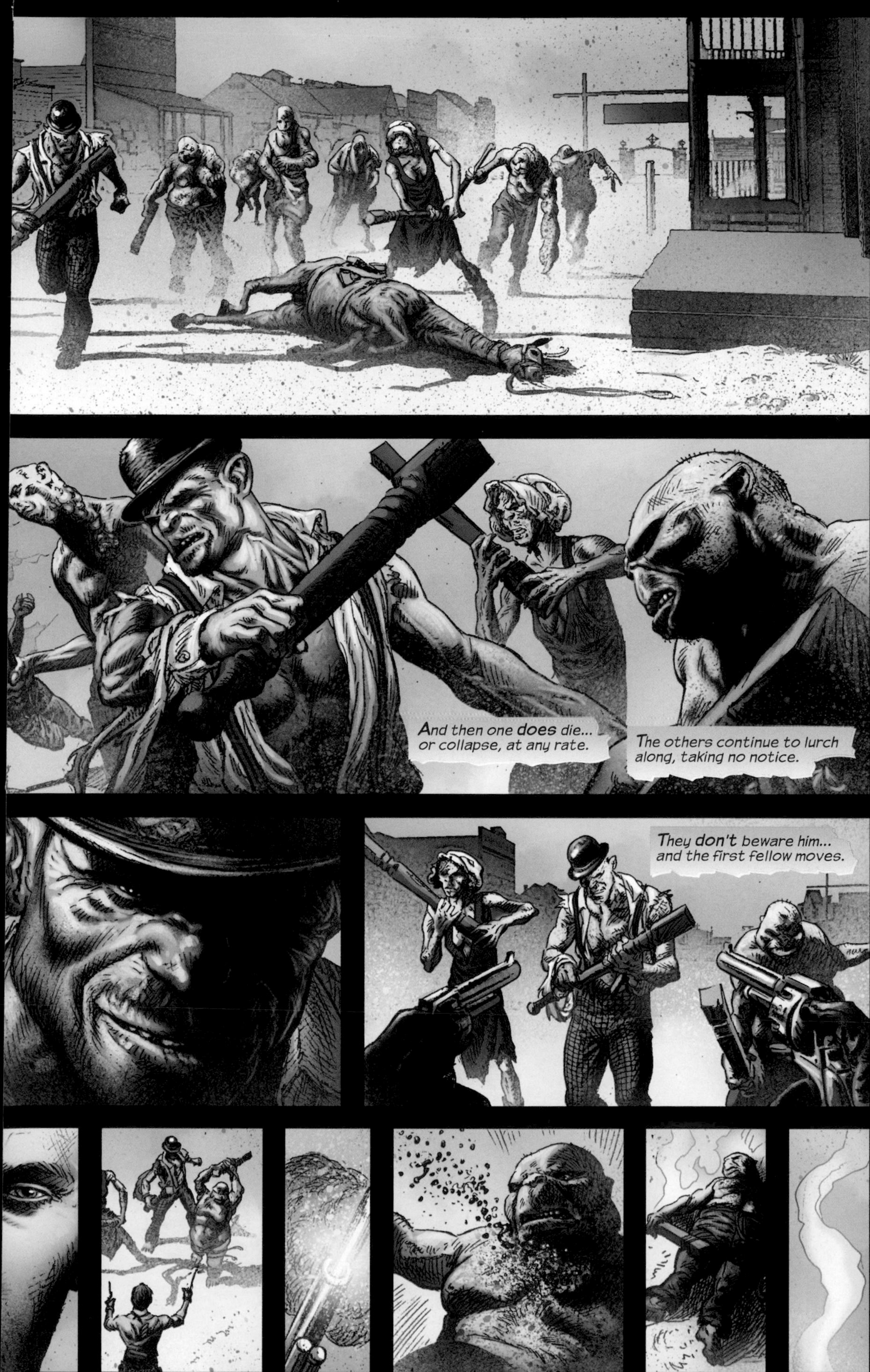
And then one does die...
or collapse, at any rate.
The others continue to lurch
along, taking no notice.
They don't beware him...
and the first fellow moves.

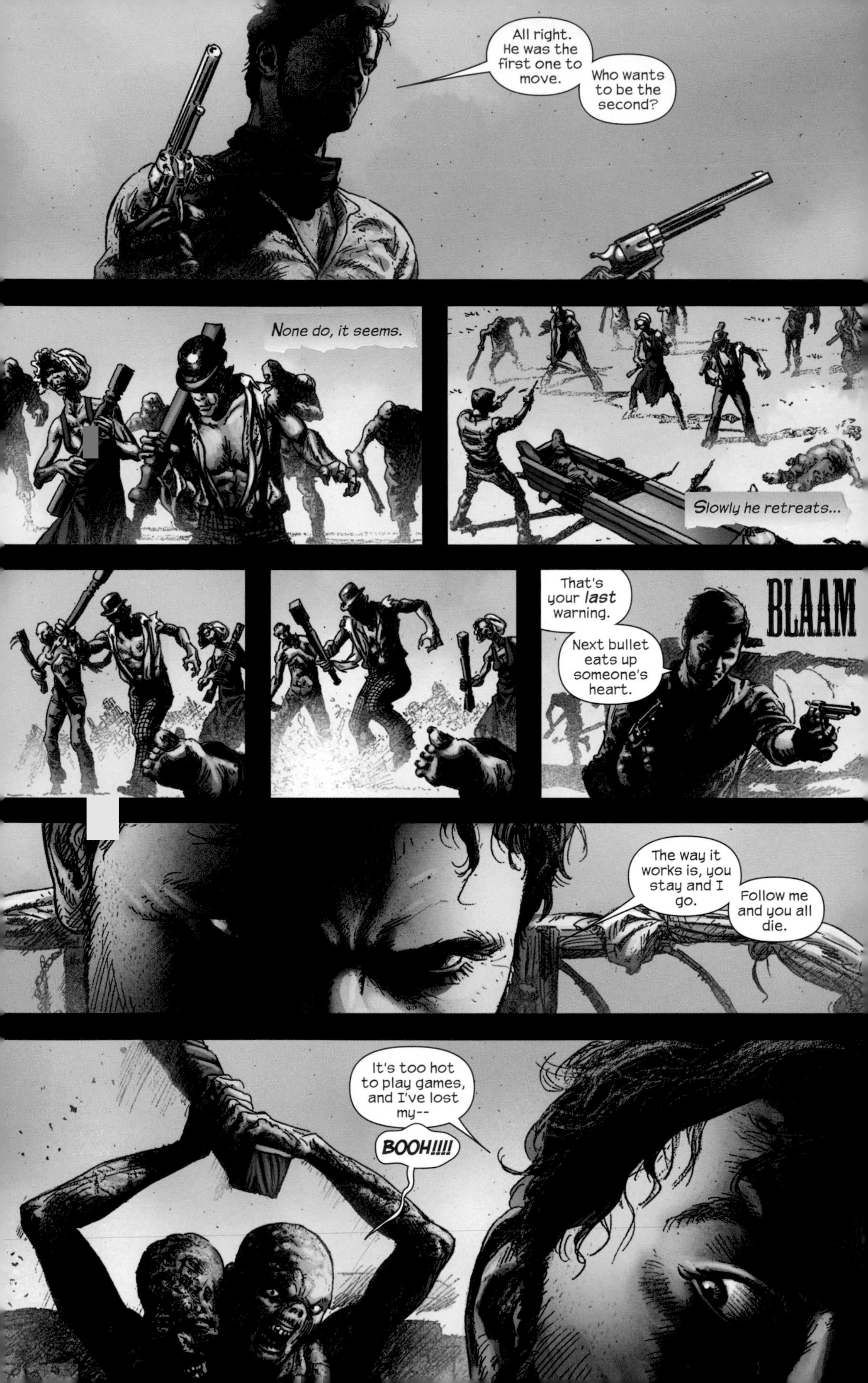
All right. He was the first one to move.
Who wants to be the second?
None do, it seems.
Slowly he retreats...
That's your *last* warning.
Next bullet eats up someone's heart.
BLAAM
The way it works is, you stay and I go.
Follow me and you all die.
It's too hot to play games, and I've lost my--
BOOH!!!!

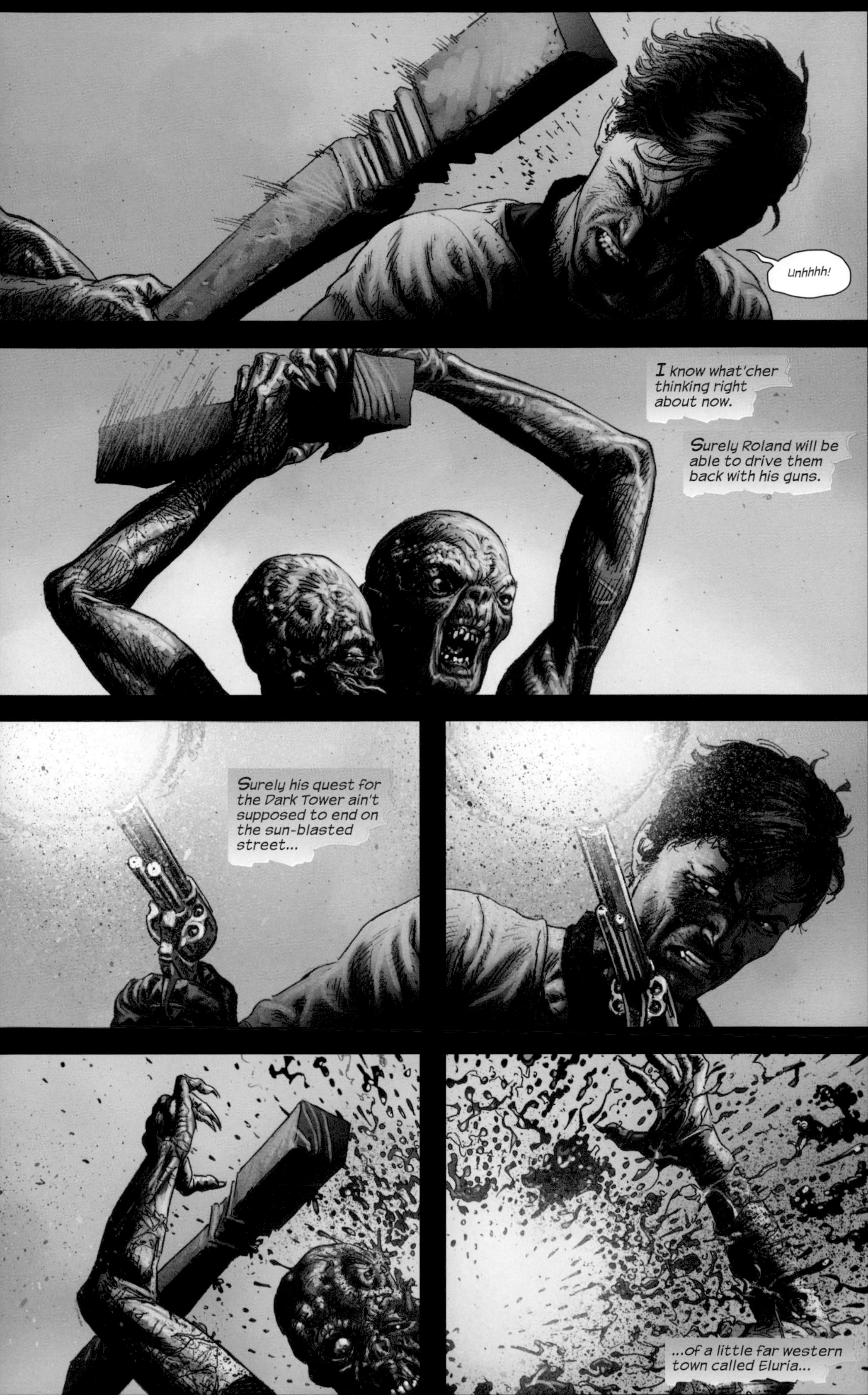
Unhhhh!
I know what'cher thinking right about now.
Surely Roland will be able to drive them back with his guns.
Surely his quest for the Dark Tower ain't supposed to end on the sun-blasted street...
...of a little far western town called Eluria...

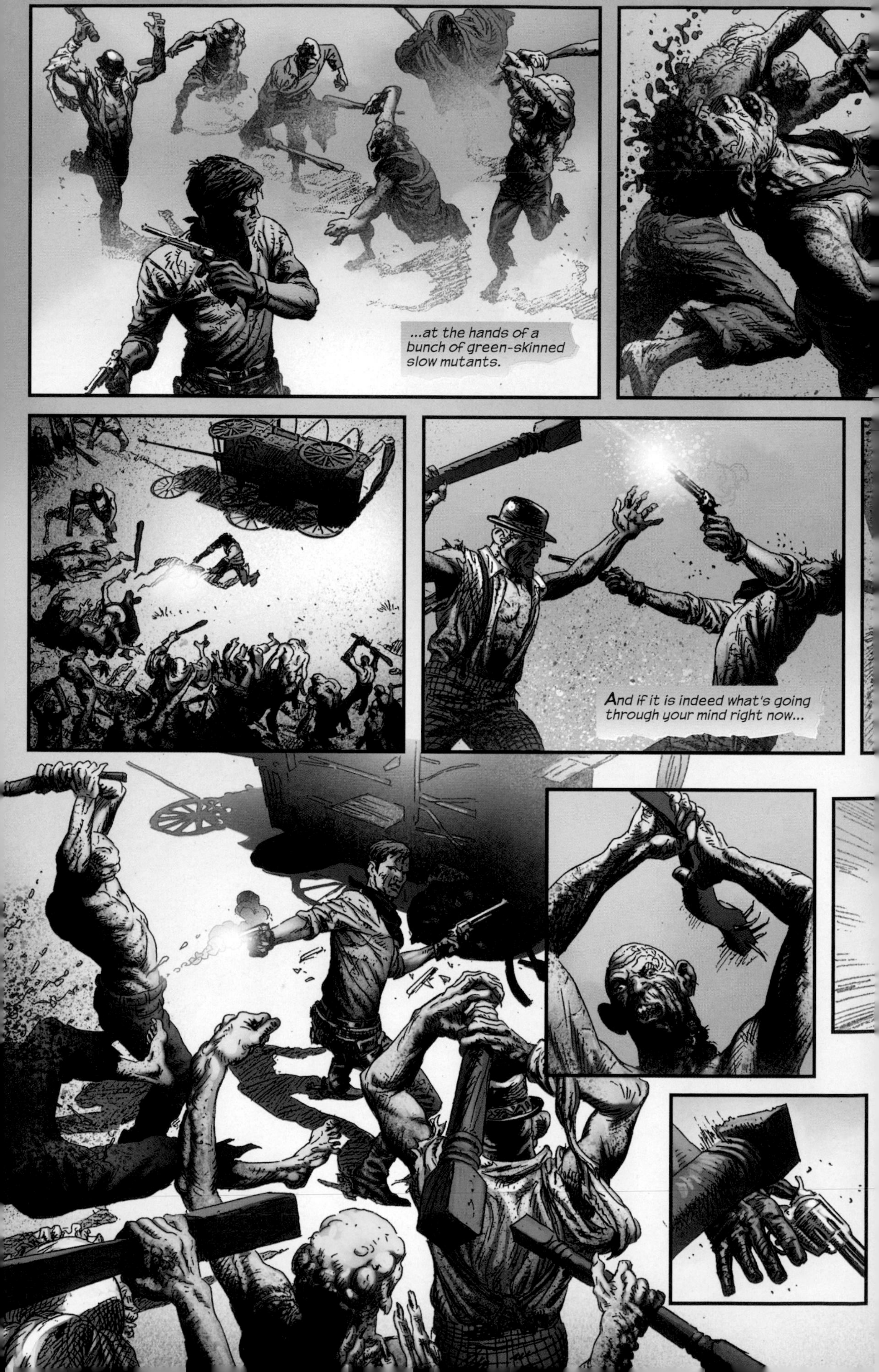
...at the hands of a bunch of green-skinned slow mutants.
And if it is indeed what's going through your mind right now...

Surely ka could not be so cruel.

...then all I have to say is:

Where the hell have ya been all this time? Ain't'cha been paying attention at all?

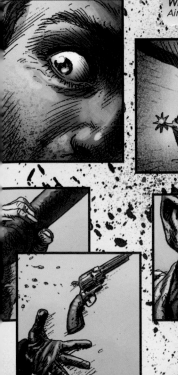

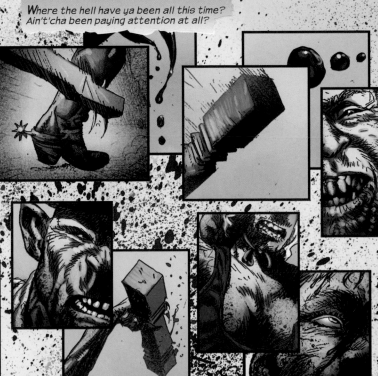

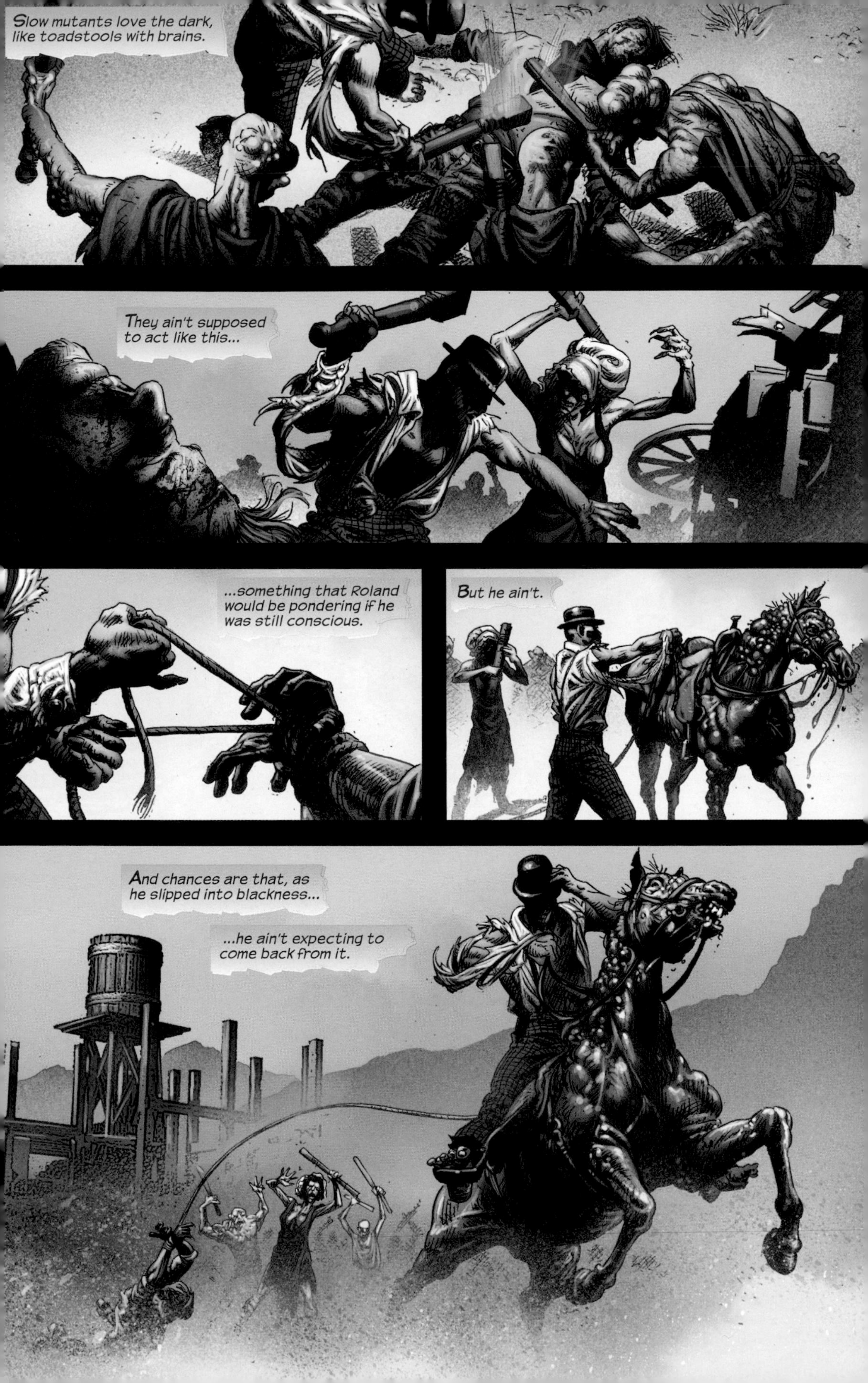
Slow mutants love the dark, like toadstools with brains.
They ain't supposed to act like this...
...something that Roland would be pondering if he was still conscious.
But he ain't.
And chances are that, as he slipped into blackness...
...he ain't expecting to come back from it.

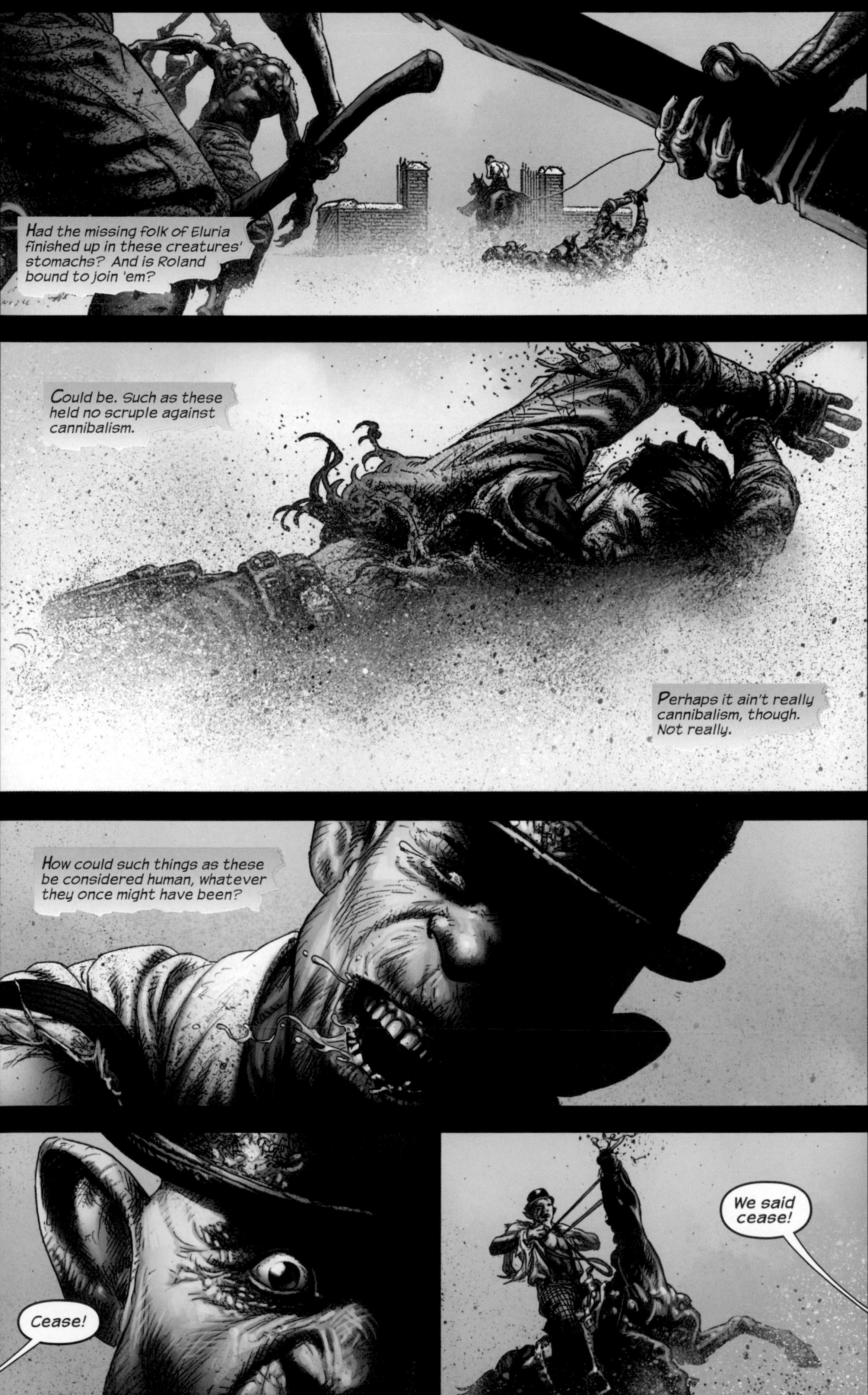
Had the missing folk of Eluria finished up in these creatures' stomachs? And is Roland bound to join 'em?
Could be. Such as these held no scruple against cannibalism.
Perhaps it ain't really cannibalism, though. Not really.
How could such things as these be considered human, whatever they once might have been?
Cease!
We said cease!

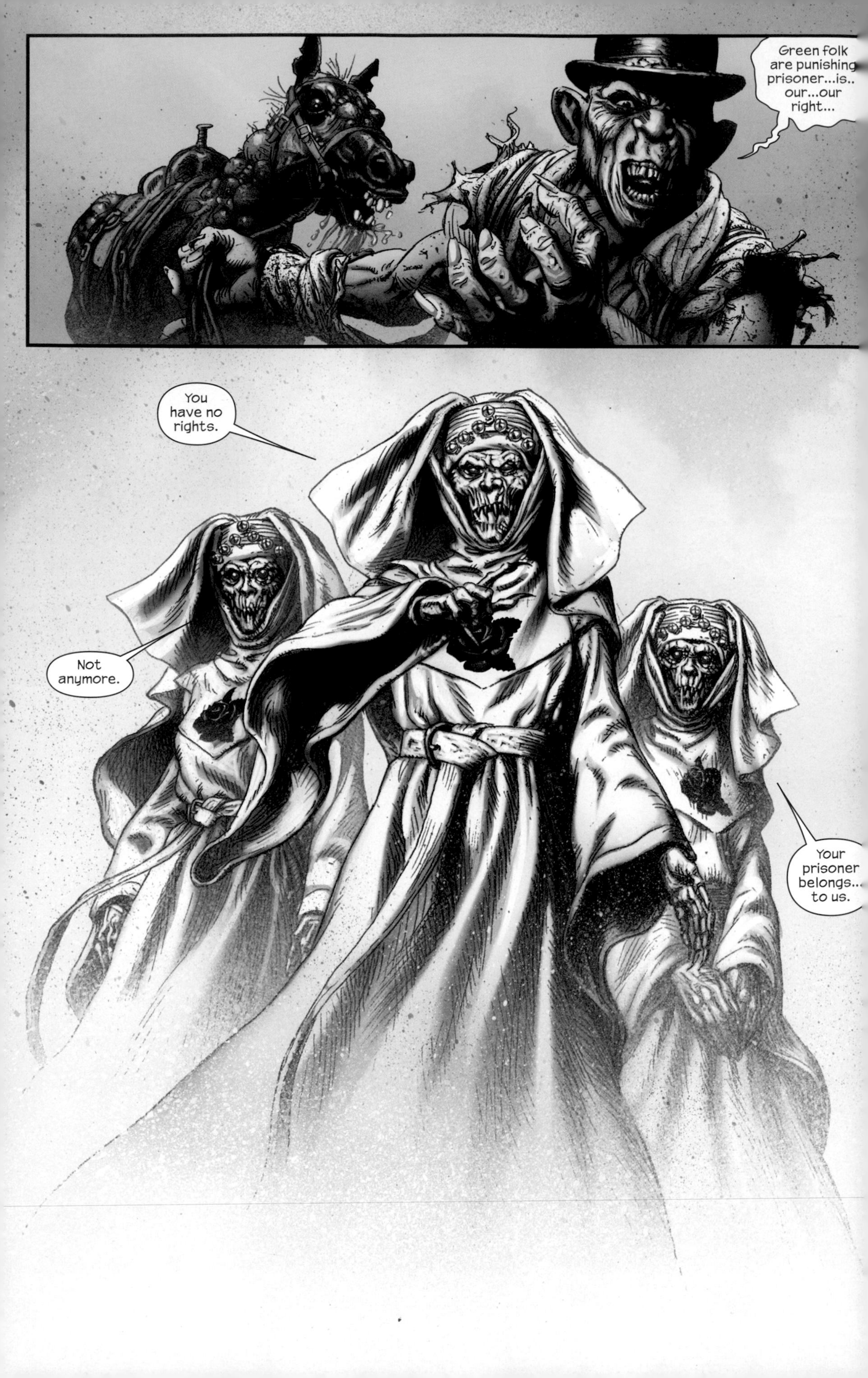
Green folk are punishing prisoner...is.. our...our right...
You have no rights.
Not anymore.
Your prisoner belongs... to us.

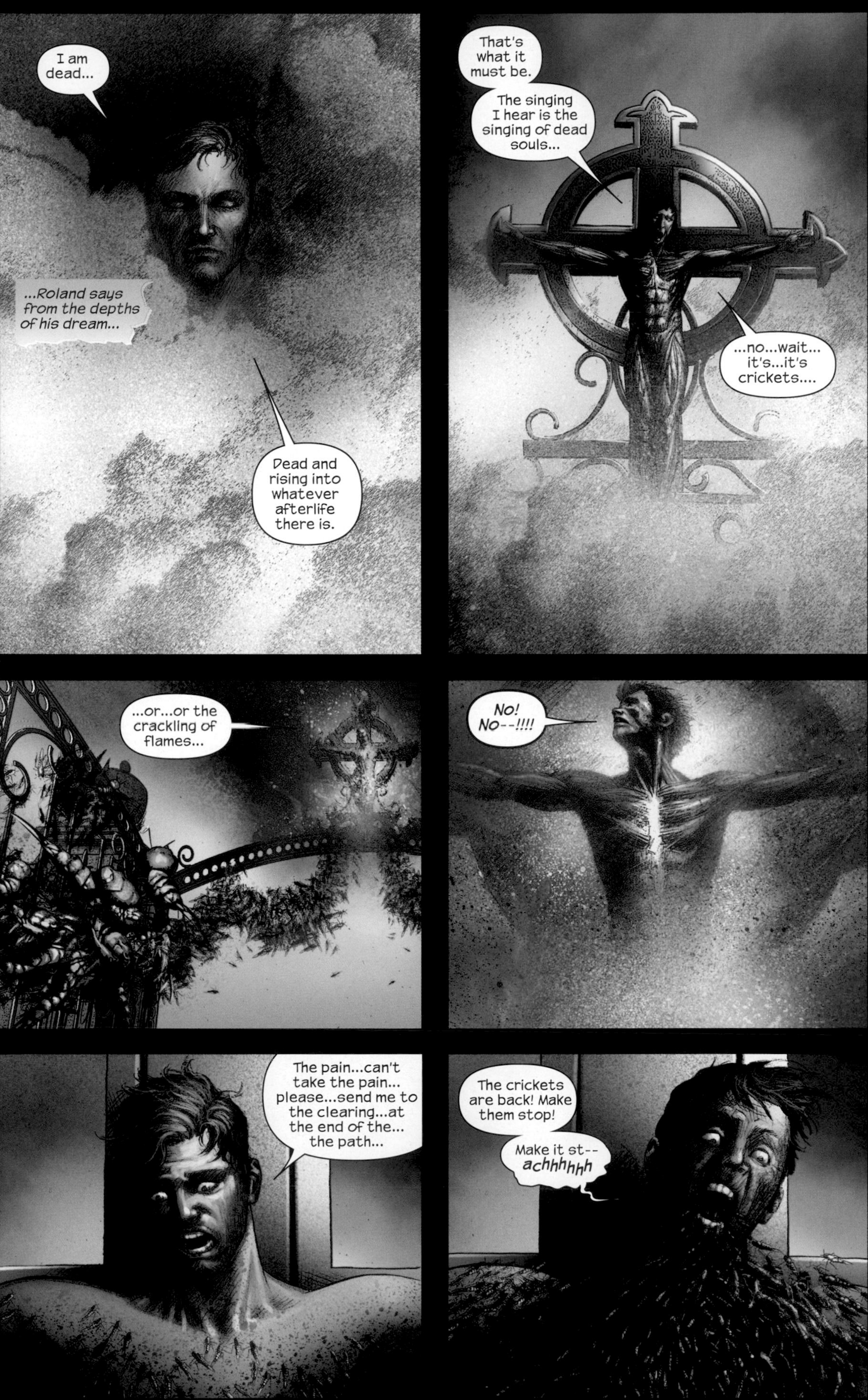
I am dead...
...Roland says from the depths of his dream...
Dead and rising into whatever afterlife there is.
That's what it must be.
The singing I hear is the singing of dead souls...
...no...wait... it's...it's crickets....
...or...or the crackling of flames...
No! No--!!!!
The pain...can't take the pain... please...send me to the clearing...at the end of the... the path...
The crickets are back! Make them stop!
Make it st-- achhhhhh

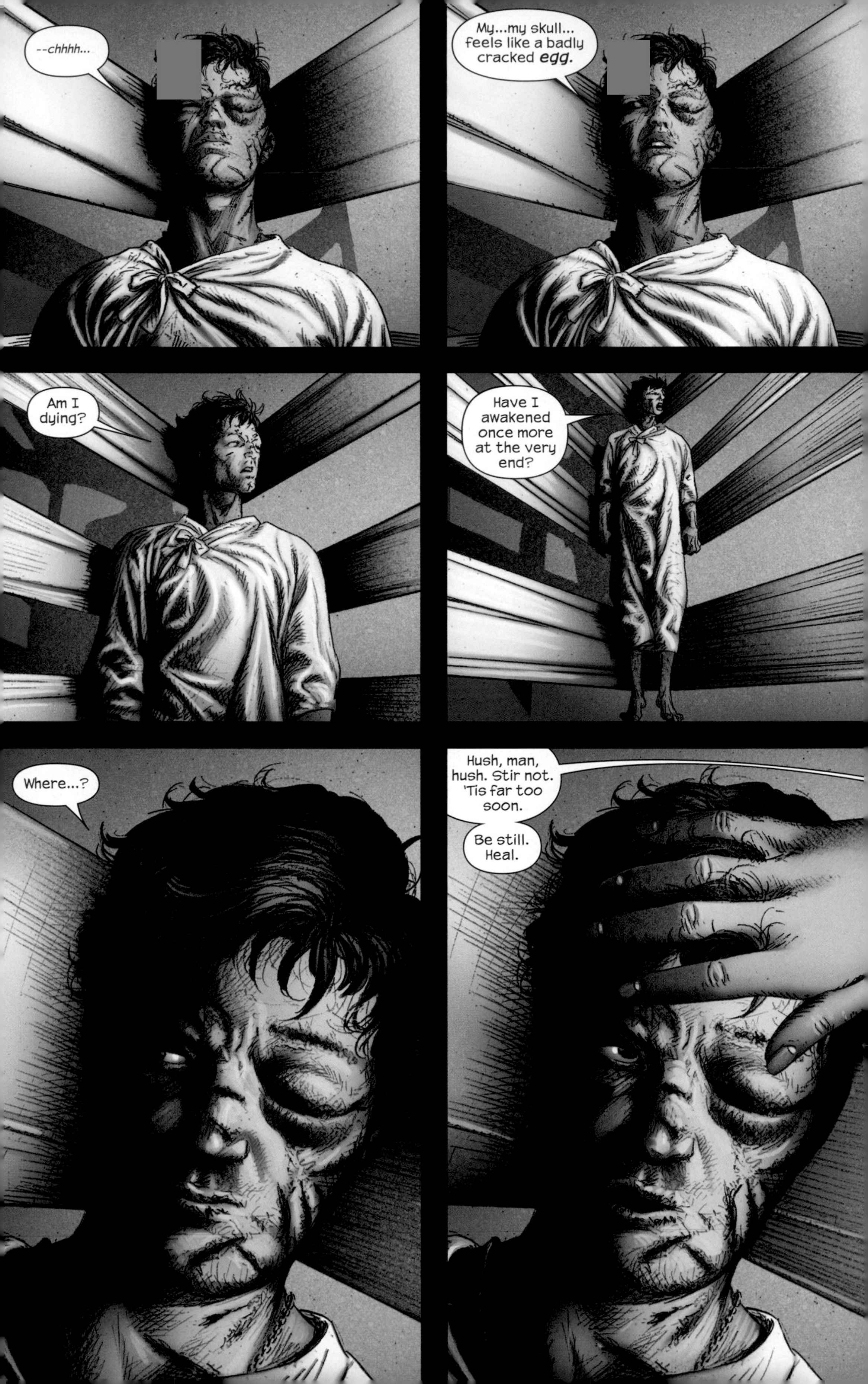
--chhhh...
My...my skull... feels like a badly cracked *egg.*
Am I dying?
Have I awakened once more at the very end?
Where...?
Hush, man, hush. Stir not. 'Tis far too soon.
Be still. Heal.

# STEPHEN KING

## THE DARK TOWER
### ~ THE GUNSLINGER ~

# THE LITTLE SISTERS
# OF ELURIA

# CHAPTER TWO

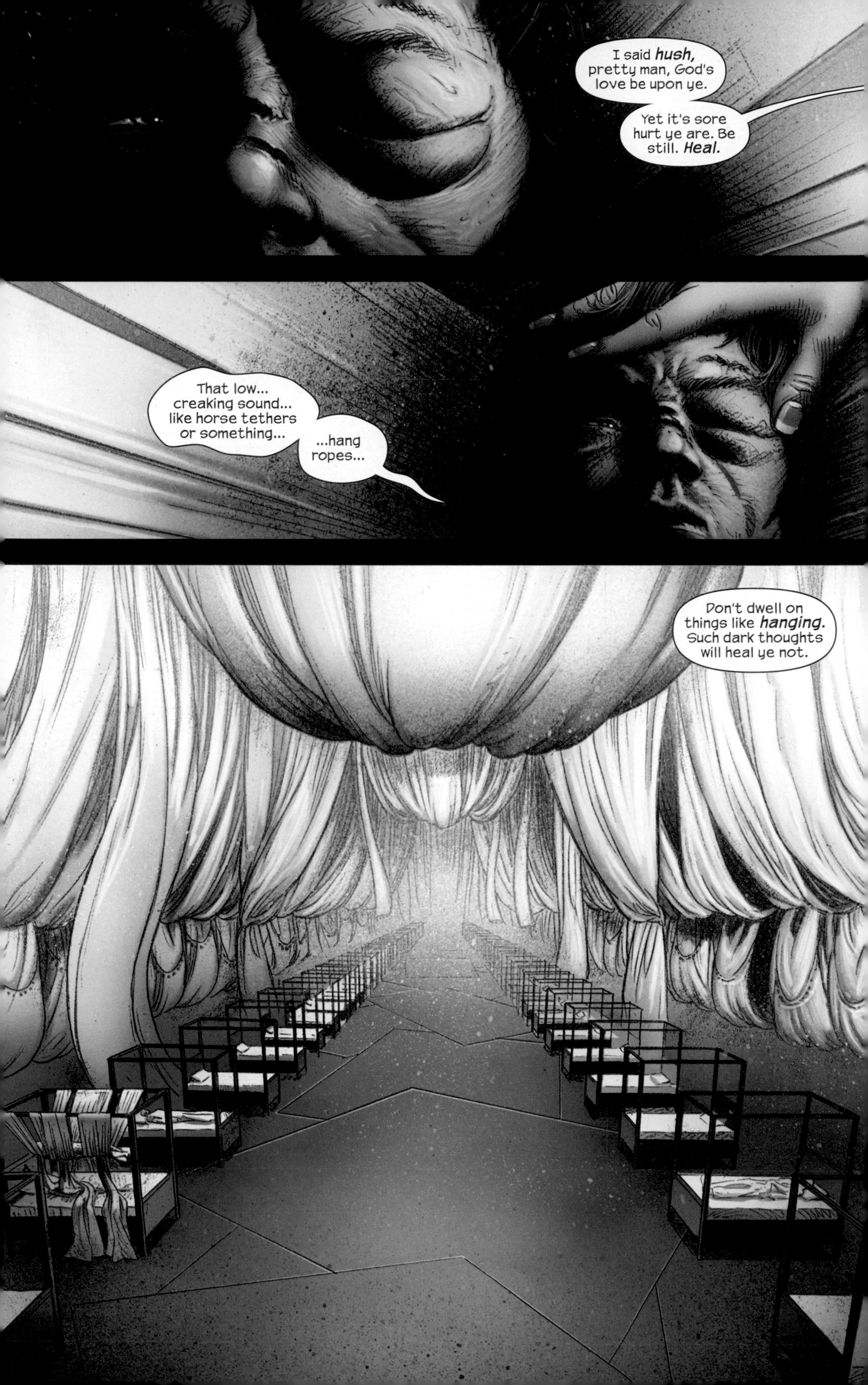
I said hush, pretty man, God's love be upon ye.
Yet it's sore hurt ye are. Be still. Heal.
That low... creaking sound... like horse tethers or something...
...hang ropes...
Don't dwell on things like hanging. Such dark thoughts will heal ye not.

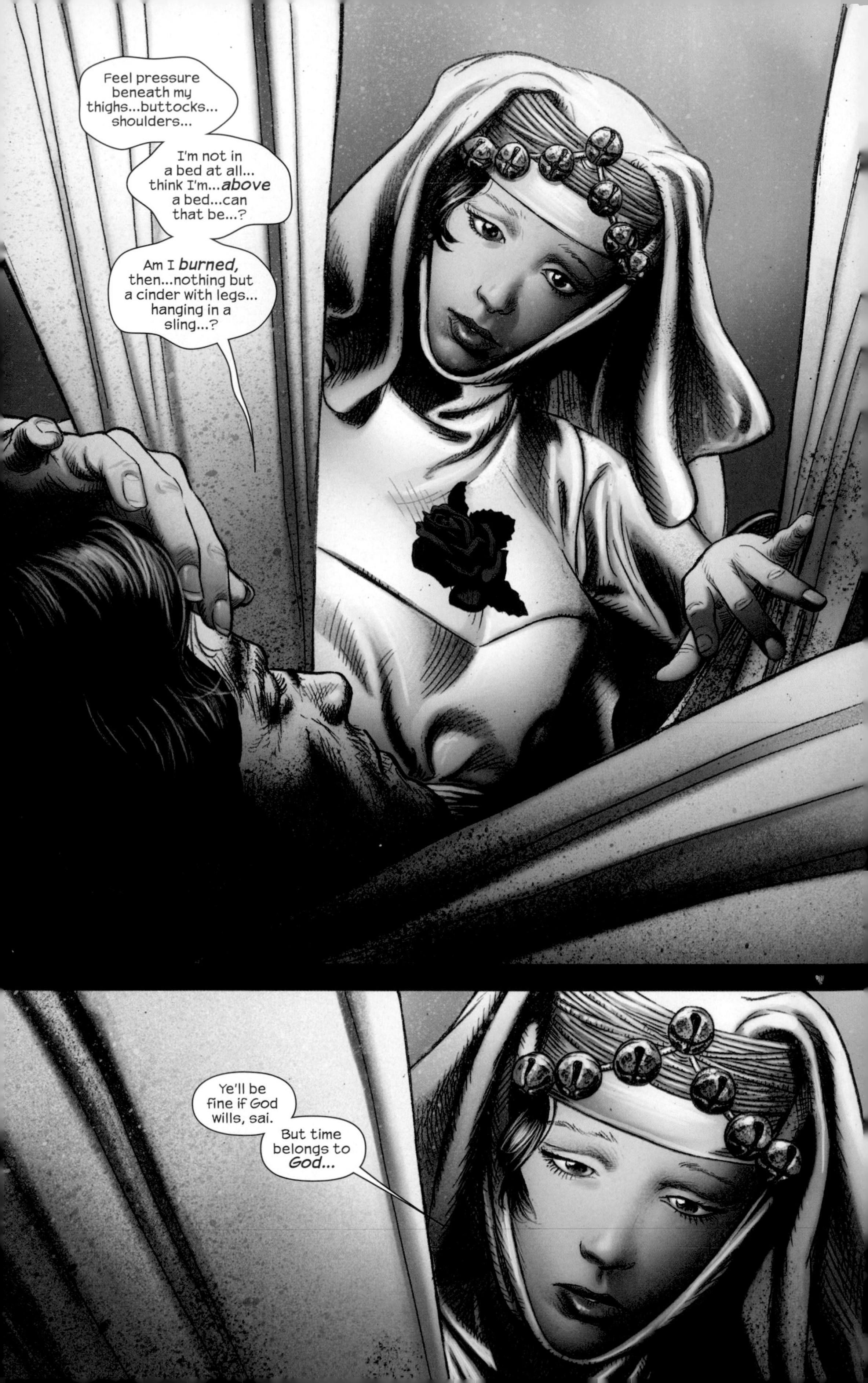
Feel pressure beneath my thighs...buttocks... shoulders...
I'm not in a bed at all... think I'm...*above* a bed...can that be...?
Am I *burned,* then...nothing but a cinder with legs... hanging in a sling...?
Ye'll be fine if God wills, sai.
But time belongs to *God...*

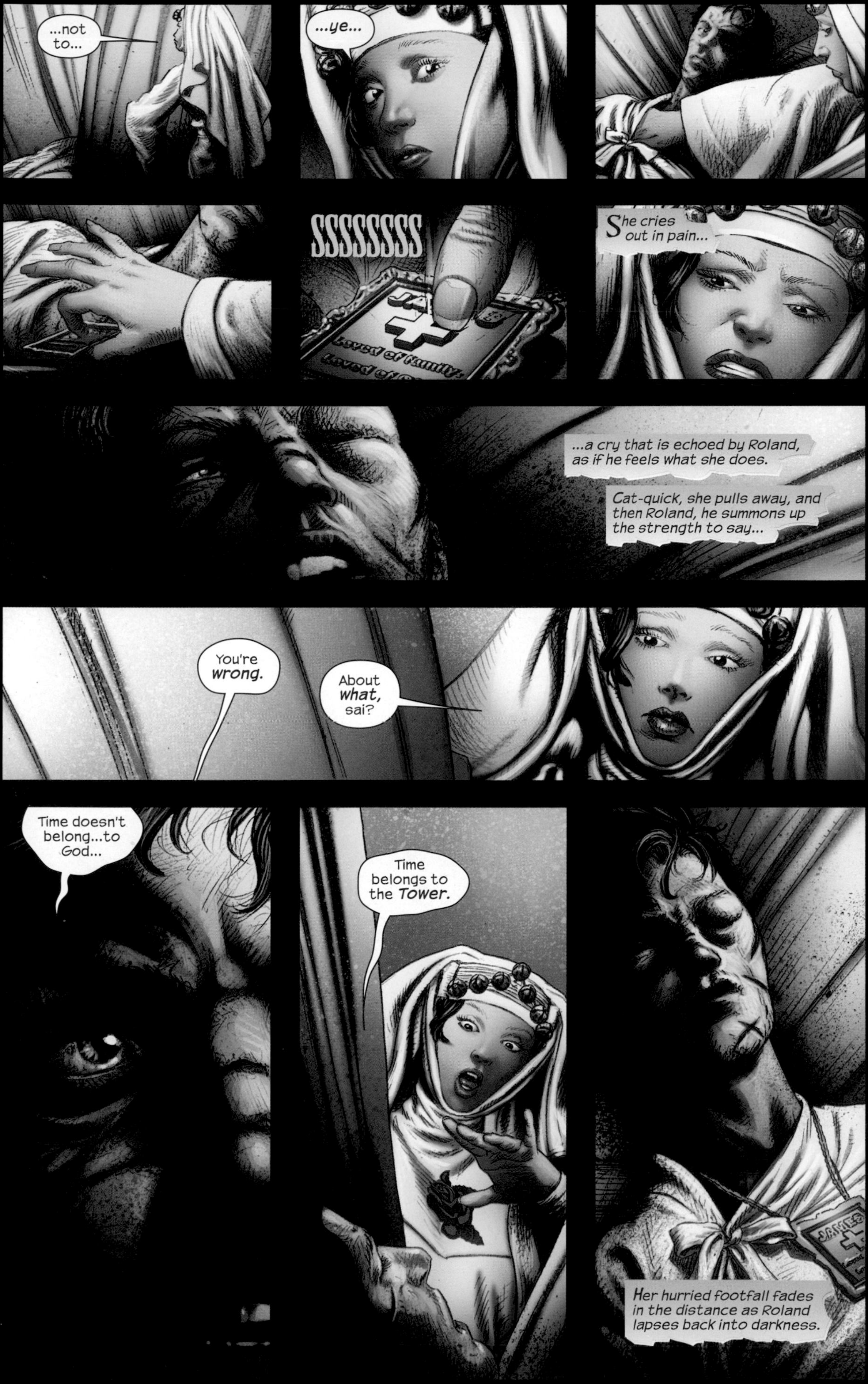
...not to...
...ye...
SSSSSSS
She cries out in pain...
...a cry that is echoed by Roland, as if he feels what she does.
Cat-quick, she pulls away, and then Roland, he summons up the strength to say...
You're wrong.
About what, sai?
Time doesn't belong...to God...
Time belongs to the Tower.
Her hurried footfall fades in the distance as Roland lapses back into darkness.

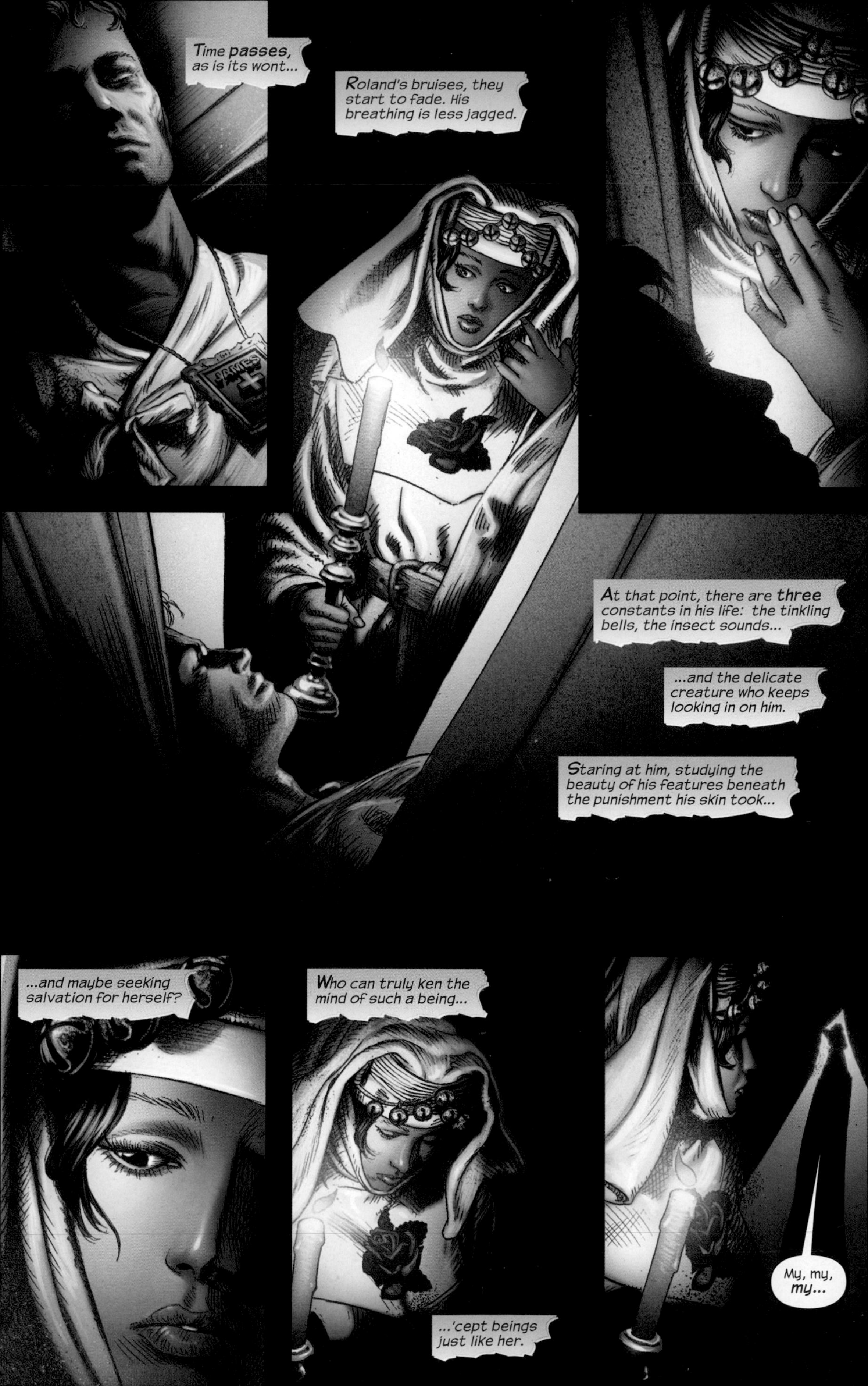
Time passes, as is its wont...
Roland's bruises, they start to fade. His breathing is less jagged.
At that point, there are three constants in his life: the tinkling bells, the insect sounds...
...and the delicate creature who keeps looking in on him.
Staring at him, studying the beauty of his features beneath the punishment his skin took...
...and maybe seeking salvation for herself?
Who can truly ken the mind of such a being...
...'cept beings just like her.
My, my, my...

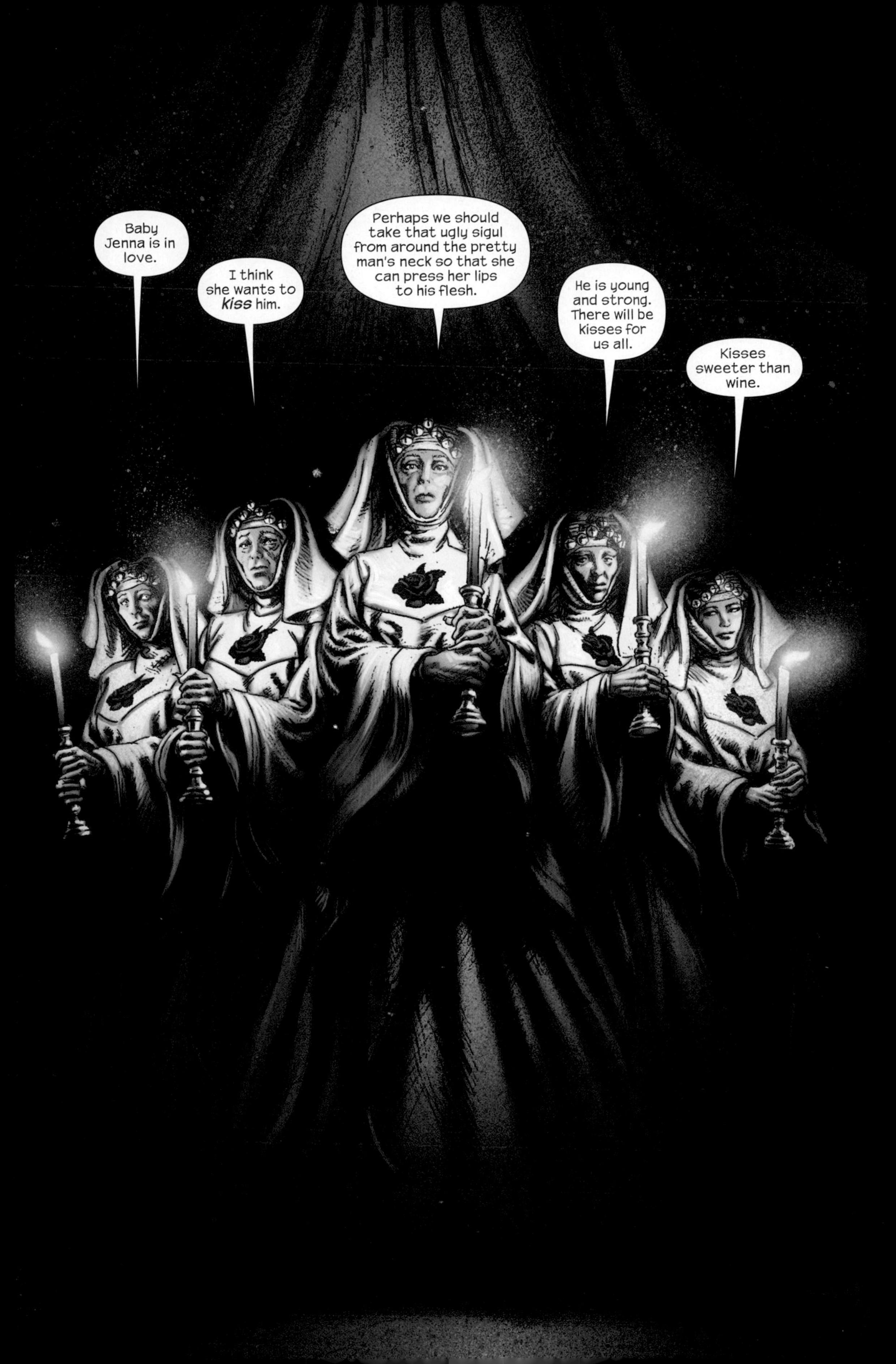
Baby Jenna is in love.
I think she wants to *kiss* him.
Perhaps we should take that ugly sigul from around the pretty man's neck so that she can press her lips to his flesh.
He is young and strong. There will be kisses for us all.
Kisses sweeter than wine.

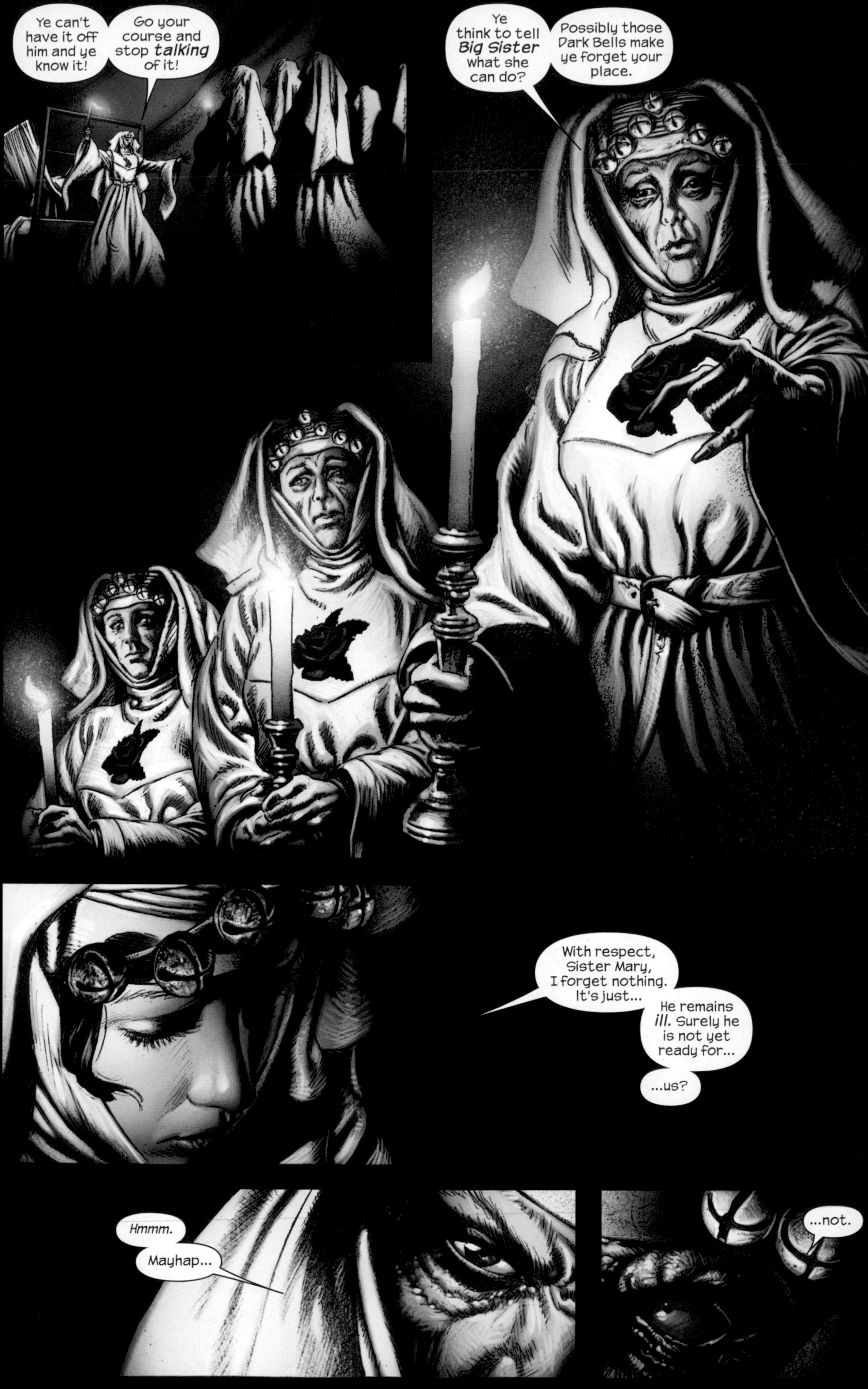
Ye can't have it off him and ye know it!
Go your course and stop *talking* of it!
Ye think to tell *Big Sister* what she can do?
Possibly those Dark Bells make ye forget your place.
With respect, Sister Mary, I forget nothing. It's just...
He remains *ill.* Surely he is not yet ready for...
...us?
*Hmmm.*
Mayhap...
...not.

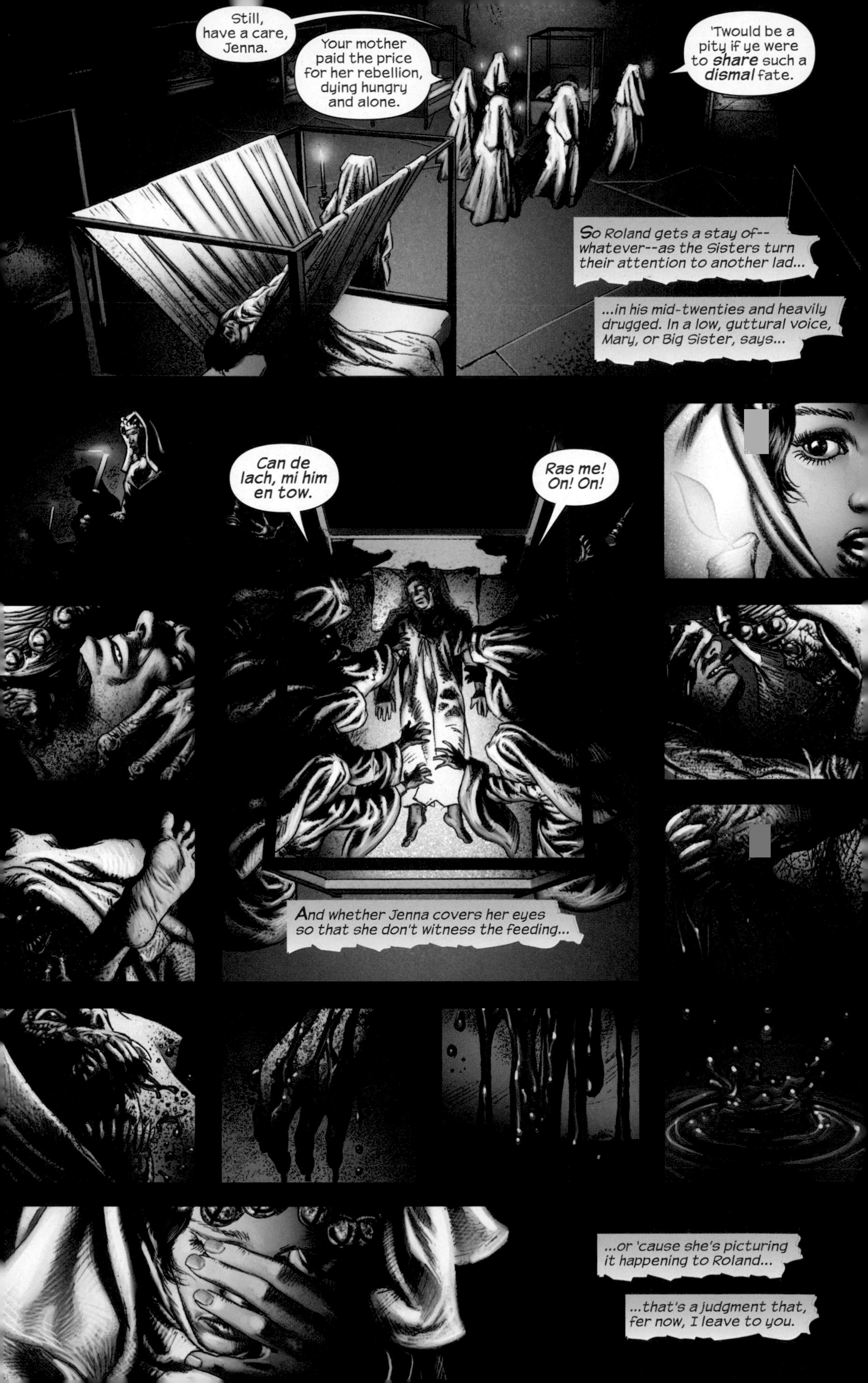
Still, have a care, Jenna.
Your mother paid the price for her rebellion, dying hungry and alone.
'Twould be a pity if ye were to **share** such a **dismal** fate.
So Roland gets a stay of--whatever--as the Sisters turn their attention to another lad...
...in his mid-twenties and heavily drugged. In a low, guttural voice, Mary, or Big Sister, says...
Can de lach, mi him en tow.
Ras me! On! On!
And whether Jenna covers her eyes so that she don't witness the feeding...
...or 'cause she's picturing it happening to Roland...
...that's a judgment that, fer now, I leave to you.

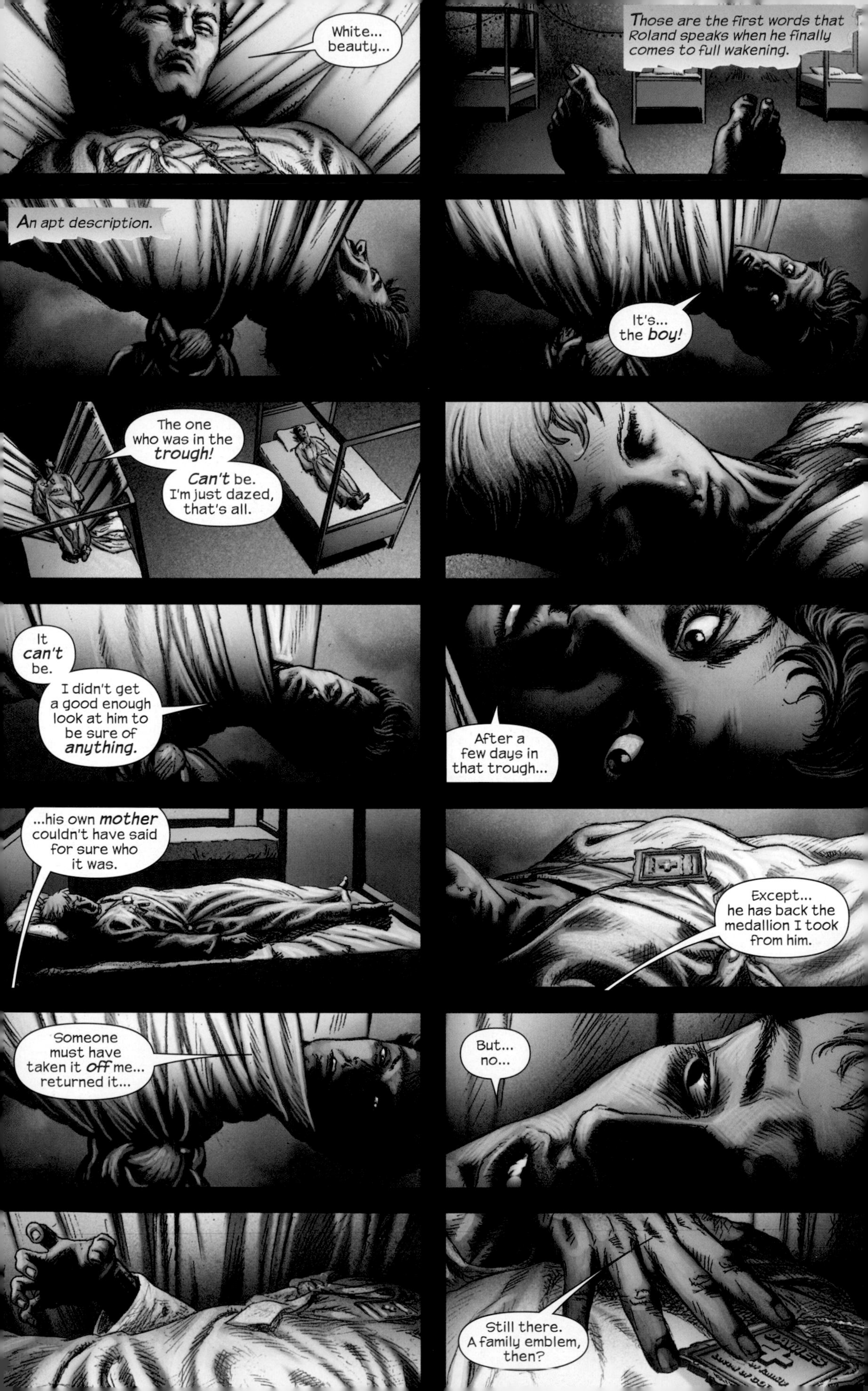
White... beauty...
Those are the first words that Roland speaks when he finally comes to full wakening.
An apt description.
It's... the *boy!*
The one who was in the *trough!*
*Can't* be. I'm just dazed, that's all.
It *can't* be.
I didn't get a good enough look at him to be sure of *anything.*
After a few days in that trough...
...his own *mother* couldn't have said for sure who it was.
Except... he has back the medallion I took from him.
Someone must have taken it *off* me... returned it...
But... no...
Still there. A family emblem, then?

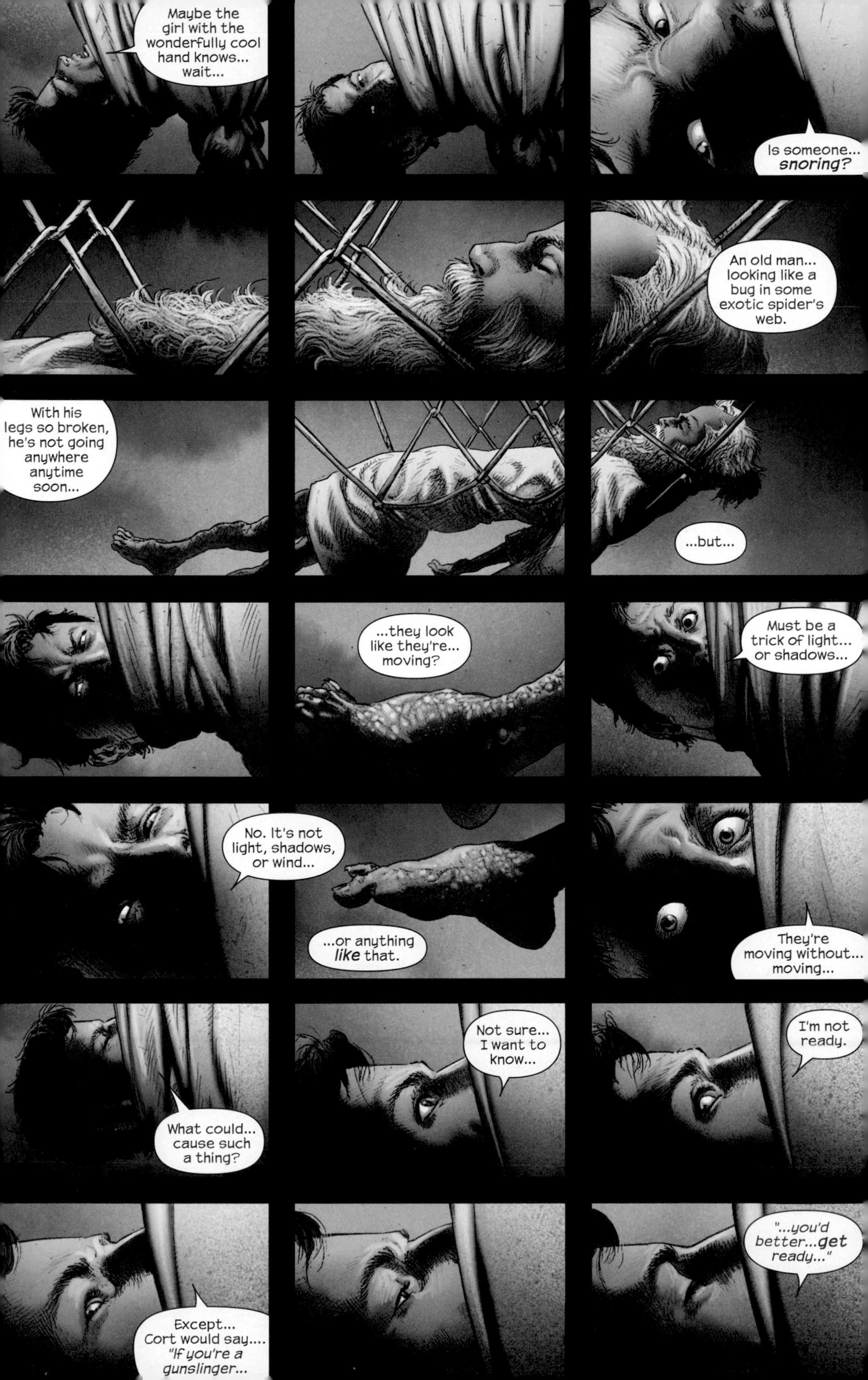

Maybe the girl with the wonderfully cool hand knows... wait...
Is someone... *snoring?*
An old man... looking like a bug in some exotic spider's web.
With his legs so broken, he's not going anywhere anytime soon...
...but...
...they look like they're... moving?
Must be a trick of light... or shadows...
No. It's not light, shadows, or wind...
...or anything *like* that.
They're moving without... moving...
What could... cause such a thing?
Not sure... I want to know...
I'm not ready.
Except... Cort would say.... *"If you're a gunslinger...*
*"...you'd better...**get** ready..."*

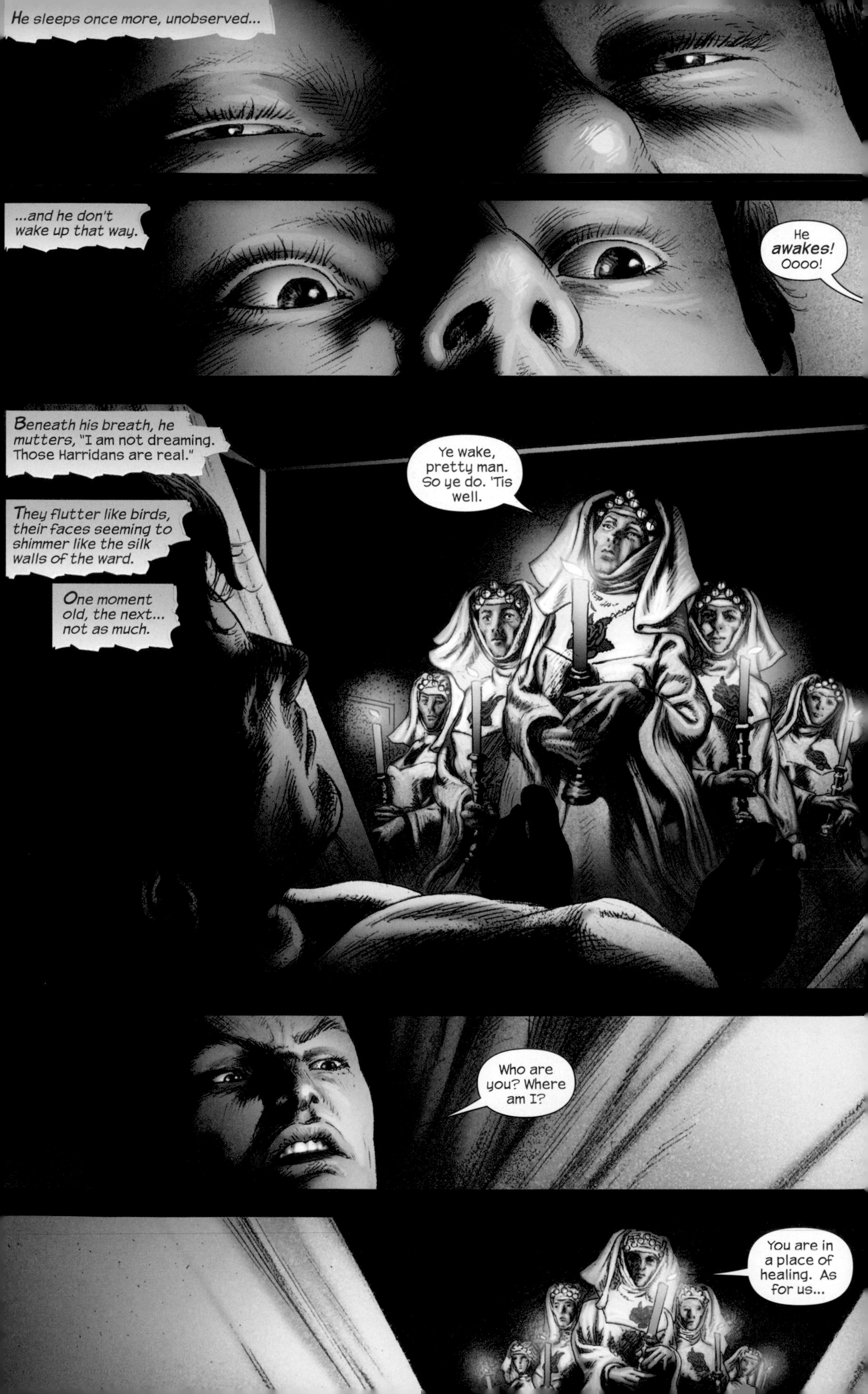

He sleeps once more, unobserved...
...and he don't wake up that way.
He *awakes!* Oooo!
Beneath his breath, he mutters, "I am not dreaming. Those Harridans are real."
Ye wake, pretty man. So ye do. 'Tis well.
They flutter like birds, their faces seeming to shimmer like the silk walls of the ward.
One moment old, the next... not as much.
Who are you? Where am I?
You are in a place of healing. As for us...

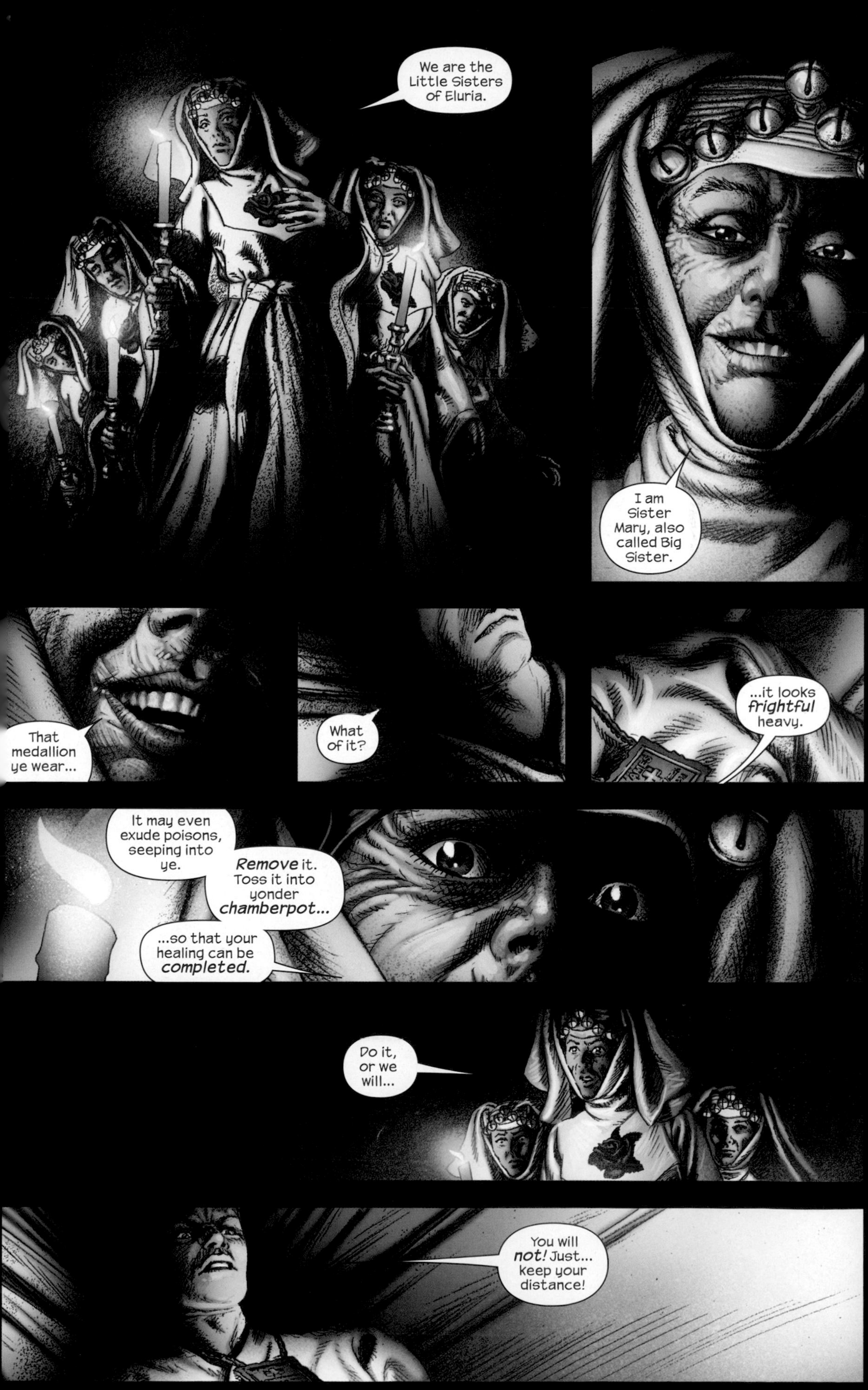
We are the Little Sisters of Eluria.
I am Sister Mary, also called Big Sister.
That medallion ye wear...
What of it?
...it looks *frightful* heavy.
It may even exude poisons, seeping into ye.
*Remove* it. Toss it into yonder *chamberpot...*
...so that your healing can be *completed.*
Do it, or we will...
You will *not!* Just... keep your distance!

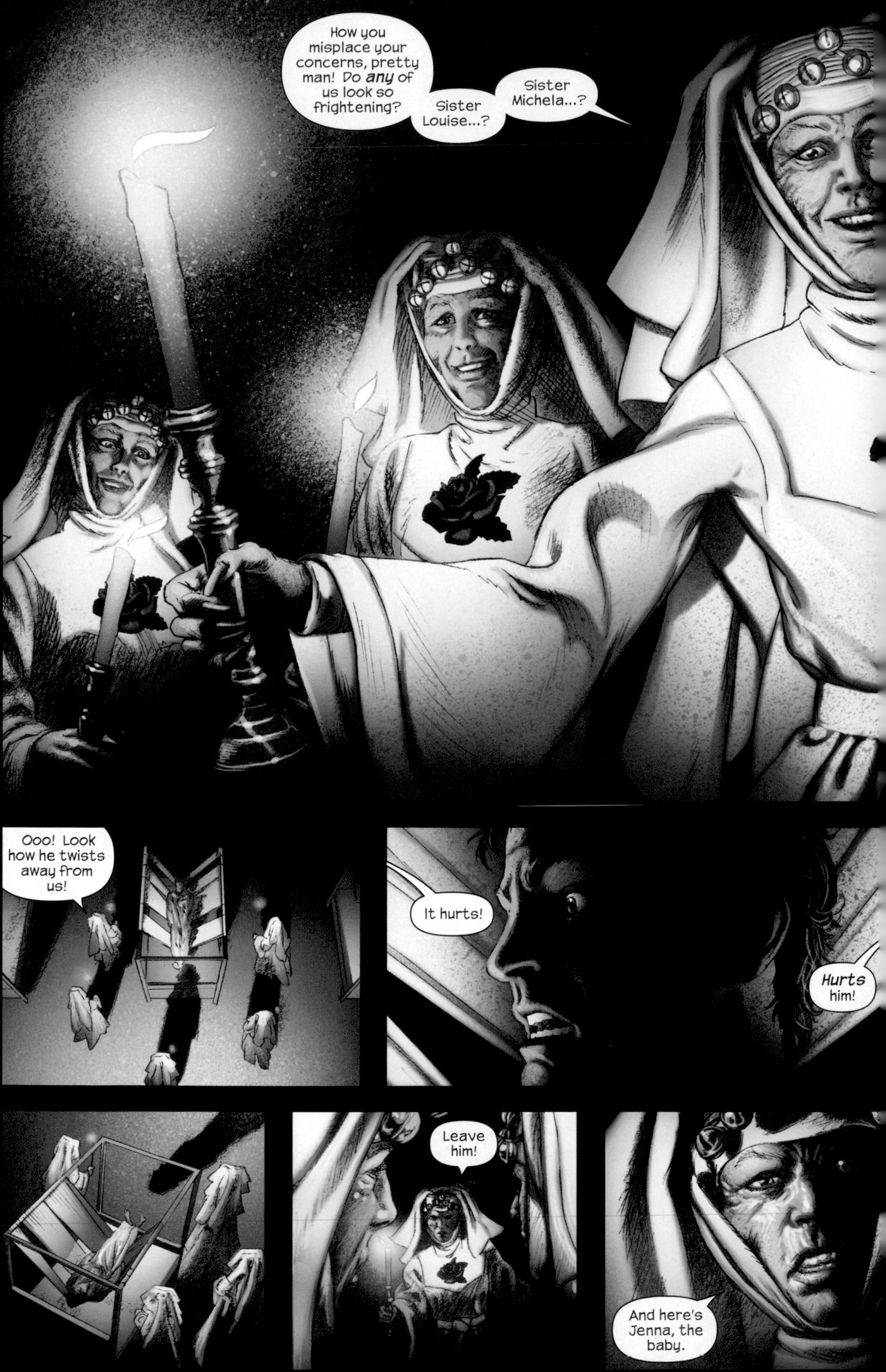
How you misplace your concerns, pretty man! Do *any* of us look so frightening?
Sister Louise...?
Sister Michela...?
Ooo! Look how he twists away from us!
It hurts!
*Hurts* him!
Leave him!
And here's Jenna, the baby.

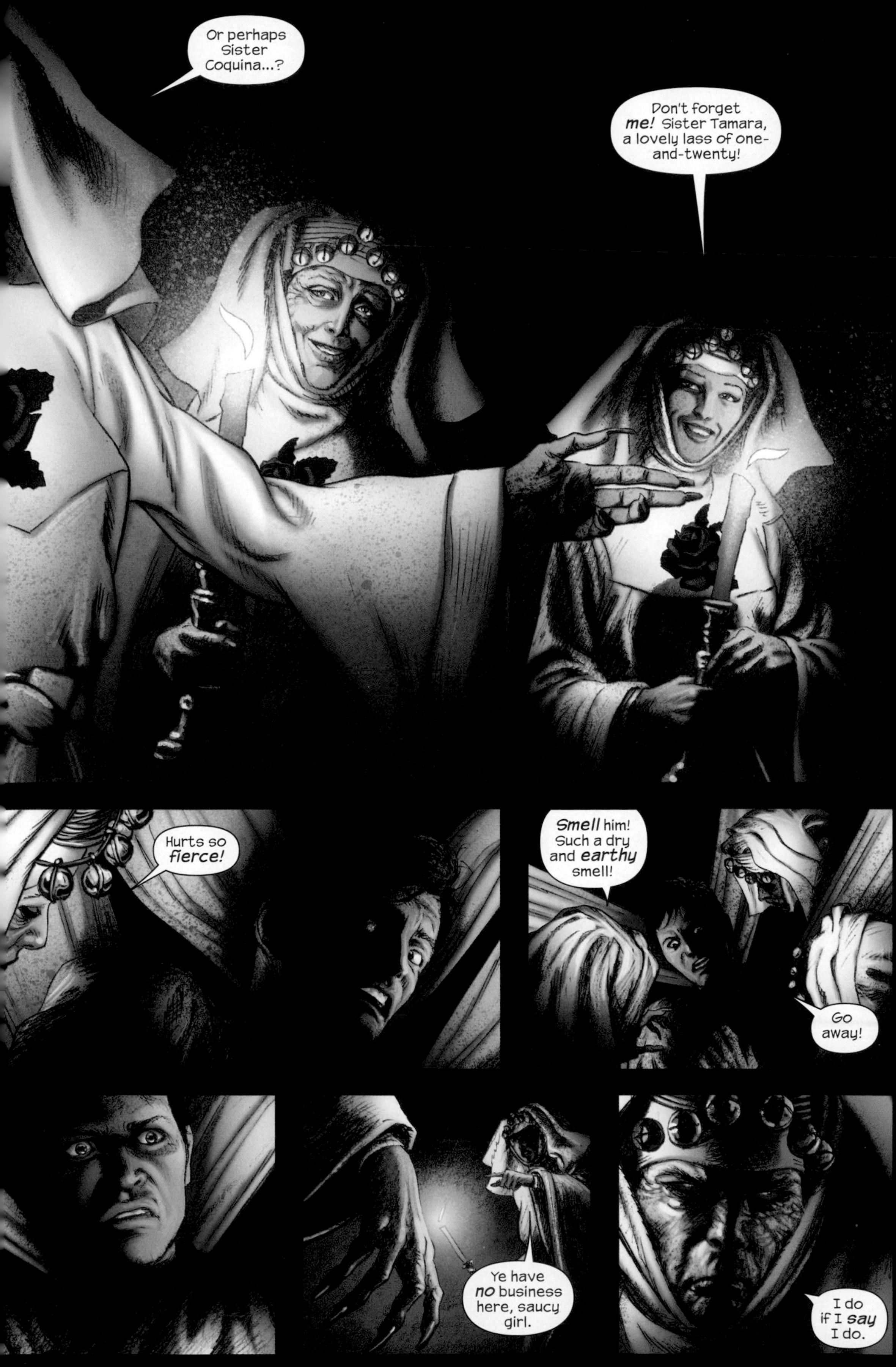
Or perhaps Sister Coquina...?
Don't forget *me!* Sister Tamara, a lovely lass of one-and-twenty!
Hurts so *fierce!*
*Smell* him! Such a dry and *earthy* smell!
Go away!
Ye have *no* business here, saucy girl.
I do if I *say* I do.

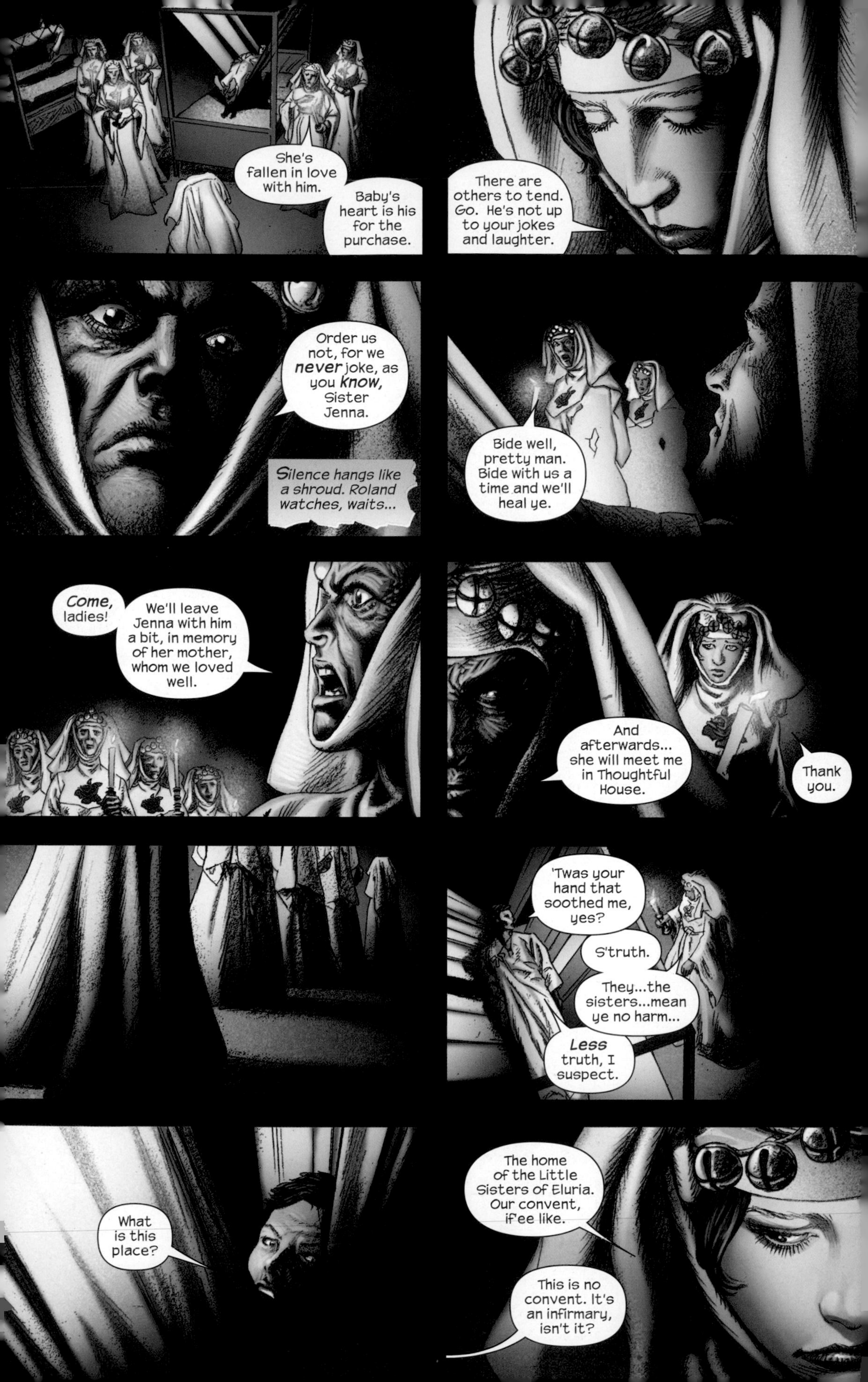
She's fallen in love with him.
Baby's heart is his for the purchase.
There are others to tend. Go. He's not up to your jokes and laughter.
Order us not, for we **never** joke, as you **know,** Sister Jenna.
*Silence hangs like a shroud. Roland watches, waits...*
Bide well, pretty man. Bide with us a time and we'll heal ye.
**Come,** ladies!
We'll leave Jenna with him a bit, in memory of her mother, whom we loved well.
And afterwards... she will meet me in Thoughtful House.
Thank you.
'Twas your hand that soothed me, yes?
S'truth.
They...the sisters...mean ye no harm...
**Less** truth, I suspect.
What is this place?
The home of the Little Sisters of Eluria. Our convent, if'ee like.
This is no convent. It's an infirmary, isn't it?

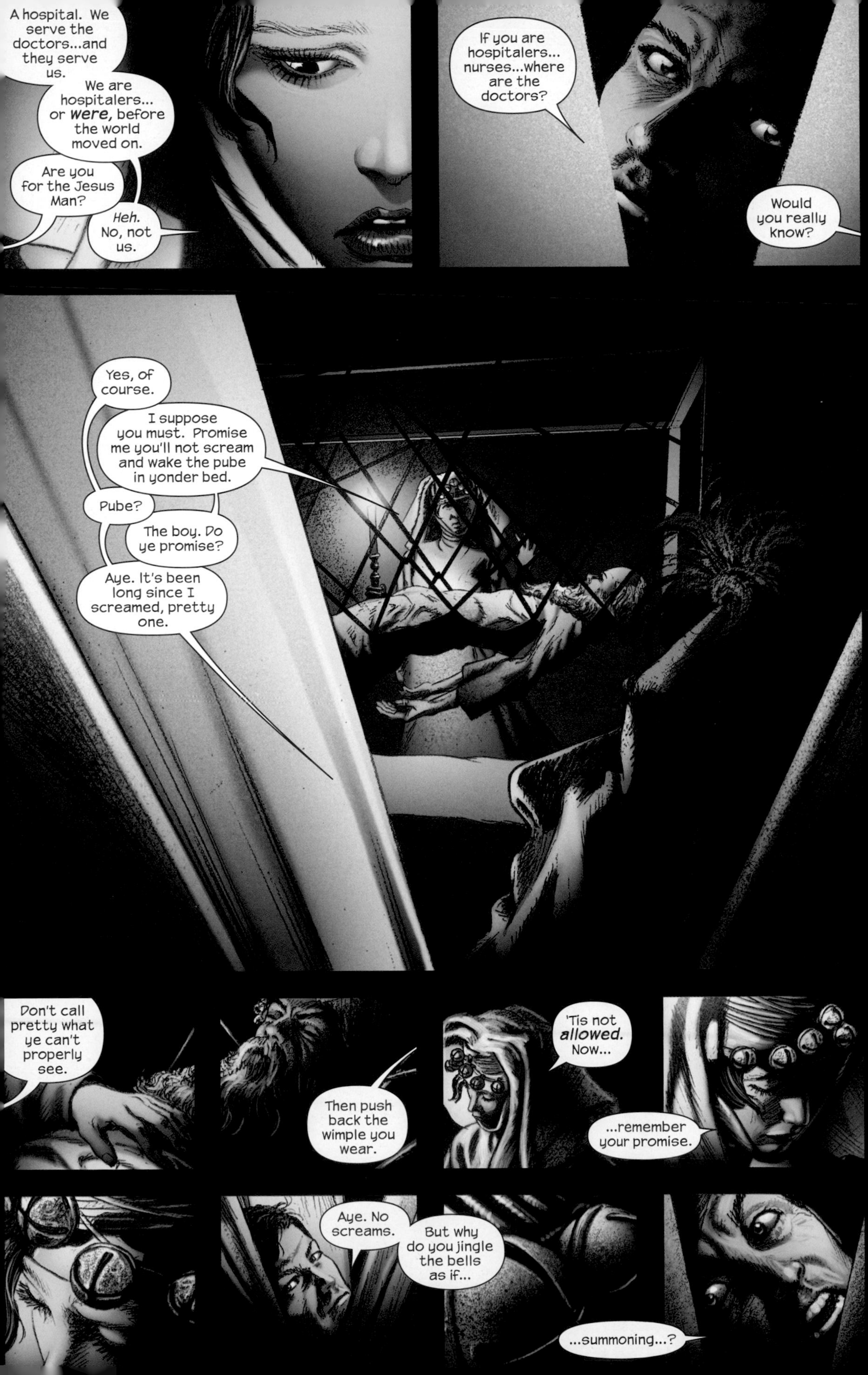
A hospital. We serve the doctors...and they serve us.
We are hospitalers... or *were,* before the world moved on.
Are you for the Jesus Man?
*Heh.* No, not us.
If you are hospitalers... nurses...where are the doctors?
Would you really know?
Yes, of course.
I suppose you must. Promise me you'll not scream and wake the pube in yonder bed.
Pube?
The boy. Do ye promise?
Aye. It's been long since I screamed, pretty one.
Don't call pretty what ye can't properly see.
Then push back the wimple you wear.
'Tis not *allowed.* Now...
...remember your promise.
Aye. No screams.
But why do you jingle the bells as if...
...summoning...?

What happens next almost **does** jerk a scream from him.

He has to bite his lip against it.

A wave of black bugs, singing fiercely...

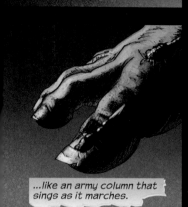

...like an army column that sings as it marches.

The bearded man does **not** sing.

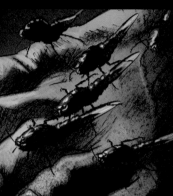

But as the bugs coat his twisted legs, he shudders and groans...

...and the young woman puts her hand on his brow and soothes him.

And in time, the bugs return to the shadows that spat them out when the bells called.

Ye did well. Yet I see how ye feel; it's on your face.

The "doctors..."

Yes. Their power is very great, but...

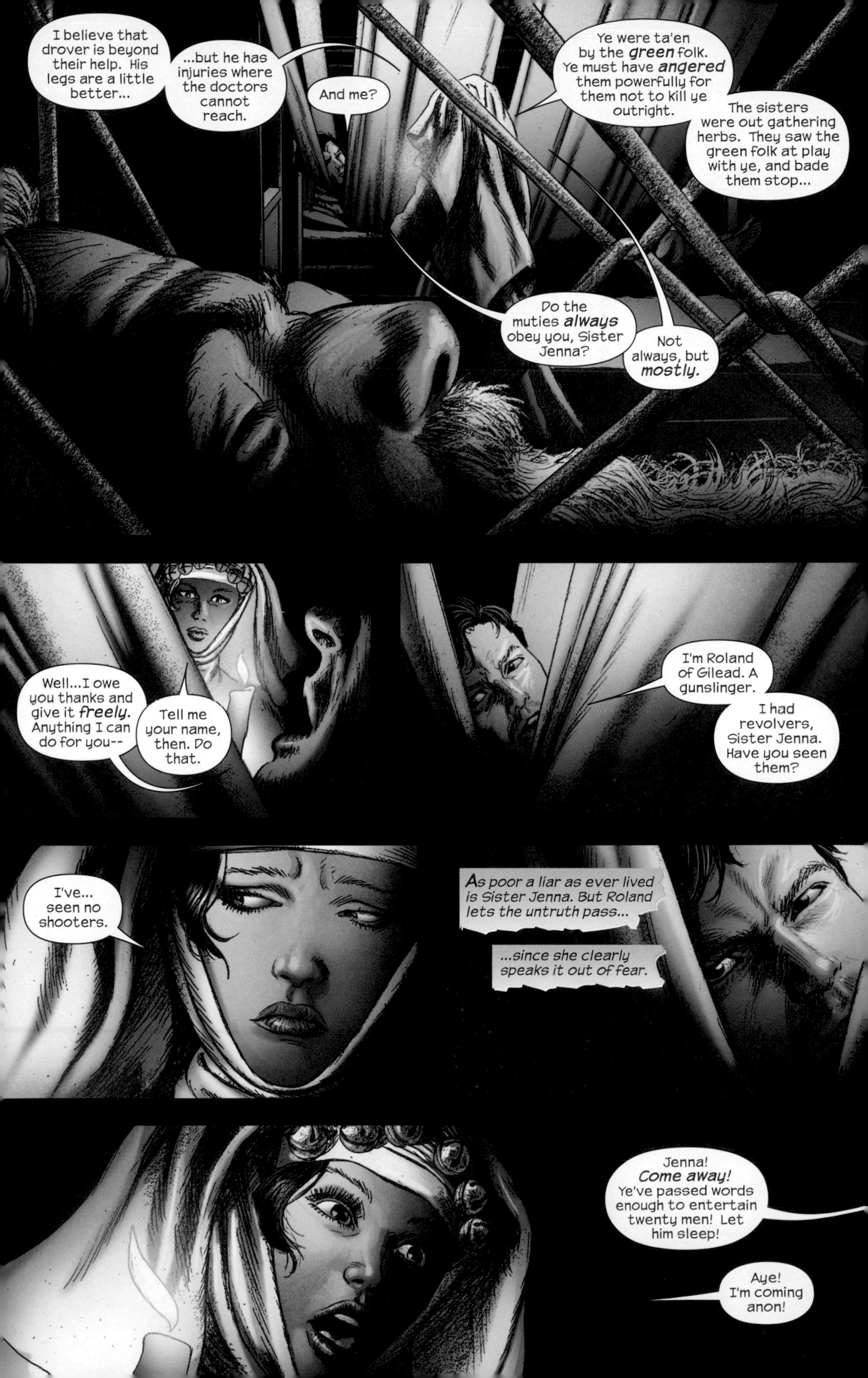

I believe that drover is beyond their help. His legs are a little better...
...but he has injuries where the doctors cannot reach.
And me?
Ye were ta'en by the green folk. Ye must have angered them powerfully for them not to kill ye outright.
The sisters were out gathering herbs. They saw the green folk at play with ye, and bade them stop...
Do the muties always obey you, Sister Jenna?
Not always, but mostly.
Well...I owe you thanks and give it freely. Anything I can do for you--
Tell me your name, then. Do that.
I'm Roland of Gilead. A gunslinger.
I had revolvers, Sister Jenna. Have you seen them?
I've... seen no shooters.
As poor a liar as ever lived is Sister Jenna. But Roland lets the untruth pass...
...since she clearly speaks it out of fear.
Jenna! Come away! Ye've passed words enough to entertain twenty men! Let him sleep!
Aye! I'm coming anon!

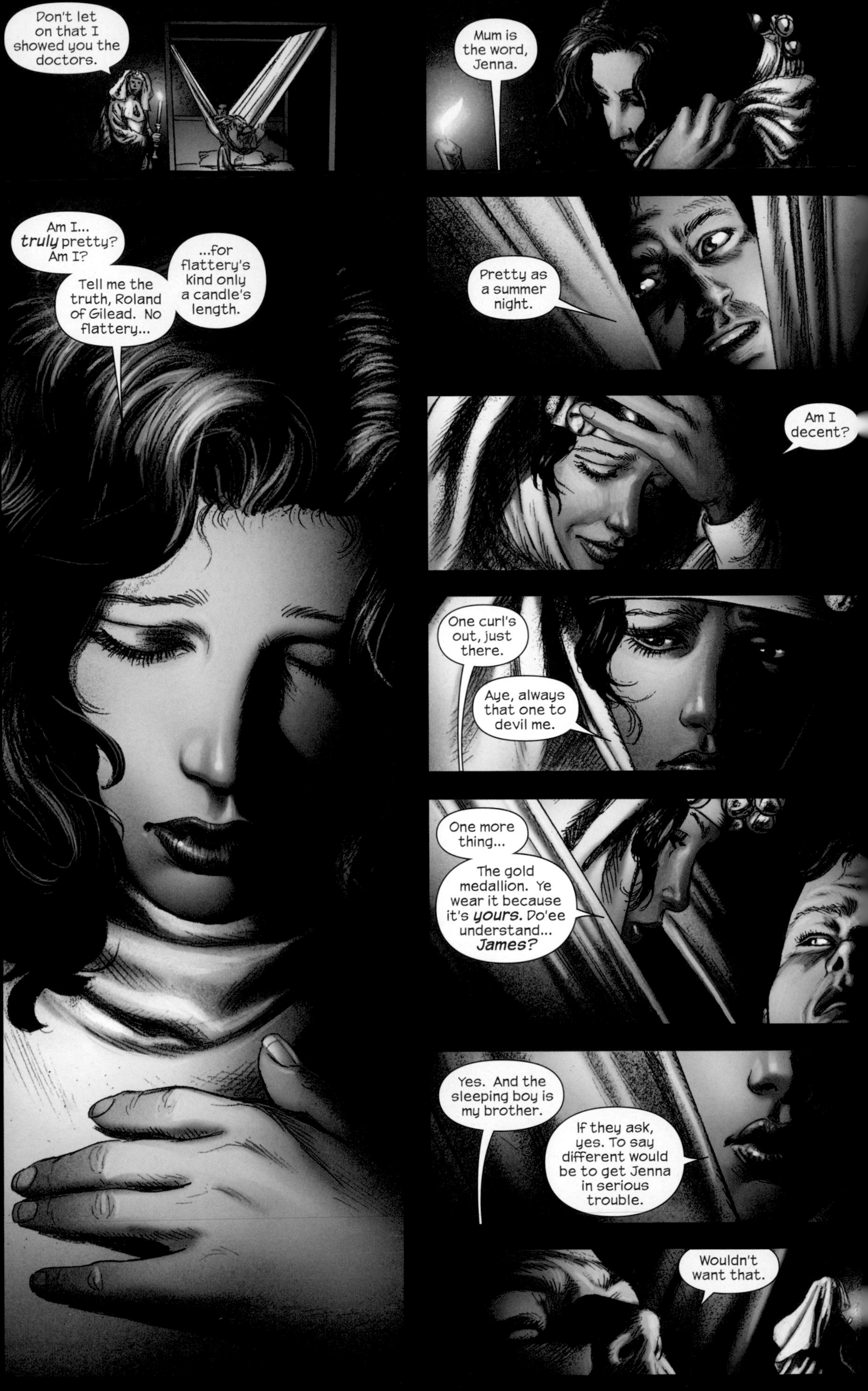

Don't let on that I showed you the doctors.
Mum is the word, Jenna.
Am I... *truly* pretty? Am I?
Tell me the truth, Roland of Gilead. No flattery...
...for flattery's kind only a candle's length.
Pretty as a summer night.
Am I decent?
One curl's out, just there.
Aye, always that one to devil me.
One more thing...
The gold medallion. Ye wear it because it's *yours.* Do'ee understand... *James?*
Yes. And the sleeping boy is my brother.
If they ask, yes. To say different would be to get Jenna in serious trouble.
Wouldn't want that.

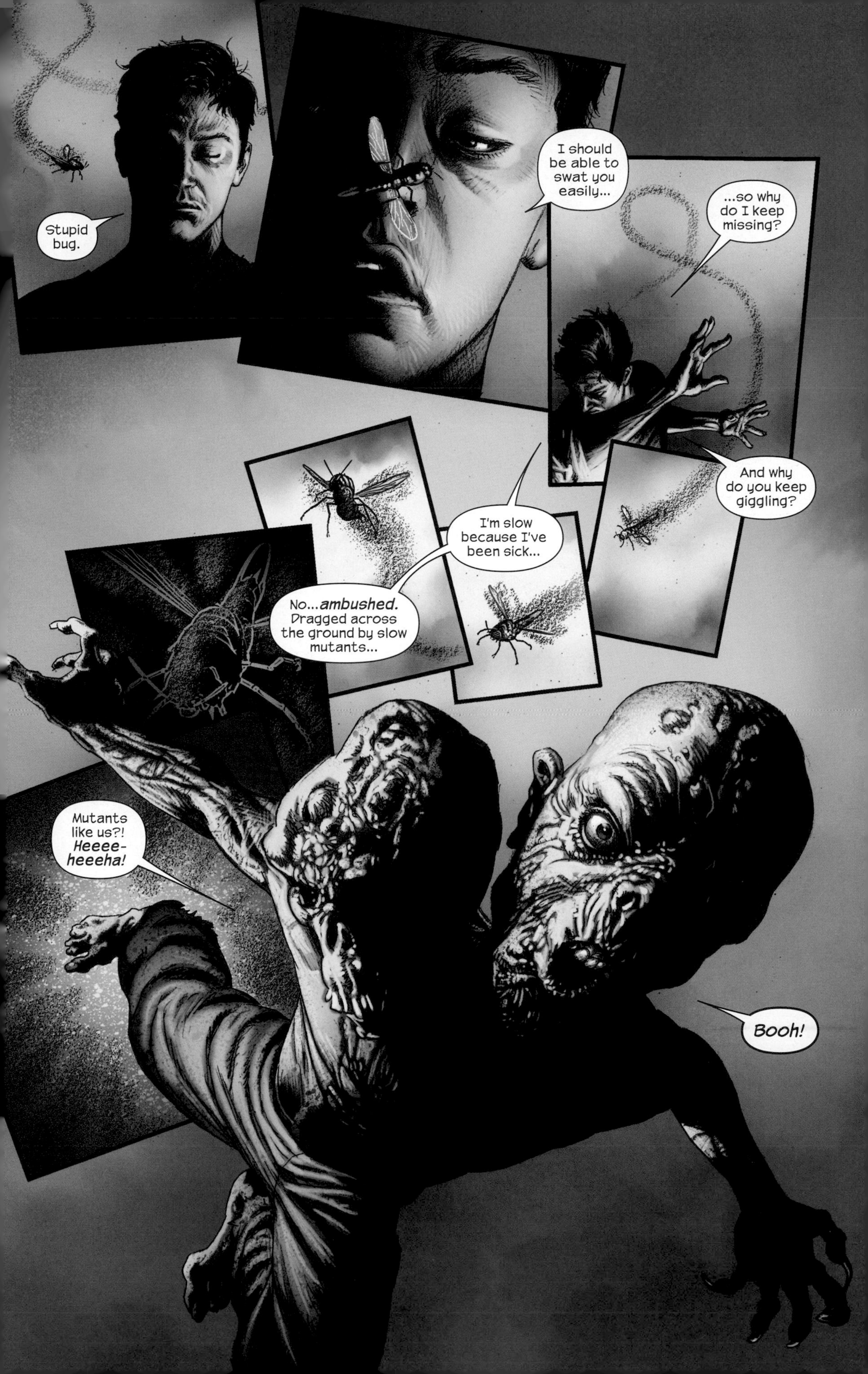
Stupid bug.
I should be able to swat you easily...
...so why do I keep missing?
And why do you keep giggling?
I'm slow because I've been sick...
No...*ambushed.* Dragged across the ground by slow mutants...
Mutants like us?! *Heeee-heeeha!*
*Booh!*

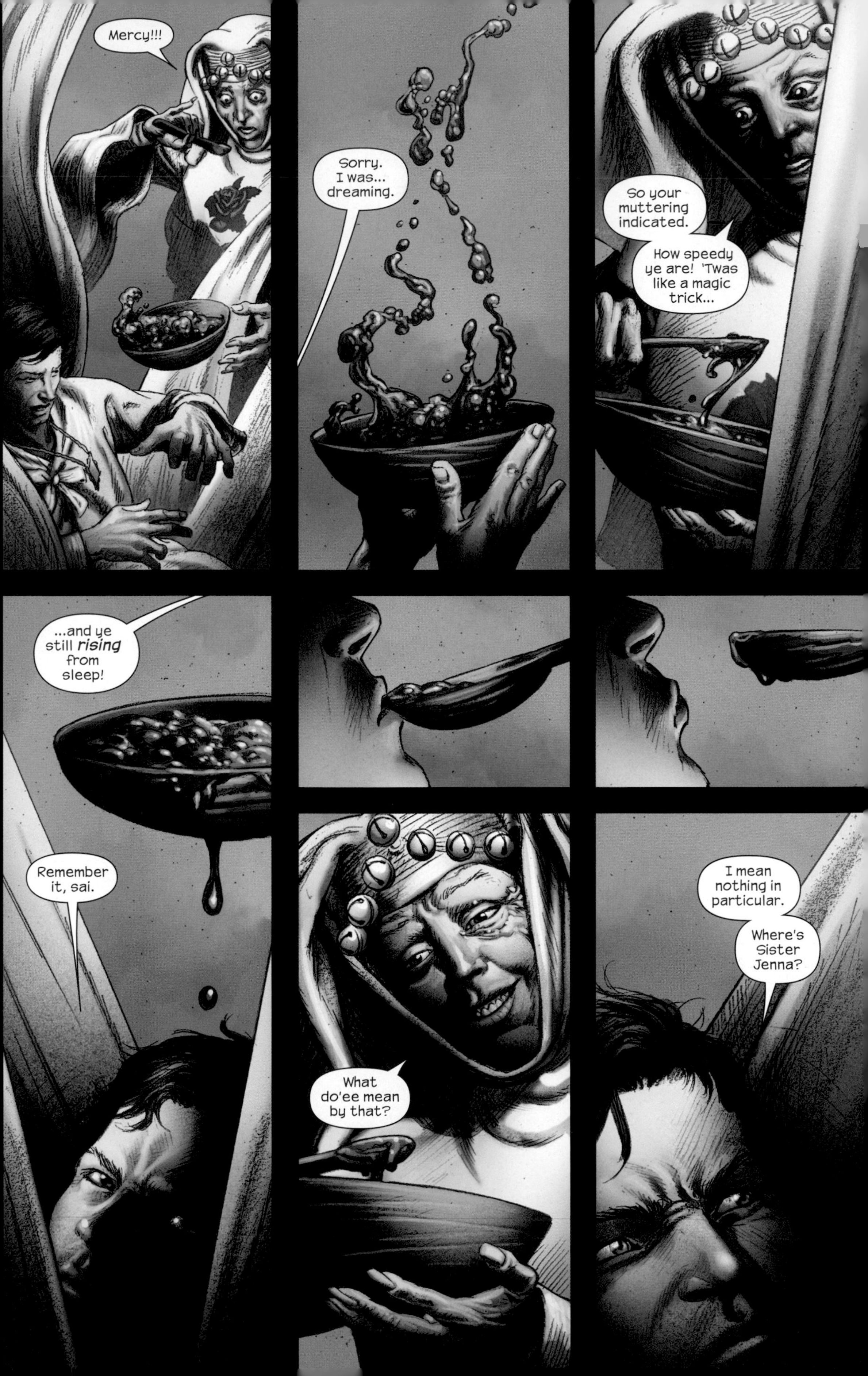
Mercy!!!
Sorry. I was... dreaming.
So your muttering indicated.
How speedy ye are! 'Twas like a magic trick...
...and ye still *rising* from sleep!
Remember it, sai.
What do'ee mean by that?
I mean nothing in particular.
Where's Sister Jenna?

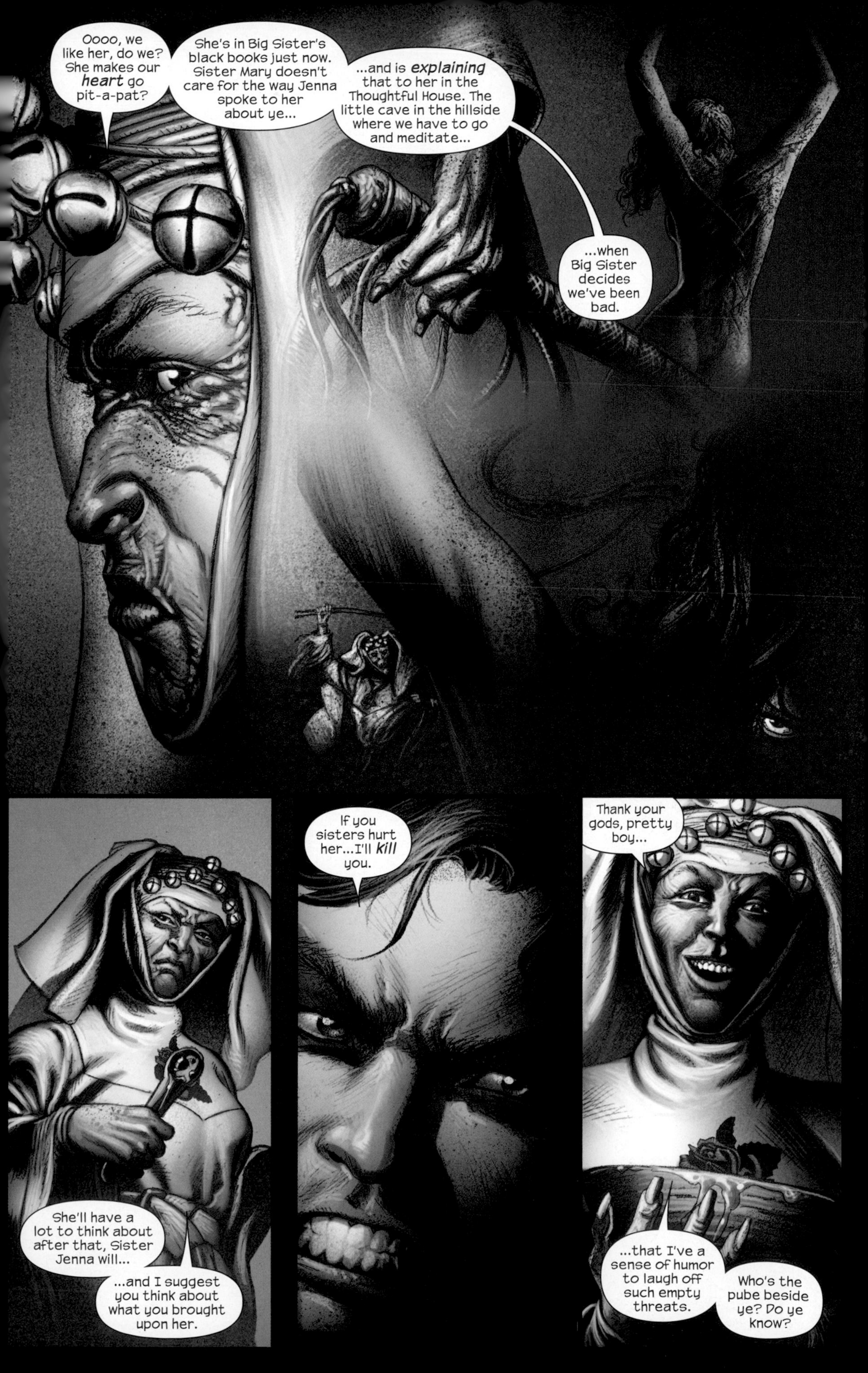
Oooo, we like her, do we? She makes our *heart* go pit-a-pat?
She's in Big Sister's black books just now. Sister Mary doesn't care for the way Jenna spoke to her about ye...
...and is *explaining* that to her in the Thoughtful House. The little cave in the hillside where we have to go and meditate...
...when Big Sister decides we've been bad.
She'll have a lot to think about after that, Sister Jenna will...
...and I suggest you think about what you brought upon her.
If you sisters hurt her...I'll *kill* you.
Thank your gods, pretty boy...
...that I've a sense of humor to laugh off such empty threats.
Who's the pube beside ye? Do ye know?

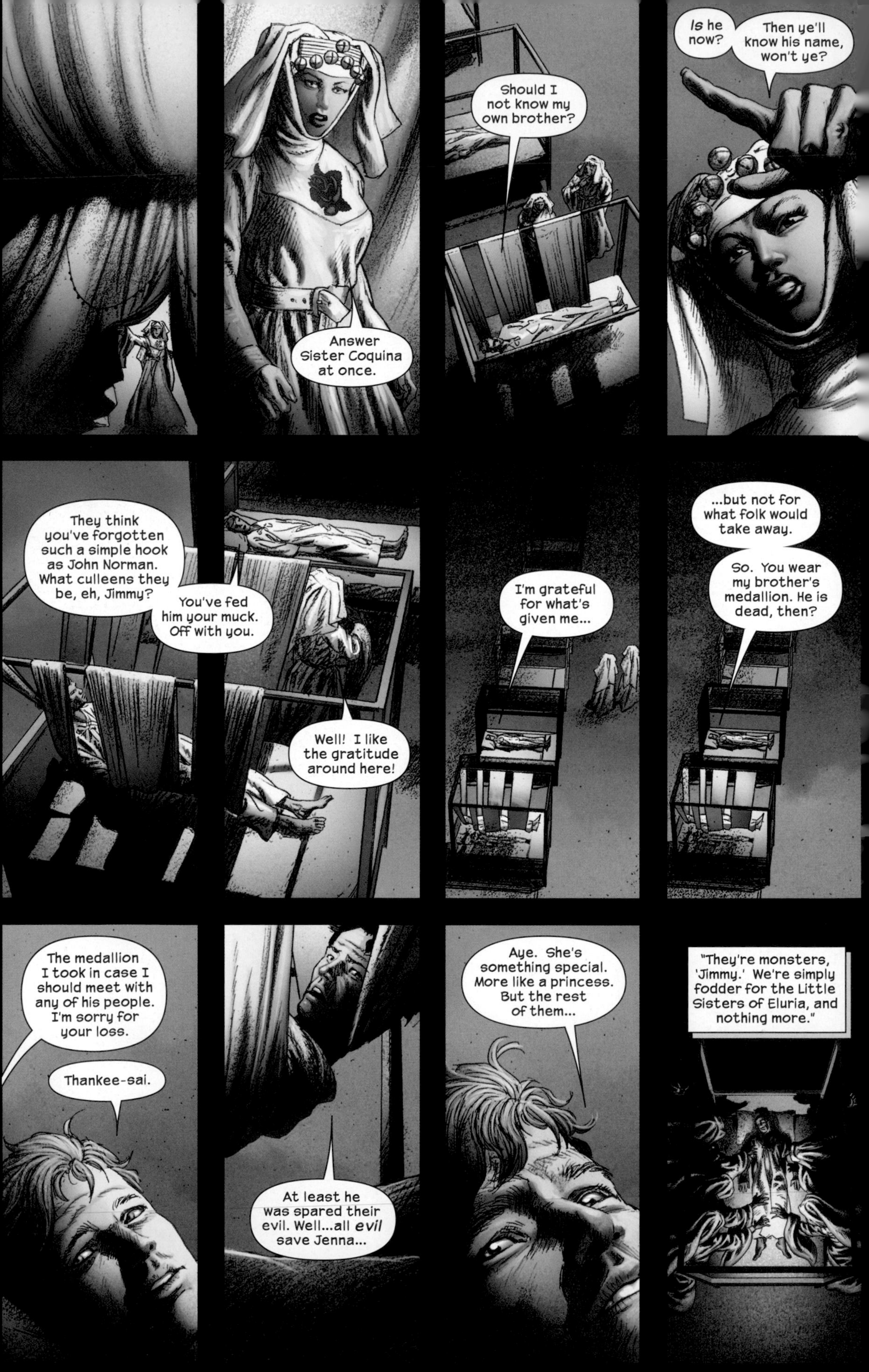
Answer Sister Coquina at once.
Should I not know my own brother?
Is he now?
Then ye'll know his name, won't ye?
They think you've forgotten such a simple hook as John Norman. What culleens they be, eh, Jimmy?
You've fed him your muck. Off with you.
Well! I like the gratitude around here!
I'm grateful for what's given me...
...but not for what folk would take away.
So. You wear my brother's medallion. He is dead, then?
The medallion I took in case I should meet with any of his people. I'm sorry for your loss.
Thankee-sai.
At least he was spared their evil. Well...all evil save Jenna...
Aye. She's something special. More like a princess. But the rest of them...
"They're monsters, 'Jimmy.' We're simply fodder for the Little Sisters of Eluria, and nothing more."

# STEPHEN KING

## THE DARK TOWER
### ~ THE GUNSLINGER ~

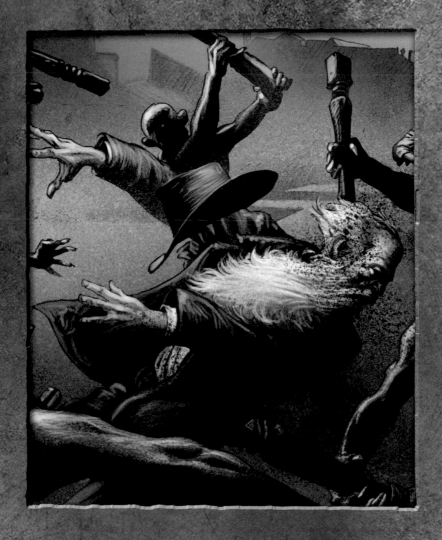

# THE LITTLE SISTERS
# OF ELURIA

# CHAPTER THREE

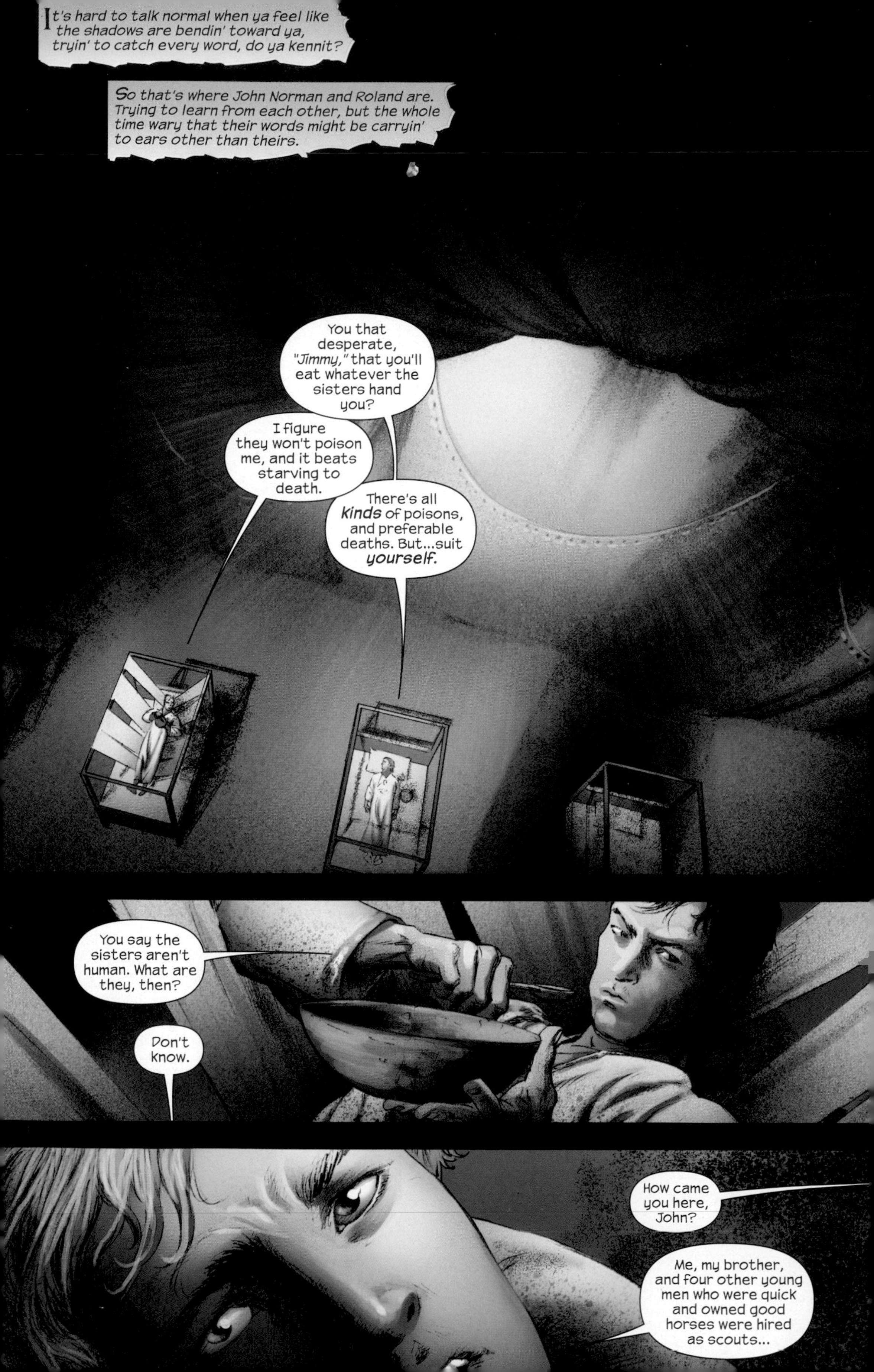
It's hard to talk normal when ya feel like the shadows are bendin' toward ya, tryin' to catch every word, do ya kennit?
So that's where John Norman and Roland are. Trying to learn from each other, but the whole time wary that their words might be carryin' to ears other than theirs.
You that desperate, "Jimmy," that you'll eat whatever the sisters hand you?
I figure they won't poison me, and it beats starving to death.
There's all kinds of poisons, and preferable deaths. But...suit yourself.
You say the sisters aren't human. What are they, then?
Don't know.
How came you here, John?
Me, my brother, and four other young men who were quick and owned good horses were hired as scouts...

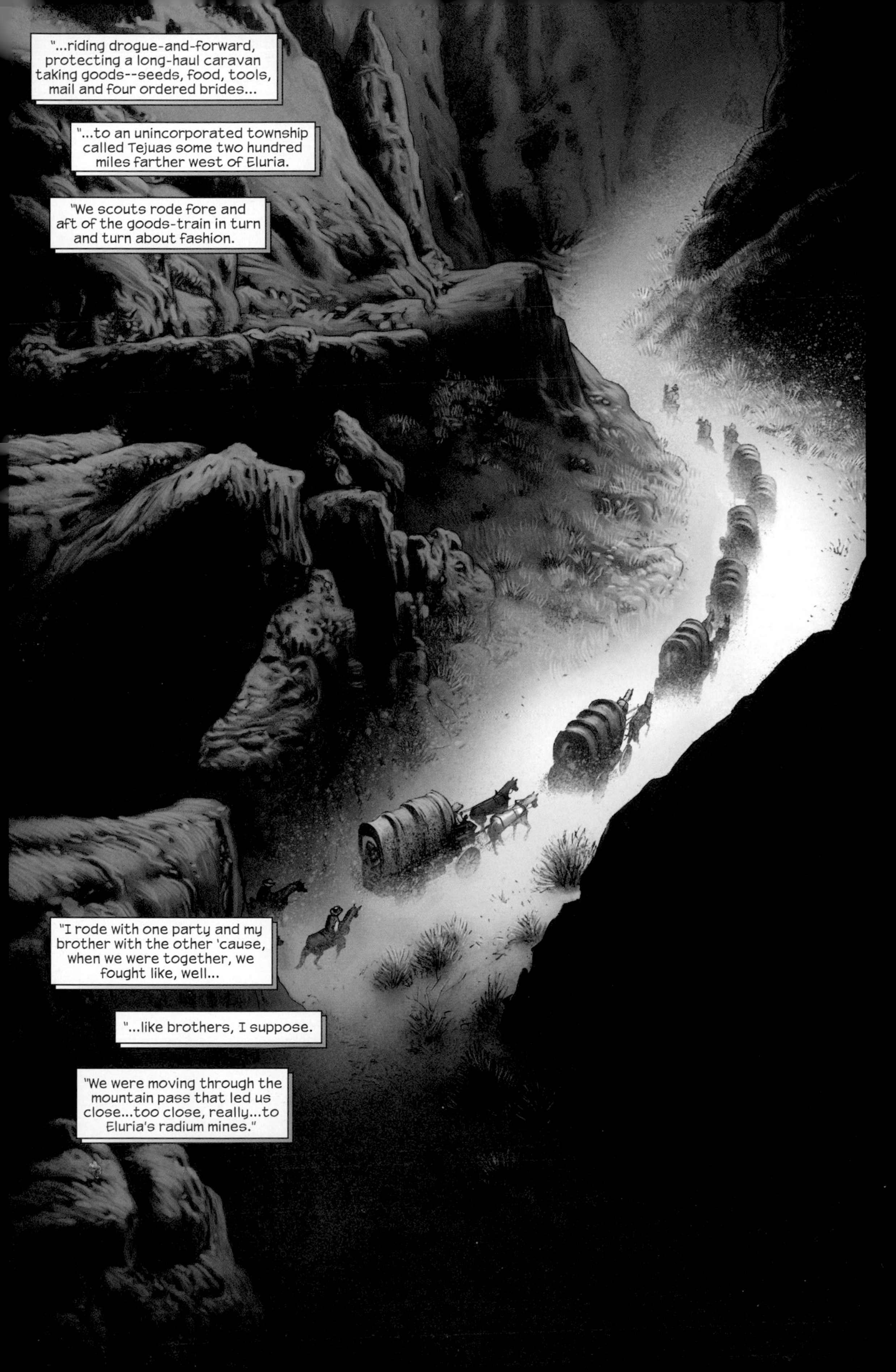
"...riding drogue-and-forward, protecting a long-haul caravan taking goods--seeds, food, tools, mail and four ordered brides...
"...to an unincorporated township called Tejuas some two hundred miles farther west of Eluria.
"We scouts rode fore and aft of the goods-train in turn and turn about fashion.
"I rode with one party and my brother with the other 'cause, when we were together, we fought like, well...
"...like brothers, I suppose.
"We were moving through the mountain pass that led us close...too close, really...to Eluria's radium mines."

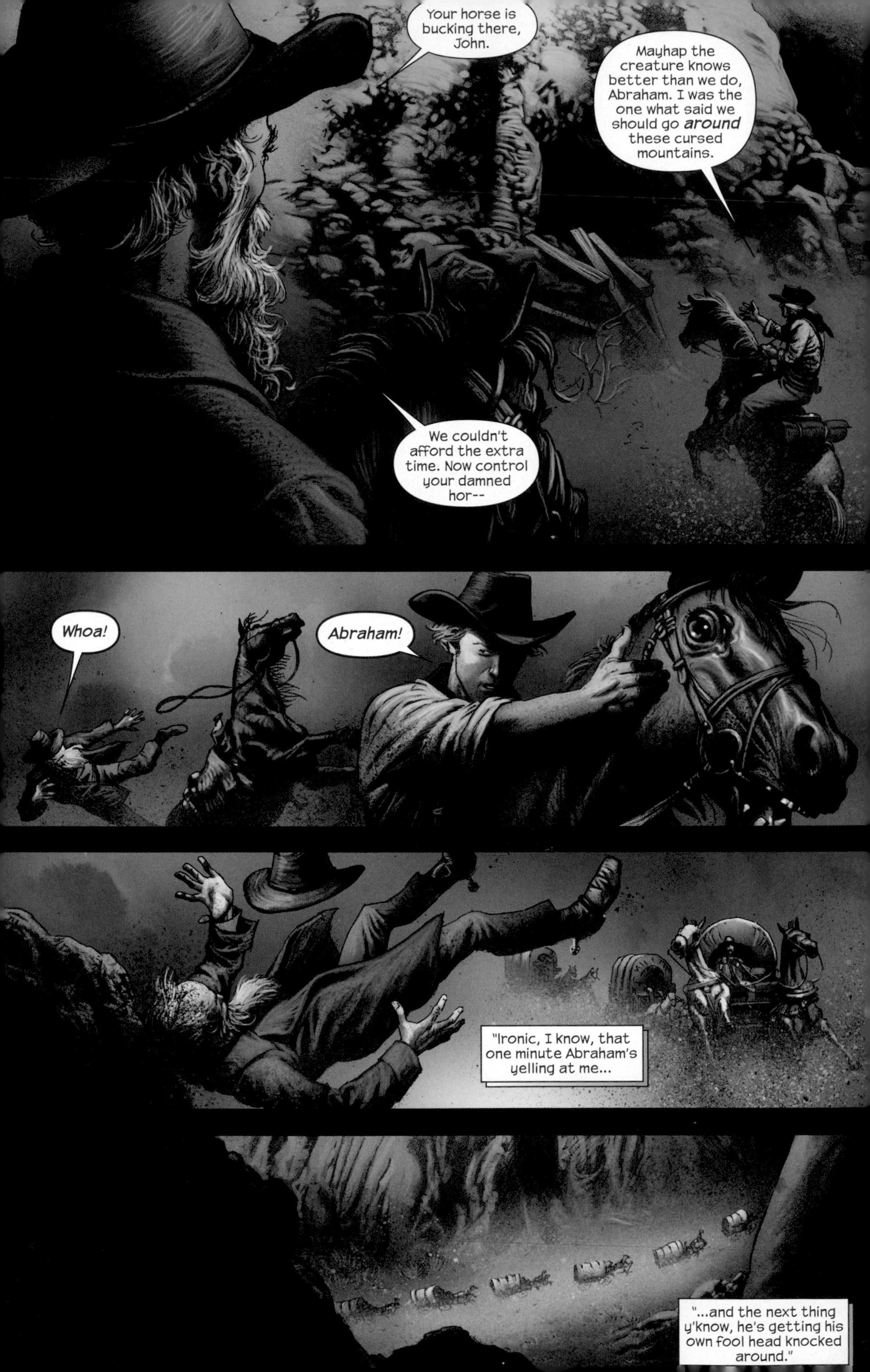
Your horse is bucking there, John.
Mayhap the creature knows better than we do, Abraham. I was the one what said we should go *around* these cursed mountains.
We couldn't afford the extra time. Now control your damned hor--
Whoa!
Abraham!
"Ironic, I know, that one minute Abraham's yelling at me...
"...and the next thing y'know, he's getting his own fool head knocked around."

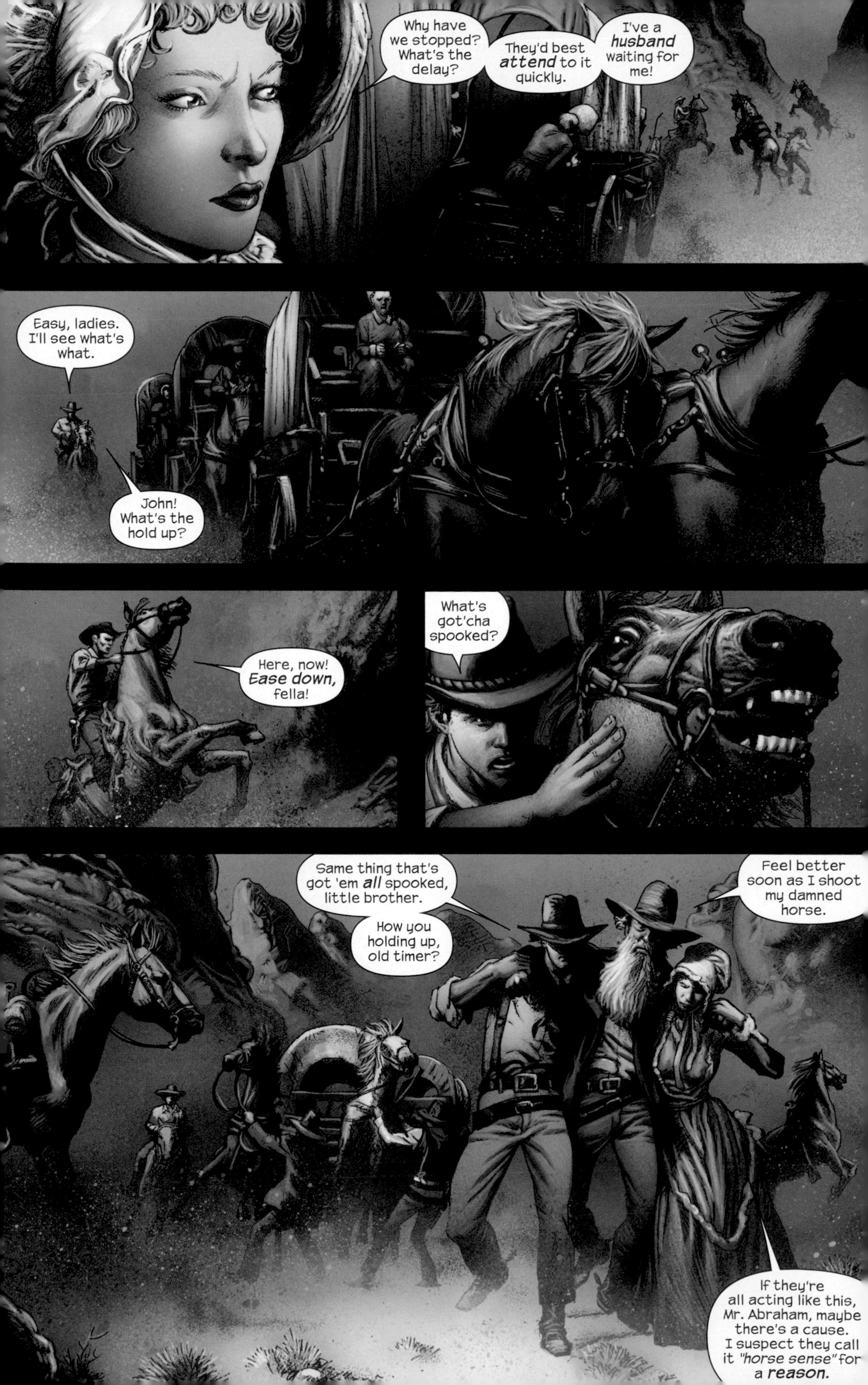
Why have we stopped? What's the delay?
They'd best attend to it quickly.
I've a husband waiting for me!
Easy, ladies. I'll see what's what.
John! What's the hold up?
Here, now! Ease down, fella!
What's got'cha spooked?
Same thing that's got 'em all spooked, little brother.
How you holding up, old timer?
Feel better soon as I shoot my damned horse.
If they're all acting like this, Mr. Abraham, maybe there's a cause. I suspect they call it "horse sense" for a reason.

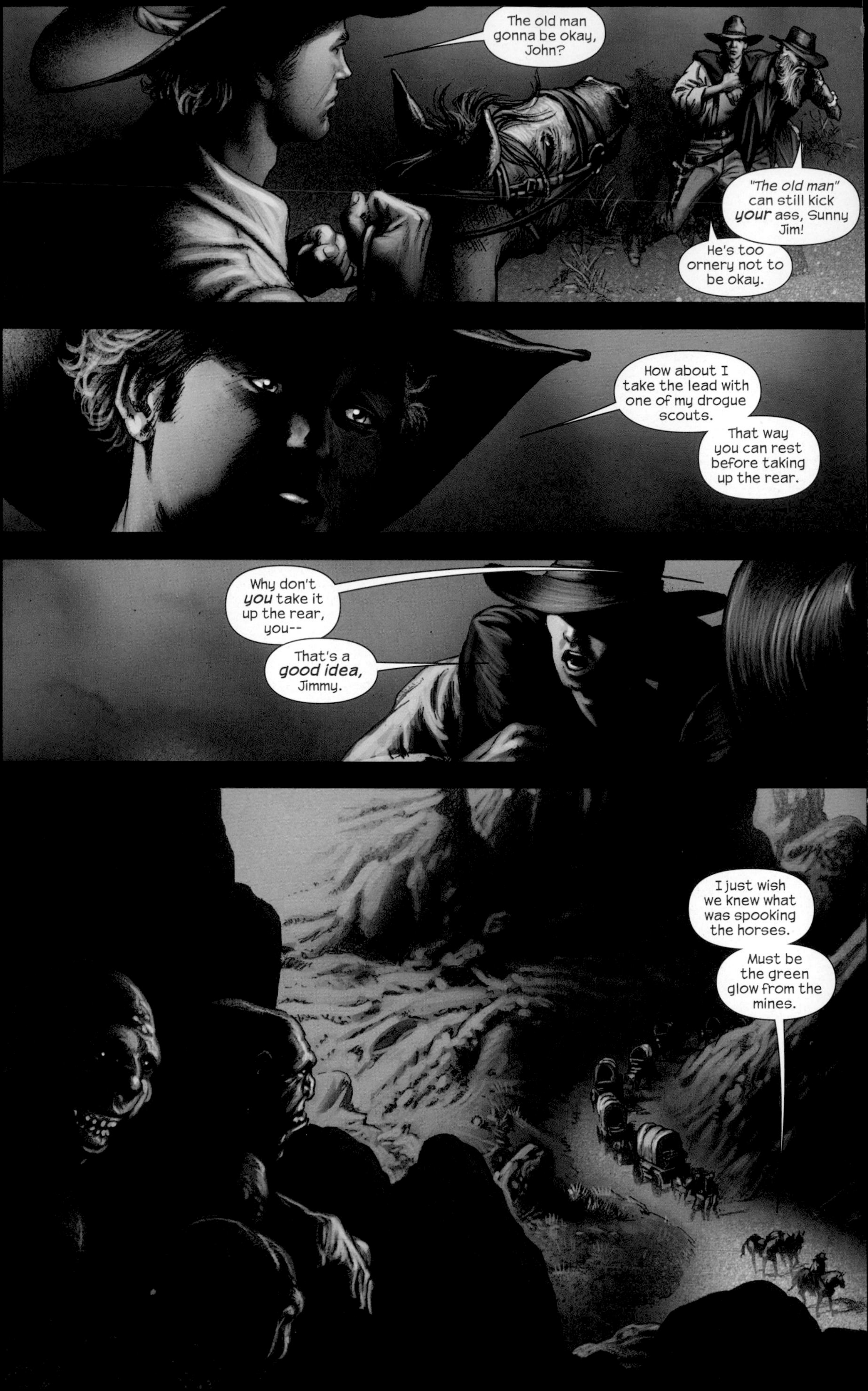
The old man gonna be okay, John?
"The old man" can still kick your ass, Sunny Jim!
He's too ornery not to be okay.
How about I take the lead with one of my drogue scouts.
That way you can rest before taking up the rear.
Why don't you take it up the rear, you--
That's a good idea, Jimmy.
I just wish we knew what was spooking the horses.
Must be the green glow from the mines.

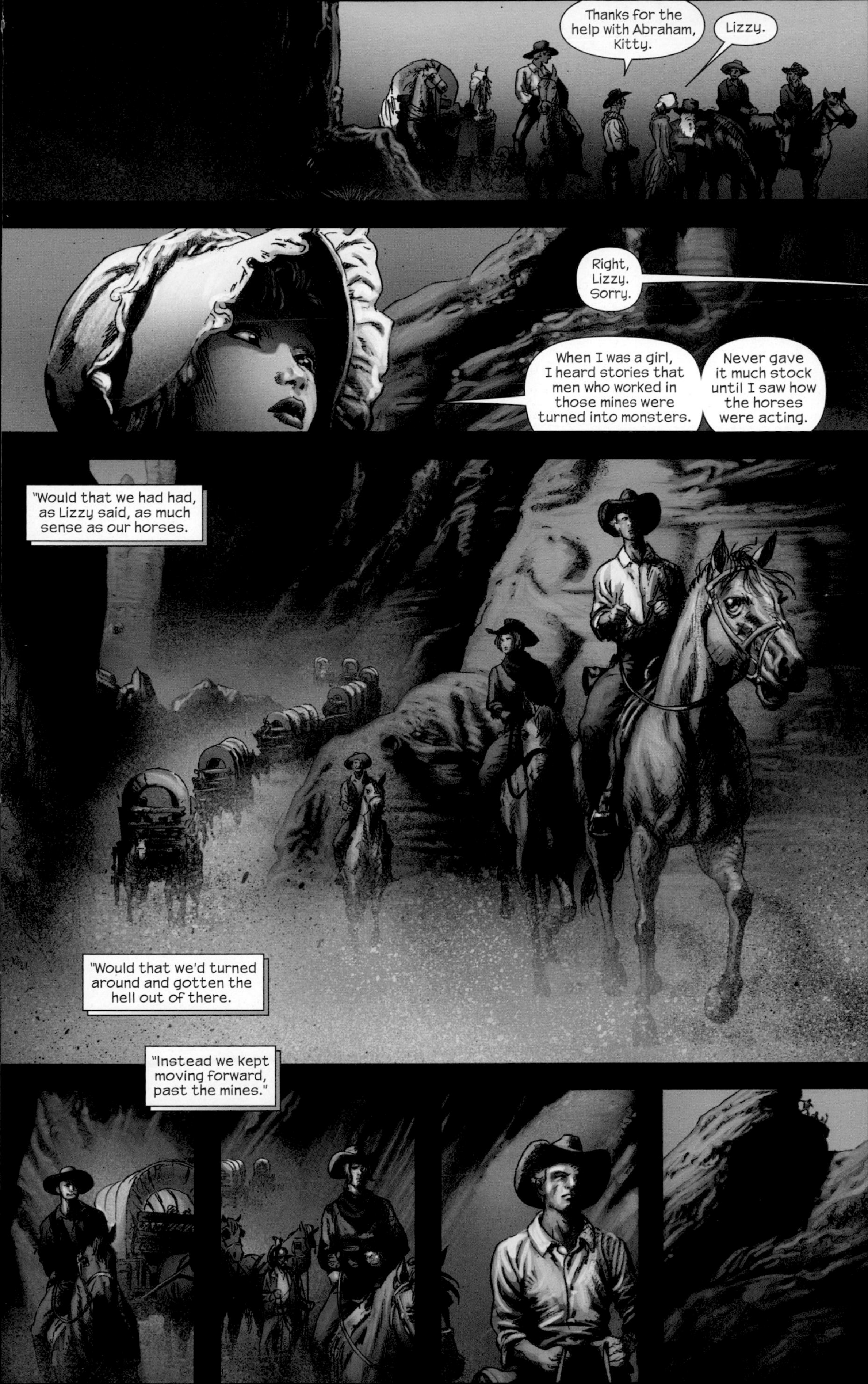
Thanks for the help with Abraham, Kitty.
Lizzy.
Right, Lizzy. Sorry.
When I was a girl, I heard stories that men who worked in those mines were turned into monsters.
Never gave it much stock until I saw how the horses were acting.
"Would that we had had, as Lizzy said, as much sense as our horses.
"Would that we'd turned around and gotten the hell out of there.
"Instead we kept moving forward, past the mines."

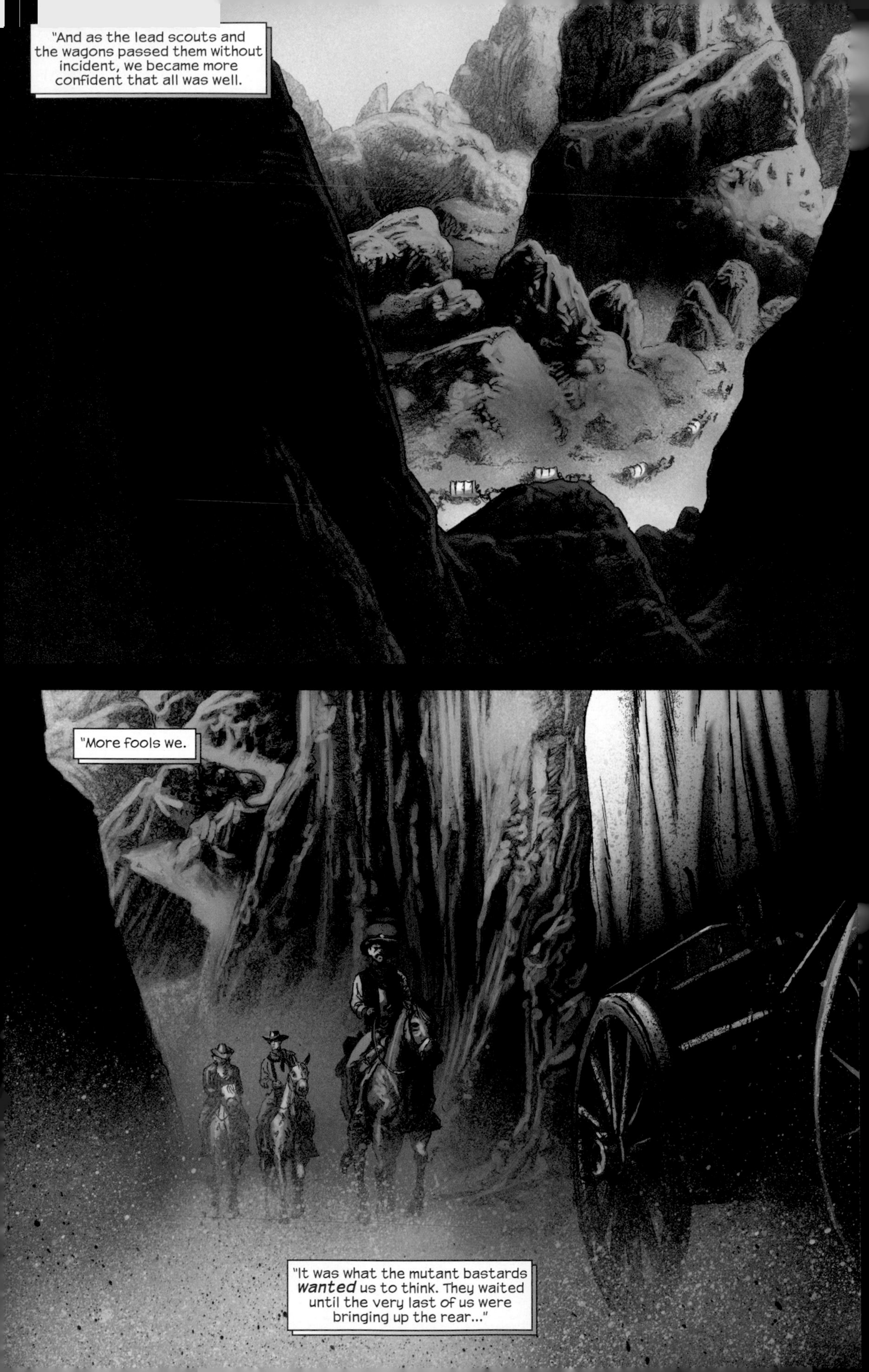
"And as the lead scouts and the wagons passed them without incident, we became more confident that all was well.
"More fools we.
"It was what the mutant bastards *wanted* us to think. They waited until the very last of us were bringing up the rear..."

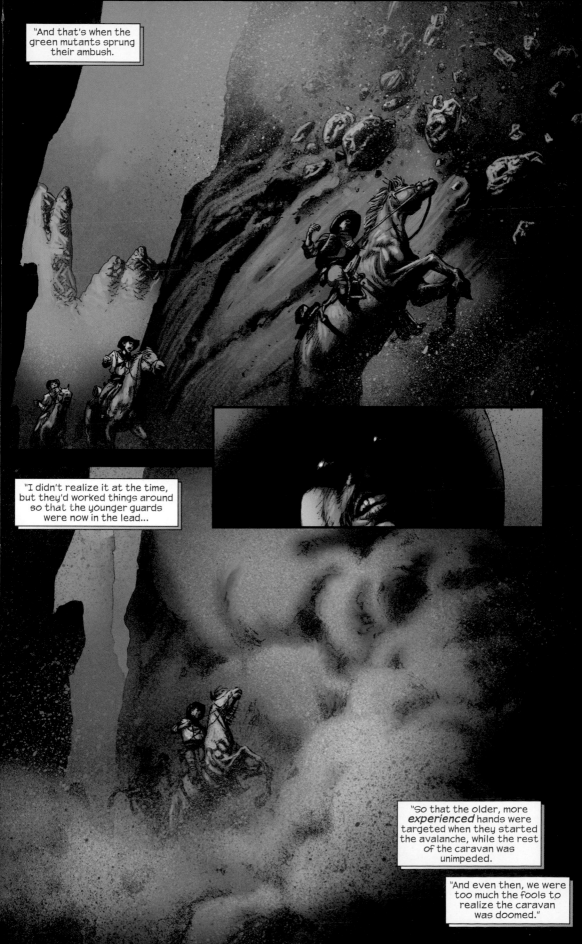

"And that's when the green mutants sprung their ambush.

"I didn't realize it at the time, but they'd worked things around so that the younger guards were now in the lead...

"So that the older, more *experienced* hands were targeted when they started the avalanche, while the rest of the caravan was unimpeded.

"And even then, we were too much the fools to realize the caravan was doomed."

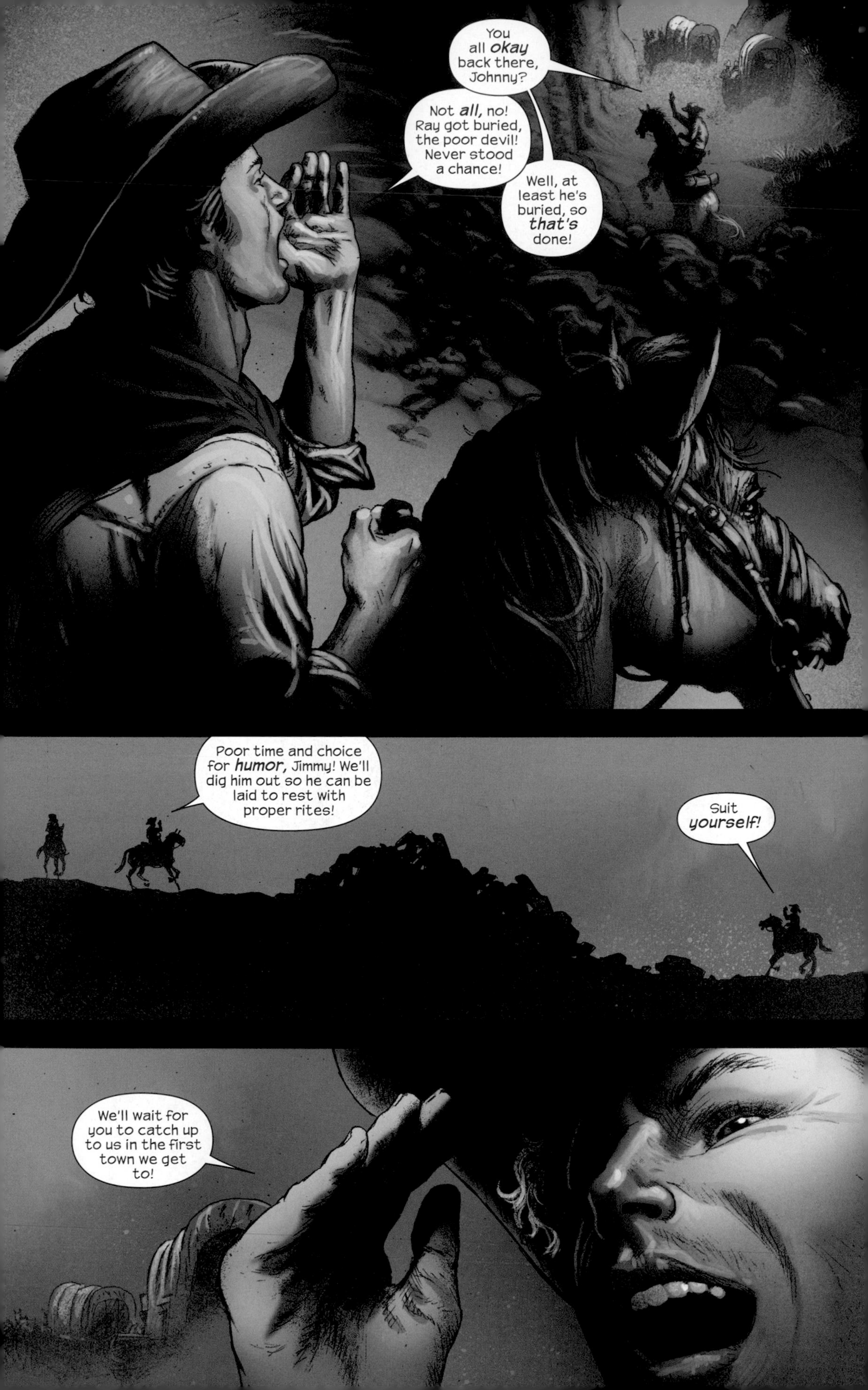
You all okay back there, Johnny?
Not all, no! Ray got buried, the poor devil! Never stood a chance!
Well, at least he's buried, so that's done!
Poor time and choice for humor, Jimmy! We'll dig him out so he can be laid to rest with proper rites!
Suit yourself!
We'll wait for you to catch up to us in the first town we get to!

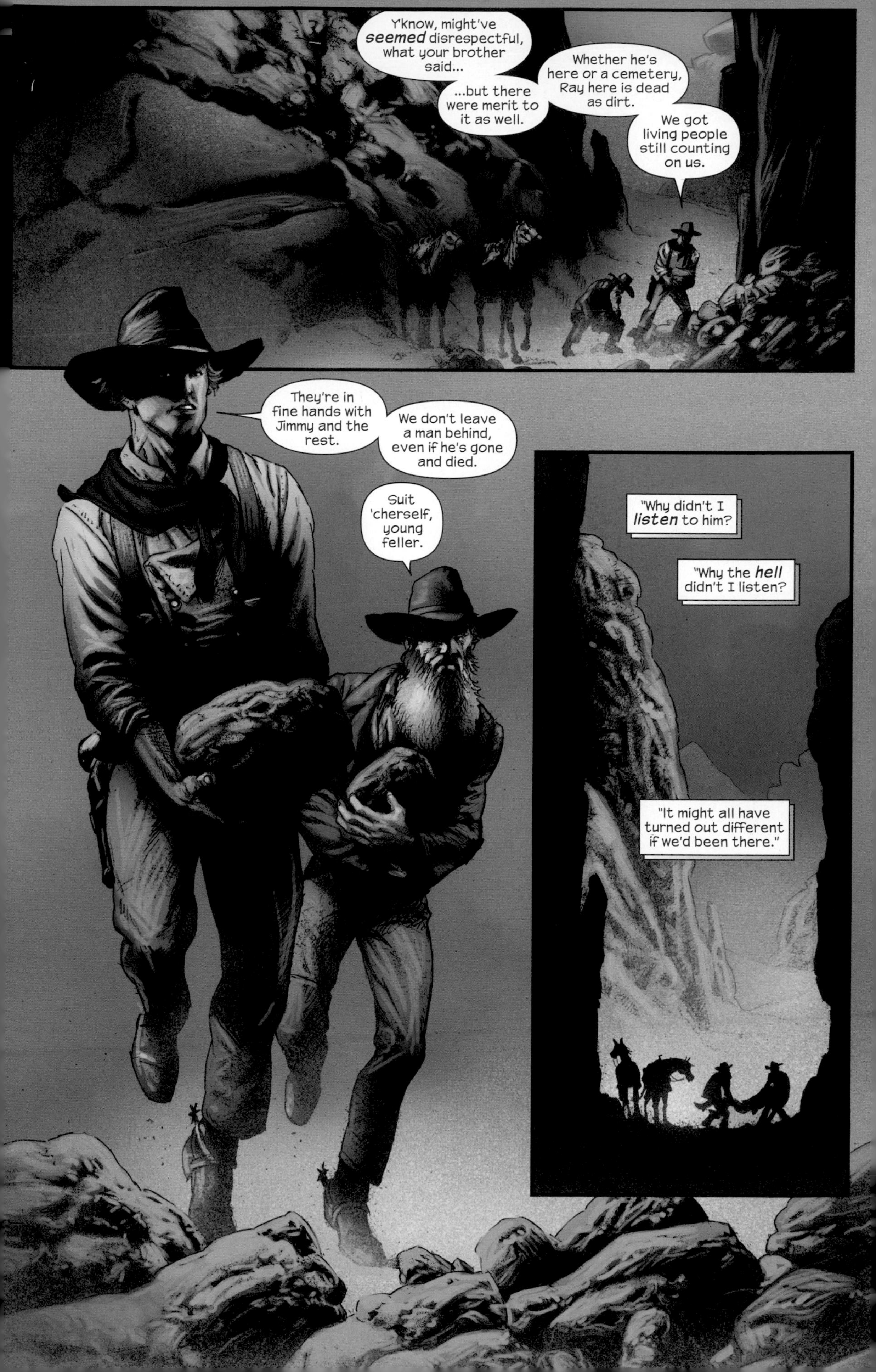
Y'know, might've seemed disrespectful, what your brother said...
...but there were merit to it as well.
Whether he's here or a cemetery, Ray here is dead as dirt.
We got living people still counting on us.
They're in fine hands with Jimmy and the rest.
We don't leave a man behind, even if he's gone and died.
Suit 'cherself, young feller.
"Why didn't I listen to him?
"Why the hell didn't I listen?
"It might all have turned out different if we'd been there."

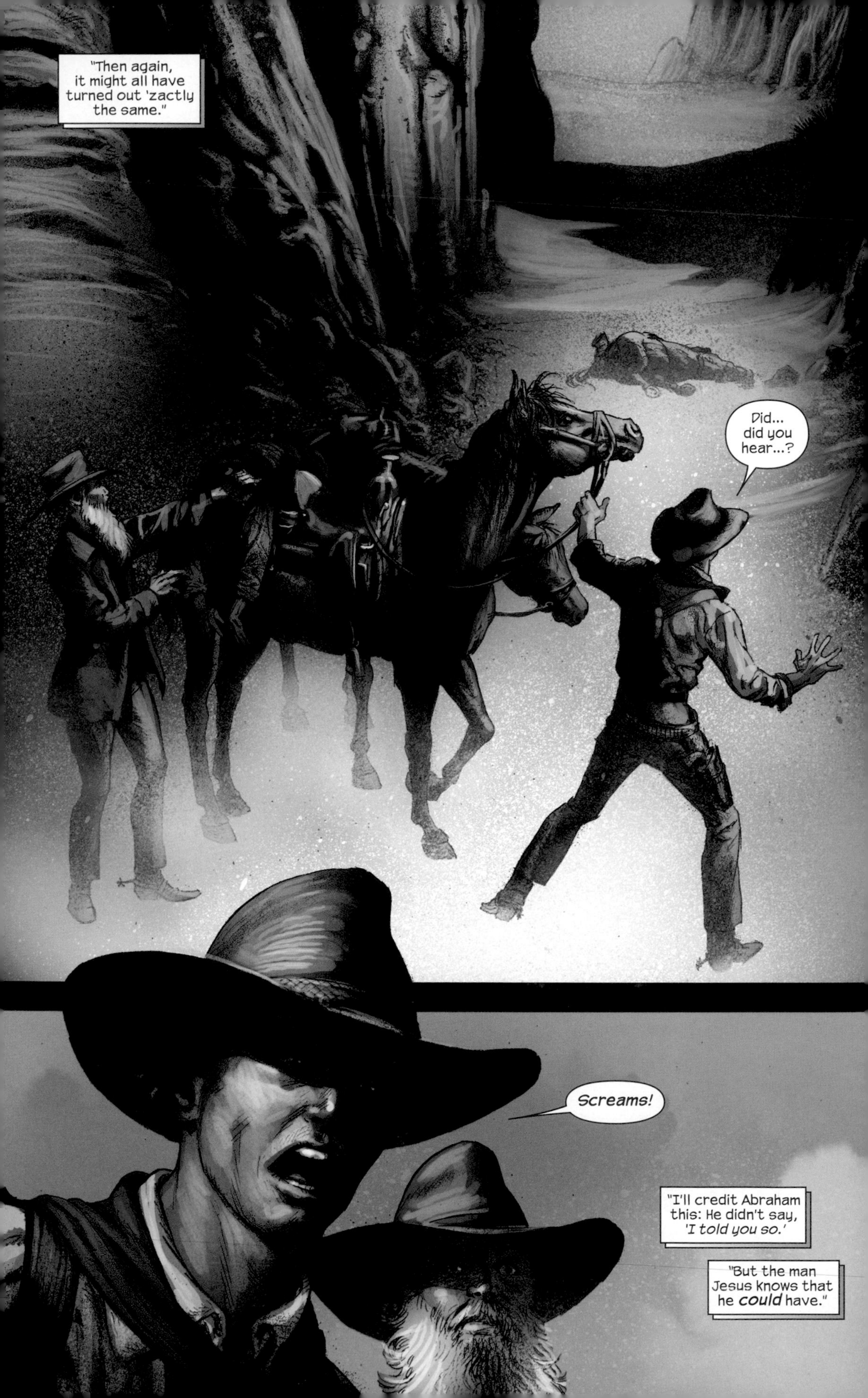
"Then again, it might all have turned out 'zactly the same."
Did... did you hear...?
Screams!
"I'll credit Abraham this: He didn't say, *'I told you so.'*
"But the man Jesus knows that he ***could*** have."

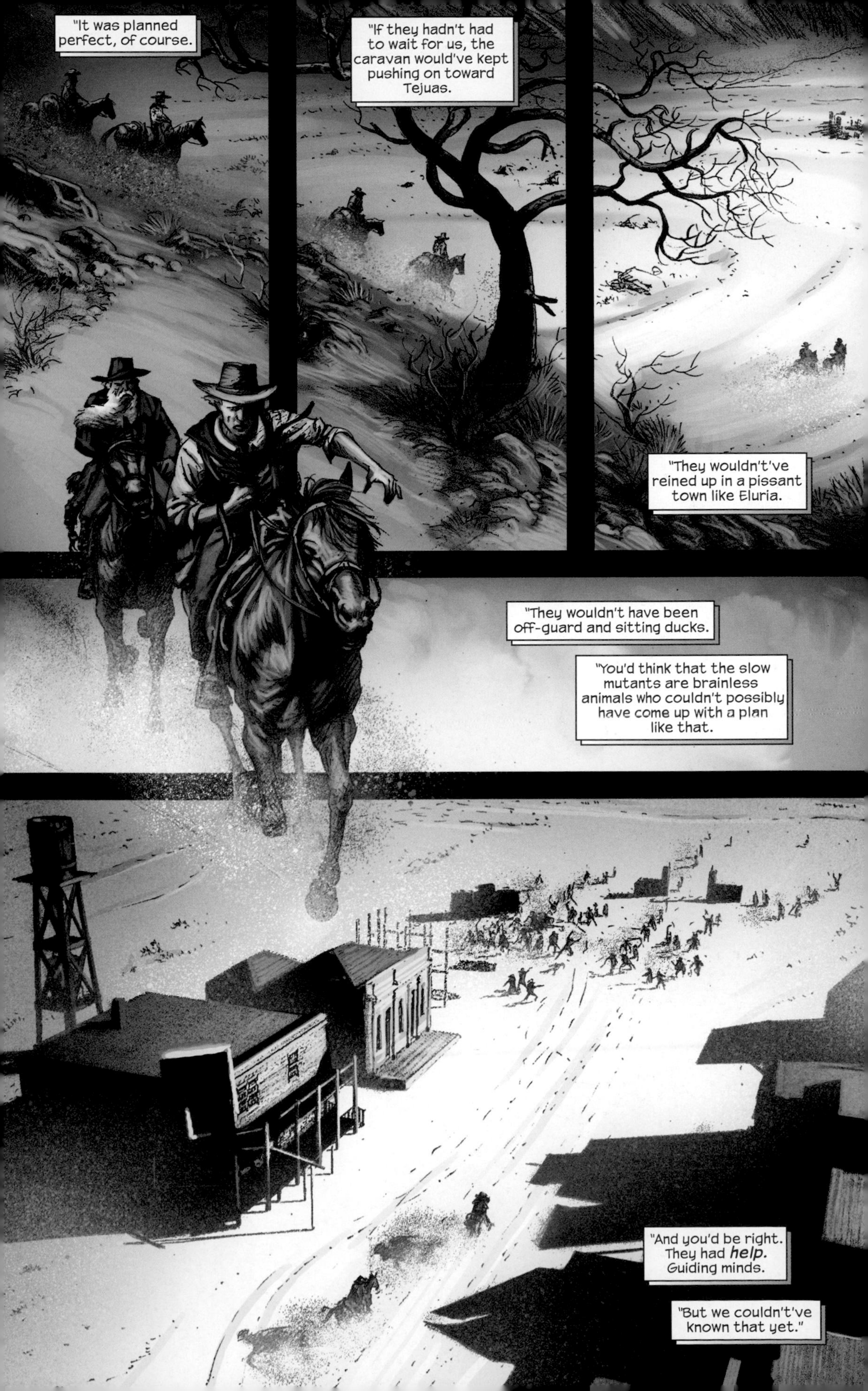
"It was planned perfect, of course.
"If they hadn't had to wait for us, the caravan would've kept pushing on toward Tejuas.
"They wouldn't've reined up in a pissant town like Eluria.
"They wouldn't have been off-guard and sitting ducks.
"You'd think that the slow mutants are brainless animals who couldn't possibly have come up with a plan like that.
"And you'd be right. They had *help.* Guiding minds.
"But we couldn't've known that yet."

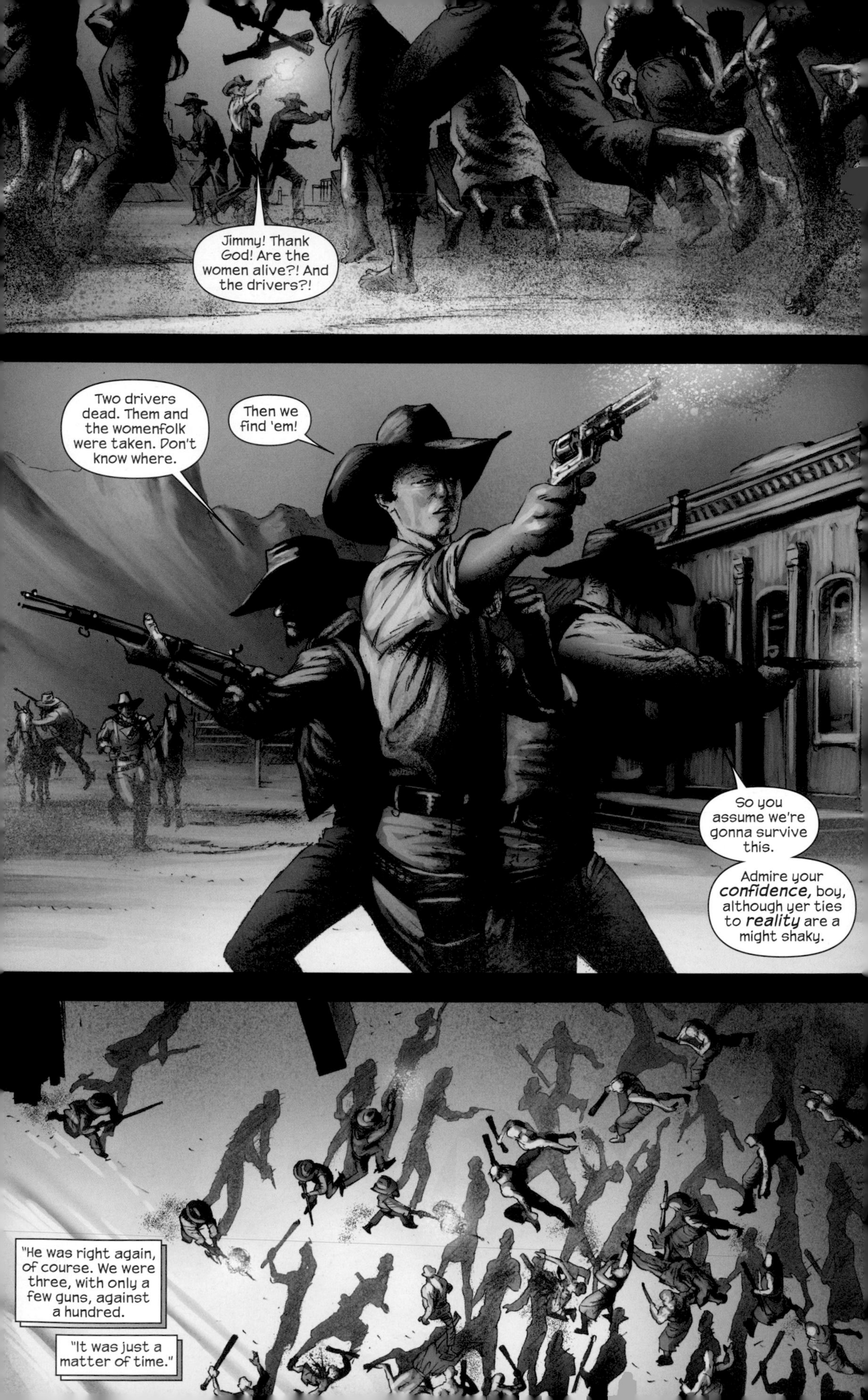
Jimmy! Thank God! Are the women alive?! And the drivers?!
Two drivers dead. Them and the womenfolk were taken. Don't know where.
Then we find 'em!
So you assume we're gonna survive this.
Admire your *confidence,* boy, although yer ties to *reality* are a might shaky.
"He was right again, of course. We were three, with only a few guns, against a hundred.
"It was just a matter of time."

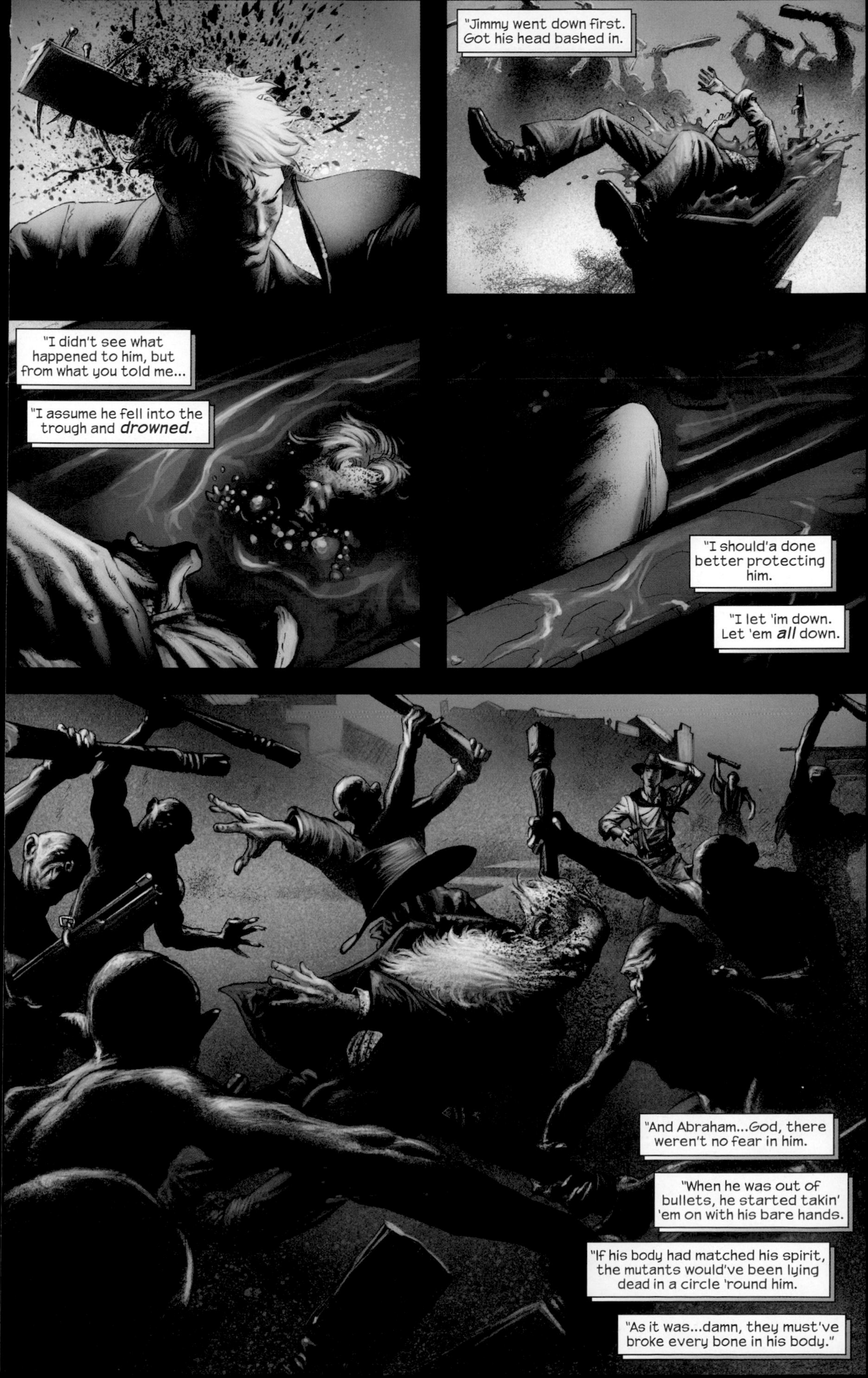
"Jimmy went down first. Got his head bashed in.
"I didn't see what happened to him, but from what you told me...
"I assume he fell into the trough and *drowned.*
"I should'a done better protecting him.
"I let 'im down. Let 'em *all* down.
"And Abraham...God, there weren't no fear in him.
"When he was out of bullets, he started takin' 'em on with his bare hands.
"If his body had matched his spirit, the mutants would've been lying dead in a circle 'round him.
"As it was...damn, they must've broke every bone in his body."

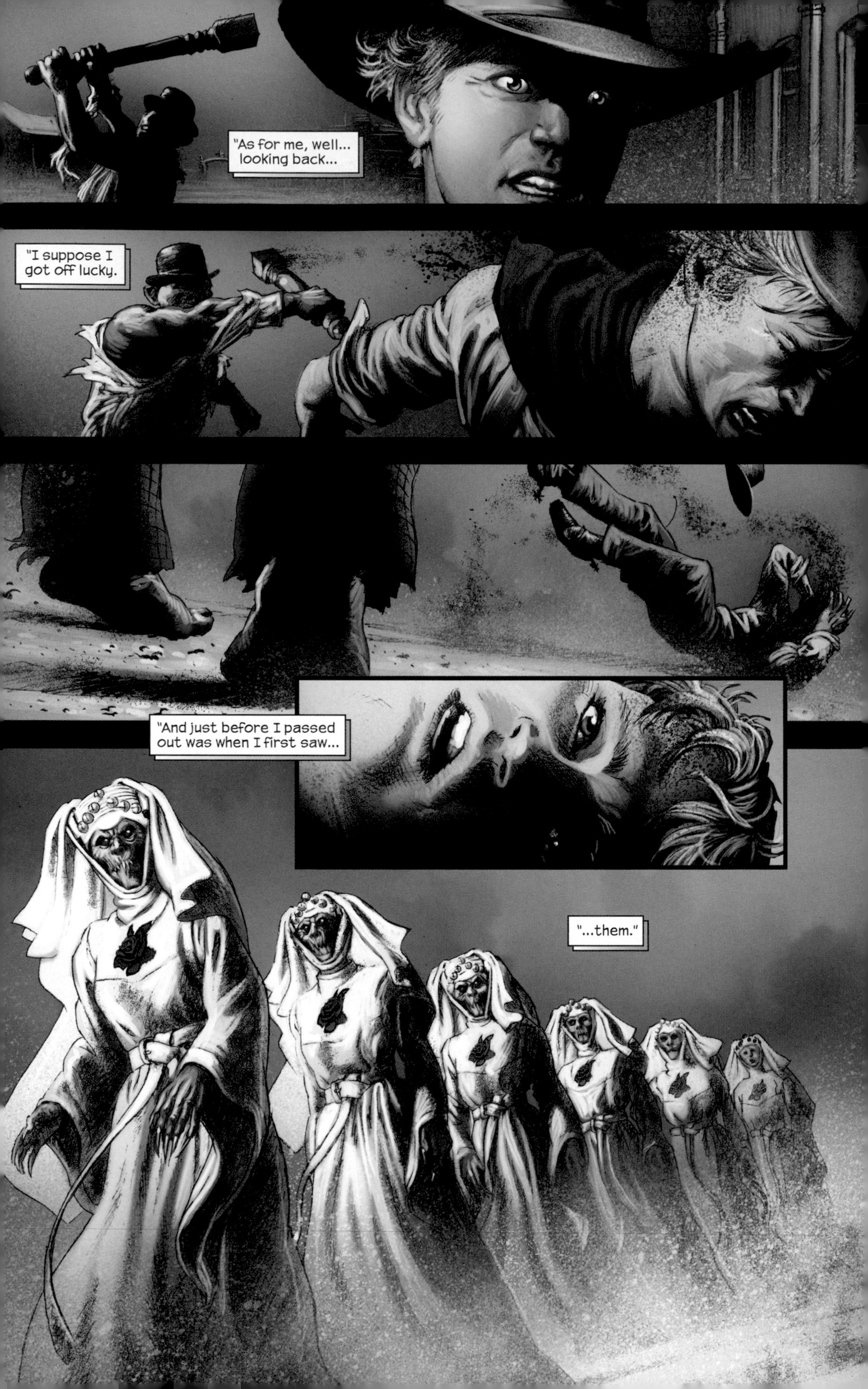
"As for me, well...
looking back...
"I suppose I
got off lucky.
"And just before I passed
out was when I first saw...
"...them."

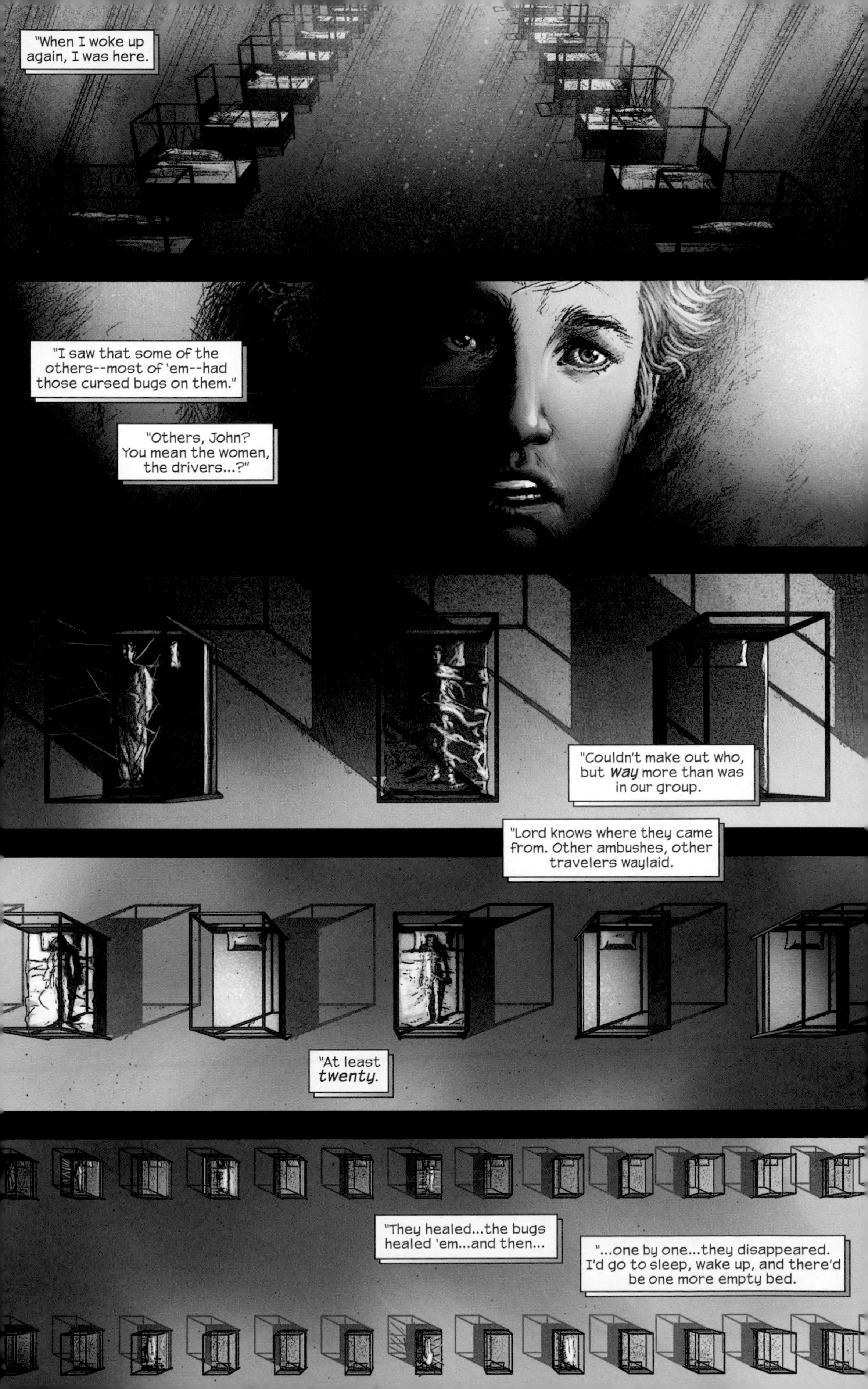
"When I woke up again, I was here.
"I saw that some of the others--most of 'em--had those cursed bugs on them."
"Others, John? You mean the women, the drivers...?"
"Couldn't make out who, but *way* more than was in our group.
"Lord knows where they came from. Other ambushes, other travelers waylaid.
"At least *twenty*.
"They healed...the bugs healed 'em...and then...
"...one by one...they disappeared. I'd go to sleep, wake up, and there'd be one more empty bed.

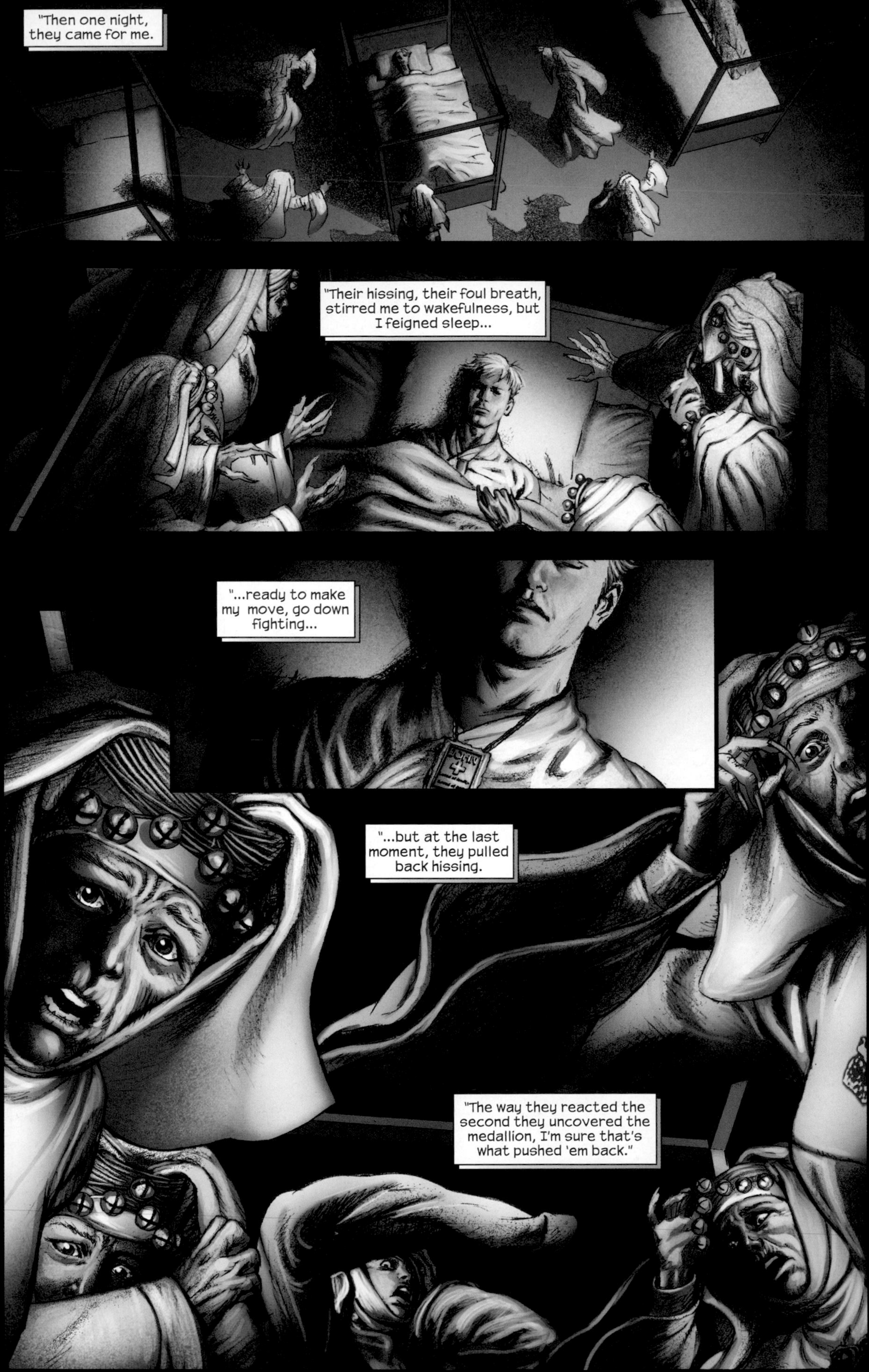
"Then one night, they came for me.
"Their hissing, their foul breath, stirred me to wakefulness, but I feigned sleep...
"...ready to make my move, go down fighting...
"...but at the last moment, they pulled back hissing.
"The way they reacted the second they uncovered the medallion, I'm sure that's what pushed 'em back."

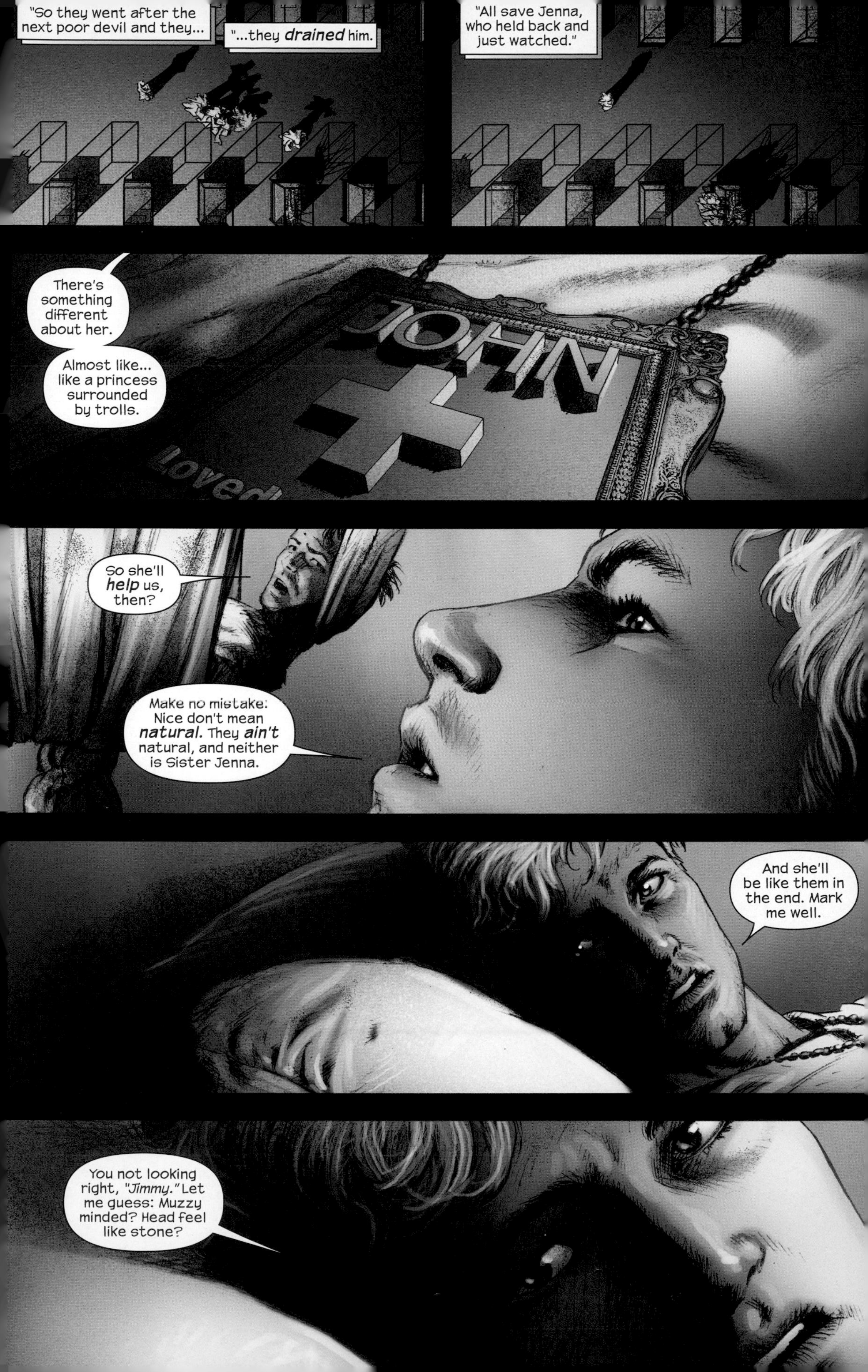
"So they went after the next poor devil and they...
"...they *drained* him.
"All save Jenna, who held back and just watched."
JOHN
Loved
There's something different about her.
Almost like... like a princess surrounded by trolls.
So she'll *help* us, then?
Make no mistake: Nice don't mean *natural.* They *ain't* natural, and neither is Sister Jenna.
And she'll be like them in the end. Mark me well.
You not looking right, "*Jimmy.*" Let me guess: Muzzy minded? Head feel like stone?

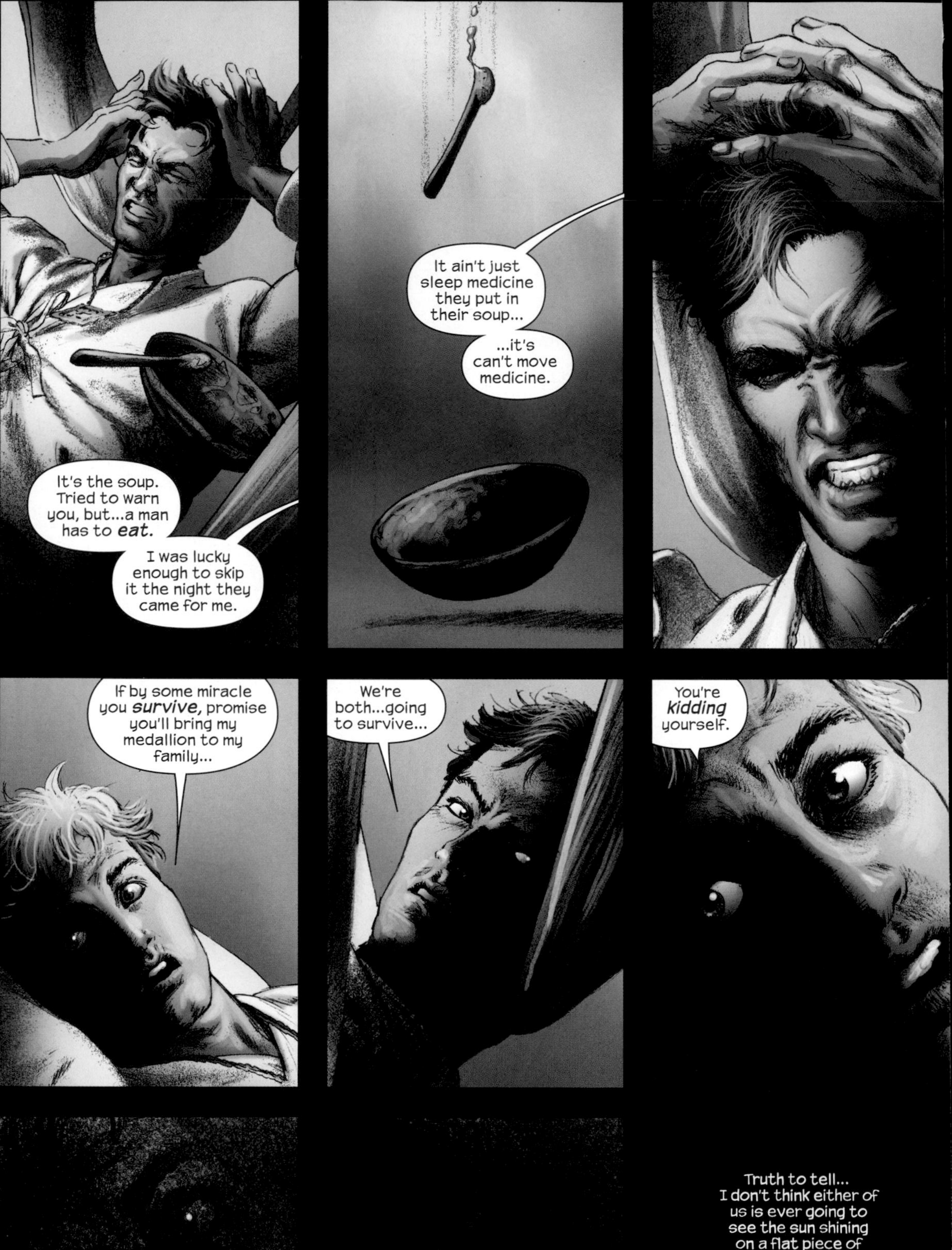

It's the soup. Tried to warn you, but...a man has to ***eat.***
I was lucky enough to skip it the night they came for me.
It ain't just sleep medicine they put in their soup...
...it's can't move medicine.
If by some miracle you ***survive,*** promise you'll bring my medallion to my family...
We're both...going to survive...
You're ***kidding*** yourself.
Truth to tell... I don't think either of us is ever going to see the sun shining on a flat piece of

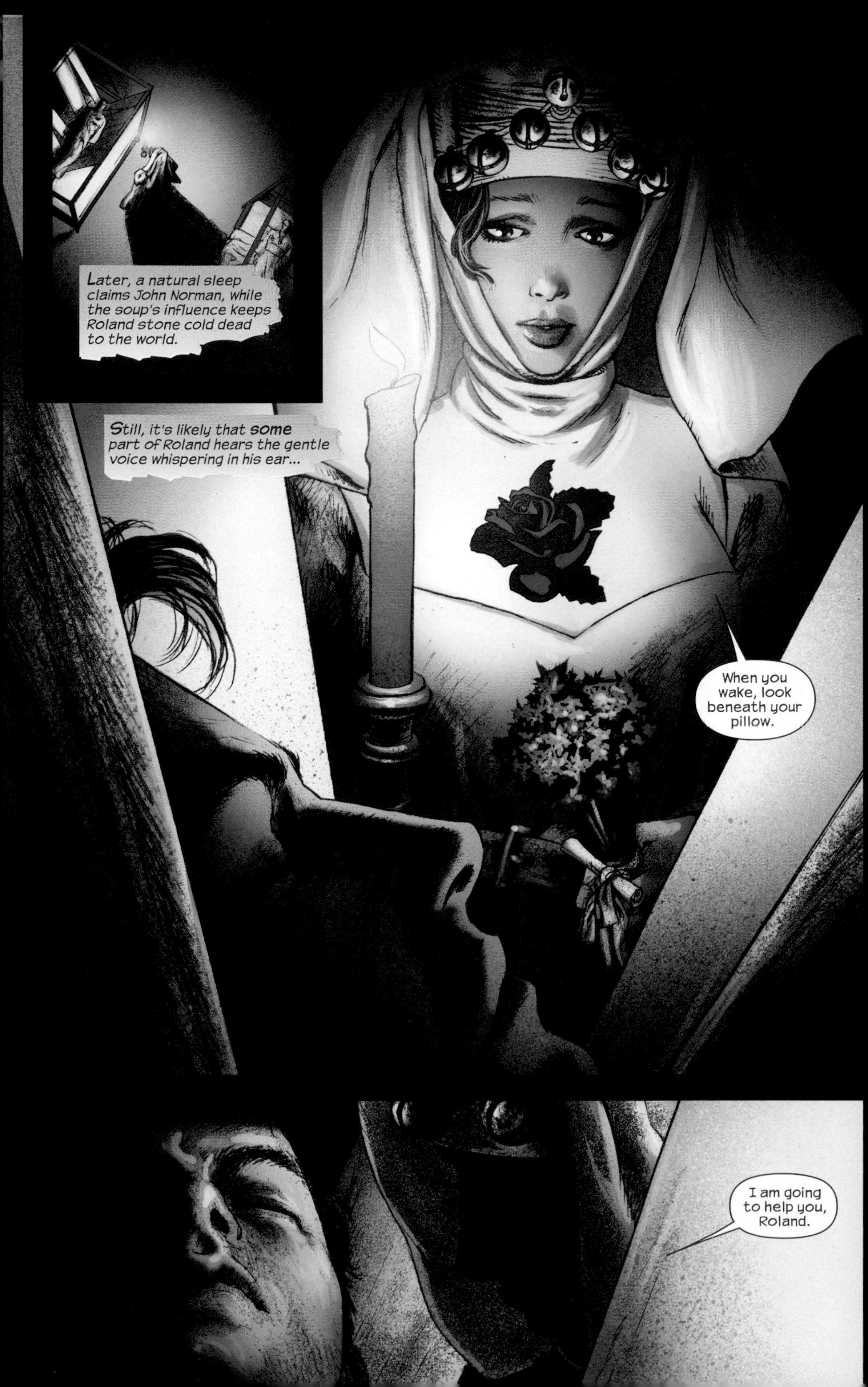
Later, a natural sleep claims John Norman, while the soup's influence keeps Roland stone cold dead to the world.
Still, it's likely that **some** part of Roland hears the gentle voice whispering in his ear...
When you wake, look beneath your pillow.
I am going to help you, Roland.

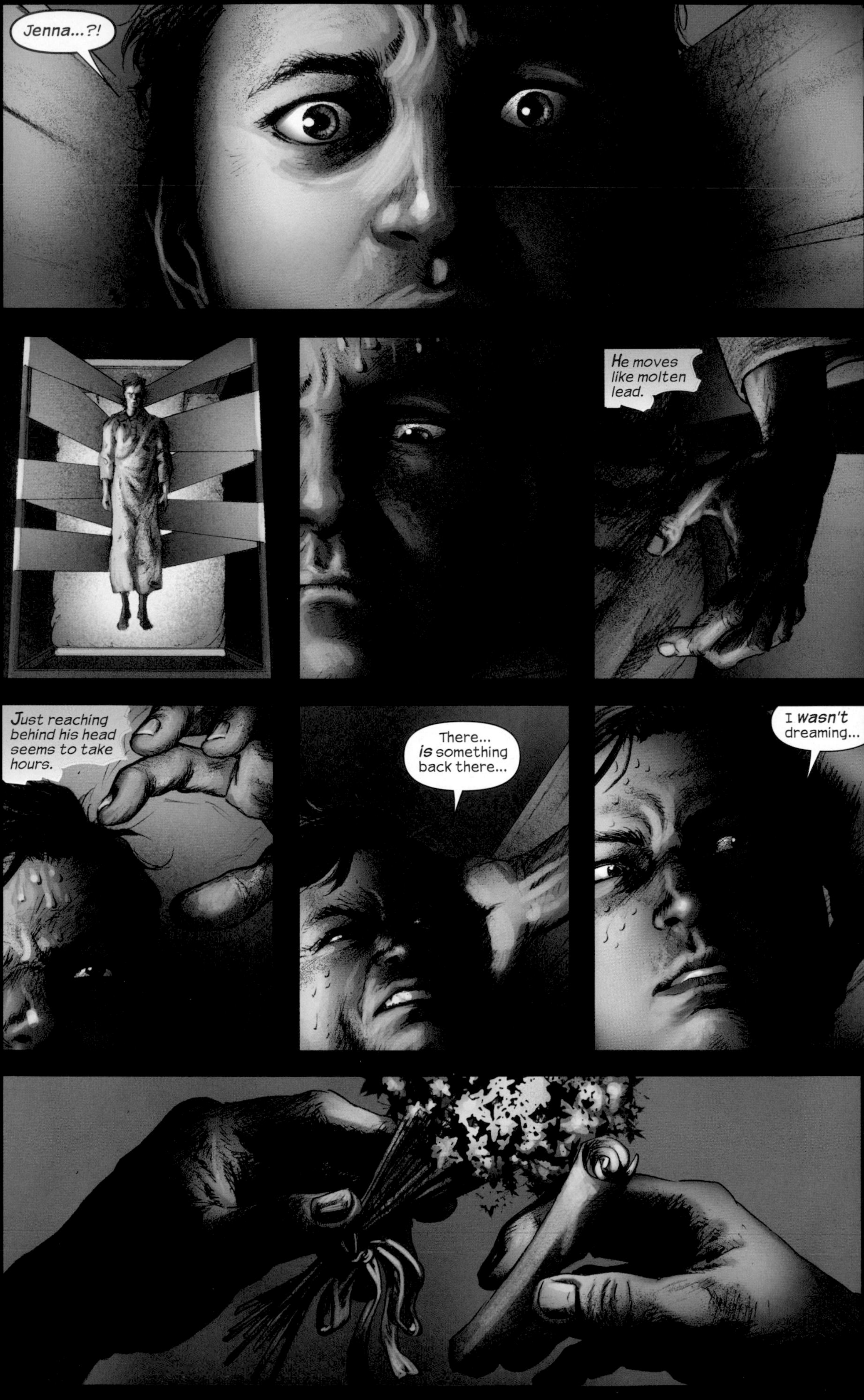
Jenna...?!
He moves like molten lead.
Just reaching behind his head seems to take hours.
There... *is* something back there...
I *wasn't* dreaming...

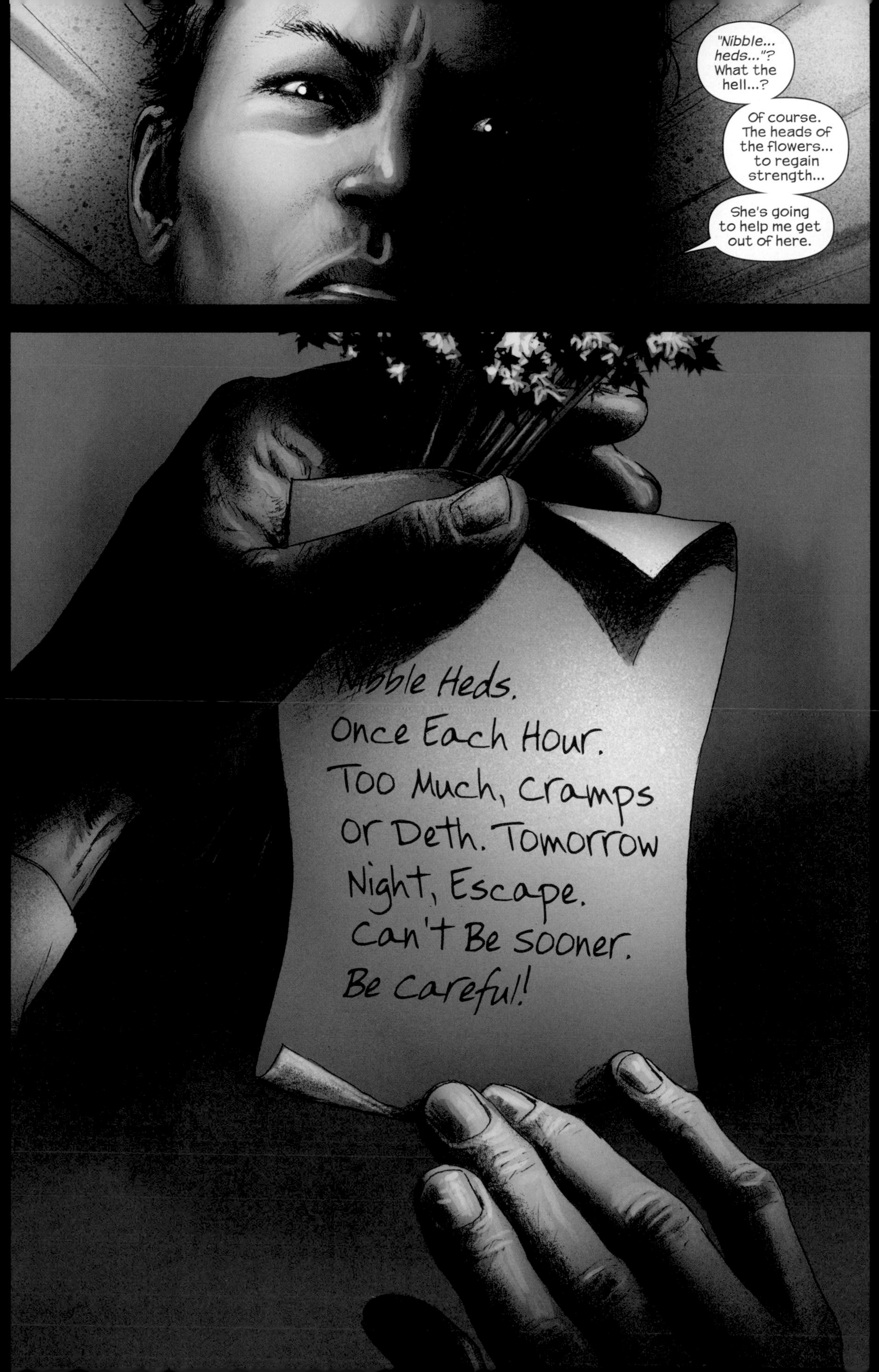
"Nibble... heds..."? What the hell...?
Of course. The heads of the flowers... to regain strength...
She's going to help me get out of here.
bble Heds.
Once Each Hour.
Too Much, Cramps
Or Deth. Tomorrow
Night, Escape.
Can't Be sooner.
Be careful!

# STEPHEN KING

## THE DARK TOWER
## ~THE GUNSLINGER~

# THE LITTLE SISTERS OF ELURIA

## CHAPTER FOUR

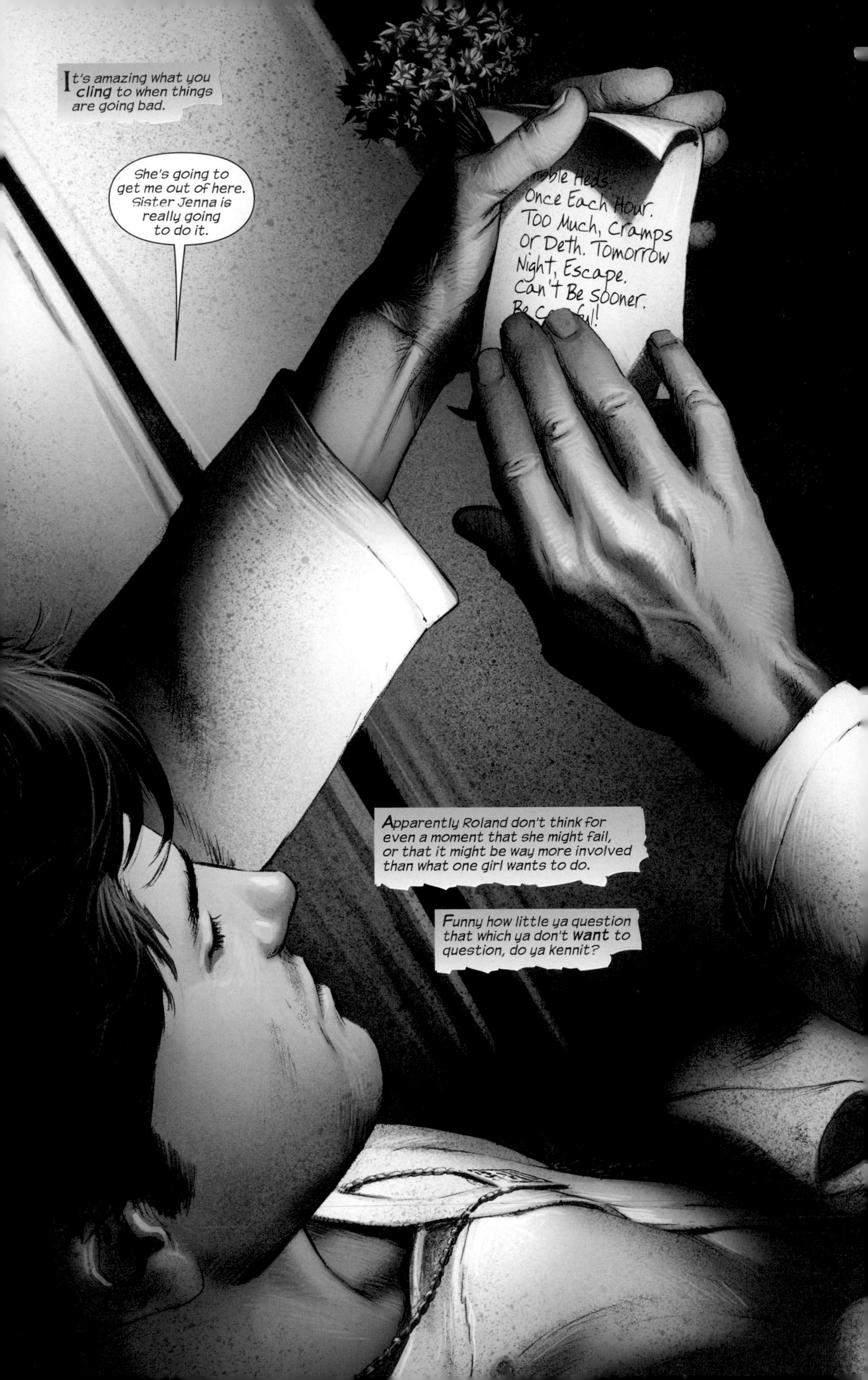

It's amazing what you cling to when things are going bad.
She's going to get me out of here. Sister Jenna is really going to do it.
Once Each Hour. Too Much, Cramps Or Deth. Tomorrow Night, Escape. Can't Be Sooner.
Apparently Roland don't think for even a moment that she might fail, or that it might be way more involved than what one girl wants to do.
Funny how little ya question that which ya don't want to question, do ya kennit?

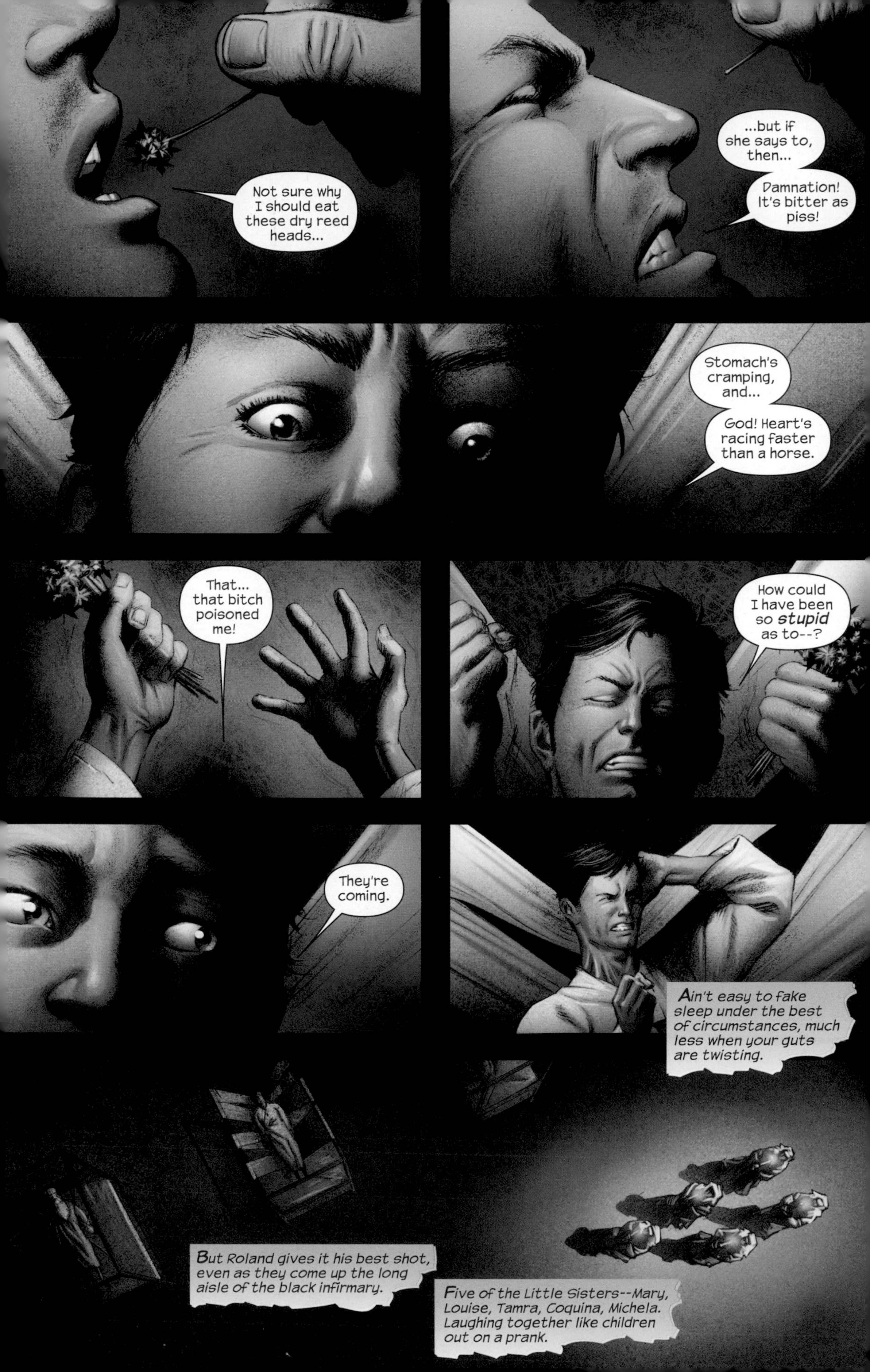
Not sure why I should eat these dry reed heads...
...but if she says to, then...
Damnation! It's bitter as piss!
Stomach's cramping, and...
God! Heart's racing faster than a horse.
That... that bitch poisoned me!
How could I have been so **stupid** as to--?
They're coming.
Ain't easy to fake sleep under the best of circumstances, much less when your guts are twisting.
But Roland gives it his best shot, even as they come up the long aisle of the black infirmary.
Five of the Little Sisters--Mary, Louise, Tamra, Coquina, Michela. Laughing together like children out on a prank.

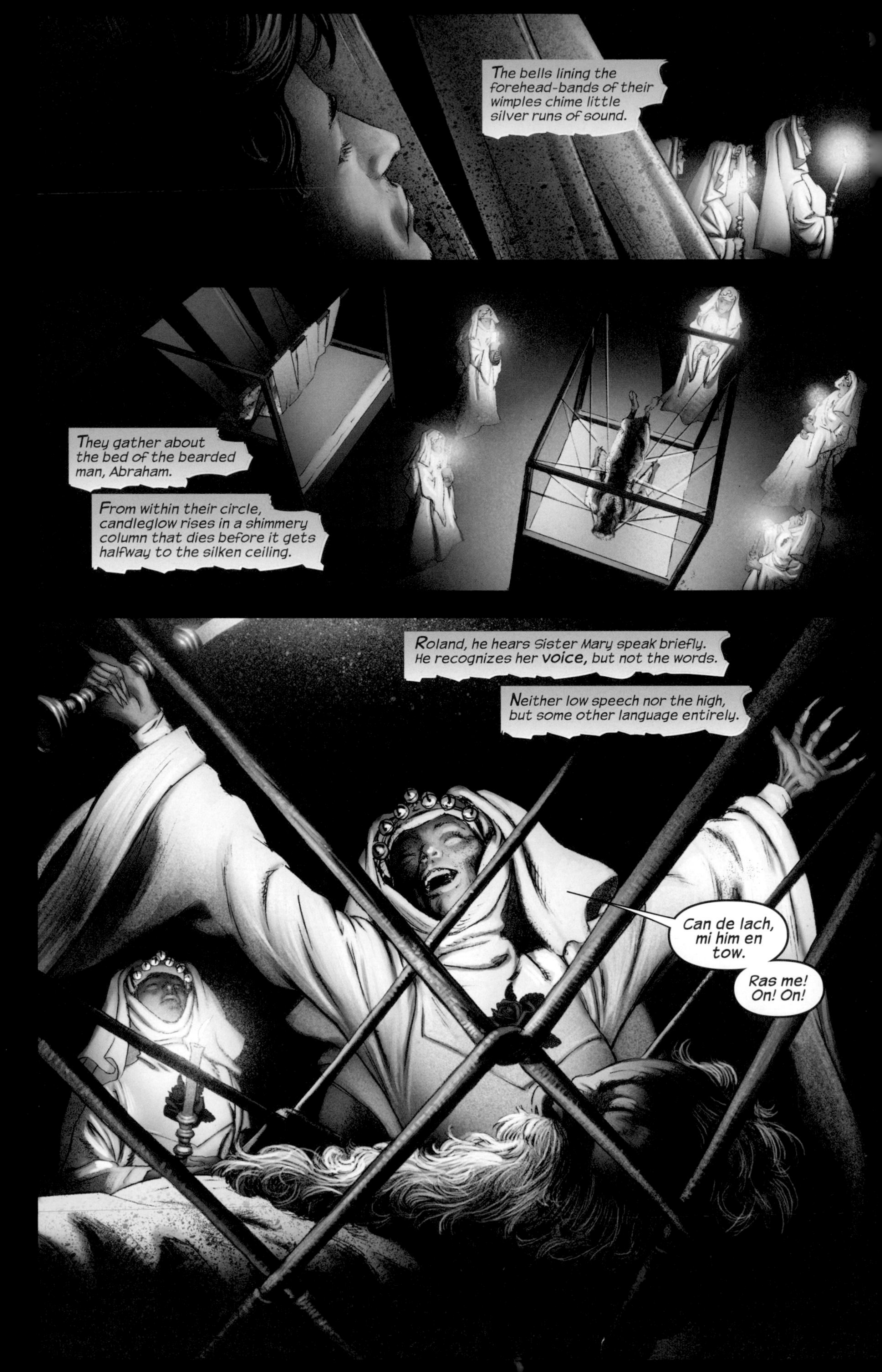
The bells lining the forehead-bands of their wimples chime little silver runs of sound.
They gather about the bed of the bearded man, Abraham.
From within their circle, candleglow rises in a shimmery column that dies before it gets halfway to the silken ceiling.
Roland, he hears Sister Mary speak briefly. He recognizes her voice, but not the words.
Neither low speech nor the high, but some other language entirely.
Can de lach, mi him en tow.
Ras me! On! On!

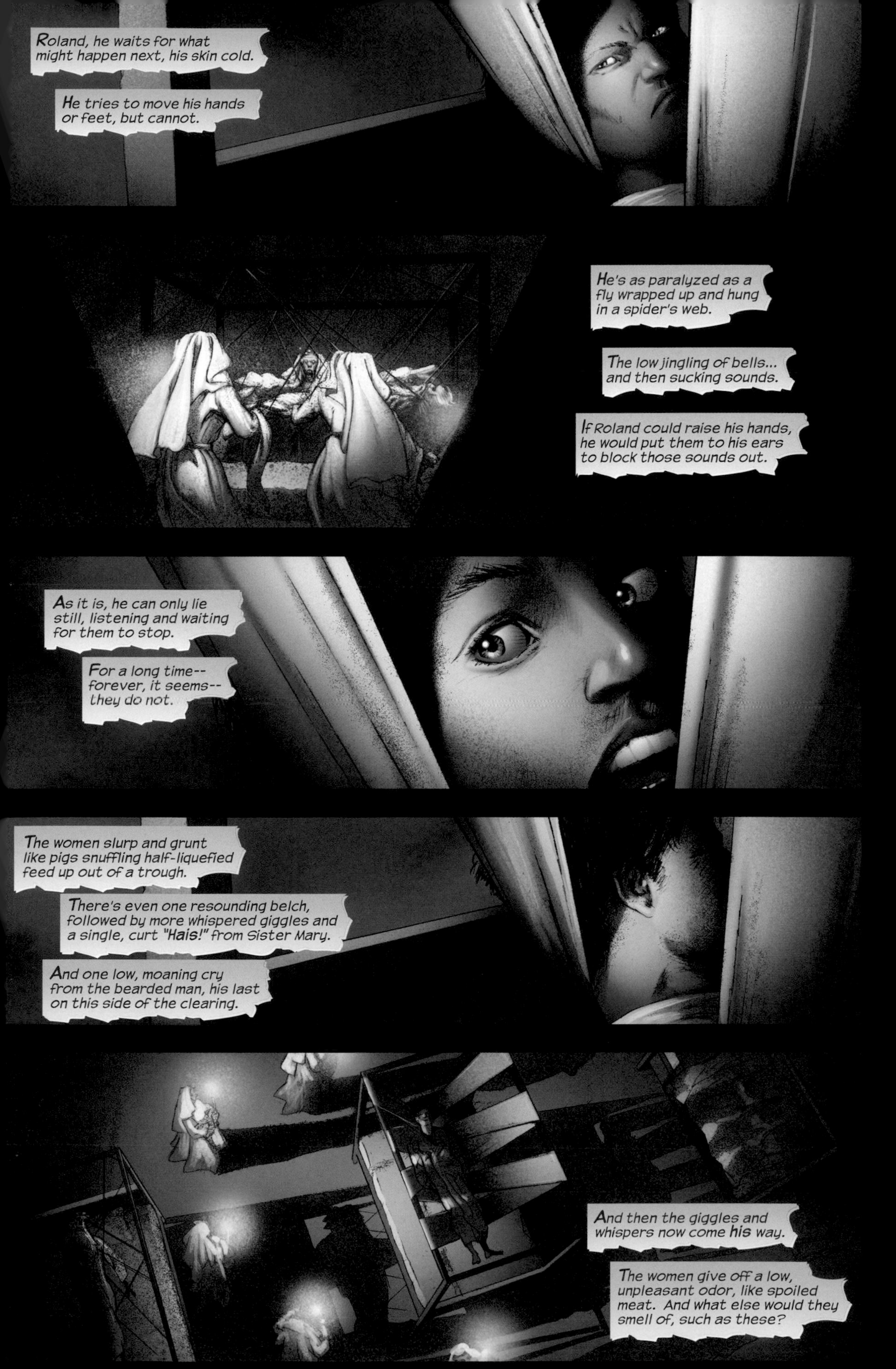
Roland, he waits for what might happen next, his skin cold.
He tries to move his hands or feet, but cannot.
He's as paralyzed as a fly wrapped up and hung in a spider's web.
The low jingling of bells... and then sucking sounds.
If Roland could raise his hands, he would put them to his ears to block those sounds out.
As it is, he can only lie still, listening and waiting for them to stop.
For a long time-- forever, it seems-- they do not.
The women slurp and grunt like pigs snuffling half-liquefied feed up out of a trough.
There's even one resounding belch, followed by more whispered giggles and a single, curt "Hais!" from Sister Mary.
And one low, moaning cry from the bearded man, his last on this side of the clearing.
And then the giggles and whispers now come his way.
The women give off a low, unpleasant odor, like spoiled meat. And what else would they smell of, such as these?

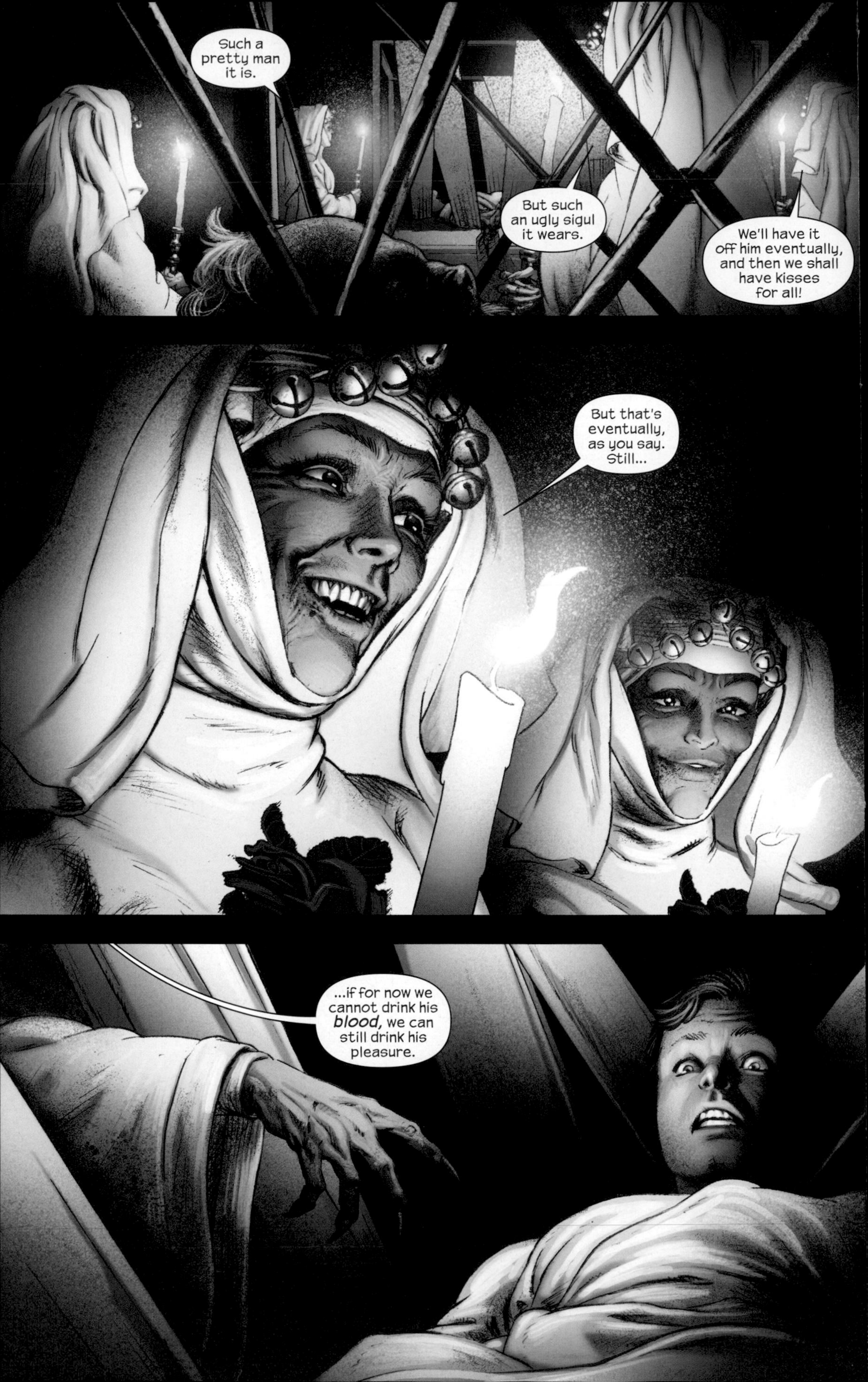
Such a pretty man it is.
But such an ugly sigul it wears.
We'll have it off him eventually, and then we shall have kisses for all!
But that's eventually, as you say. Still...
...if for now we cannot drink his *blood,* we can still drink his pleasure.

Turns out not all of him is paralyzed, after all.

Part of him had, in fact, arisen at the sound of their voices and now stood tall.

A hand reaches beneath the bed dress...

...and touches his, uhm...*tower*...

...encircles it, *caresses* it.

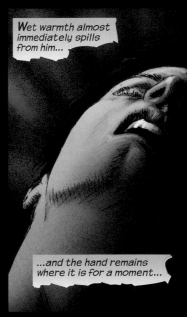

Wet warmth almost immediately spills from him...

...and the hand remains where it is for a moment...

...before letting him go.

Giggles, soft as wind.

Chiming bells.

Share the power, Sisters. Enough for all.

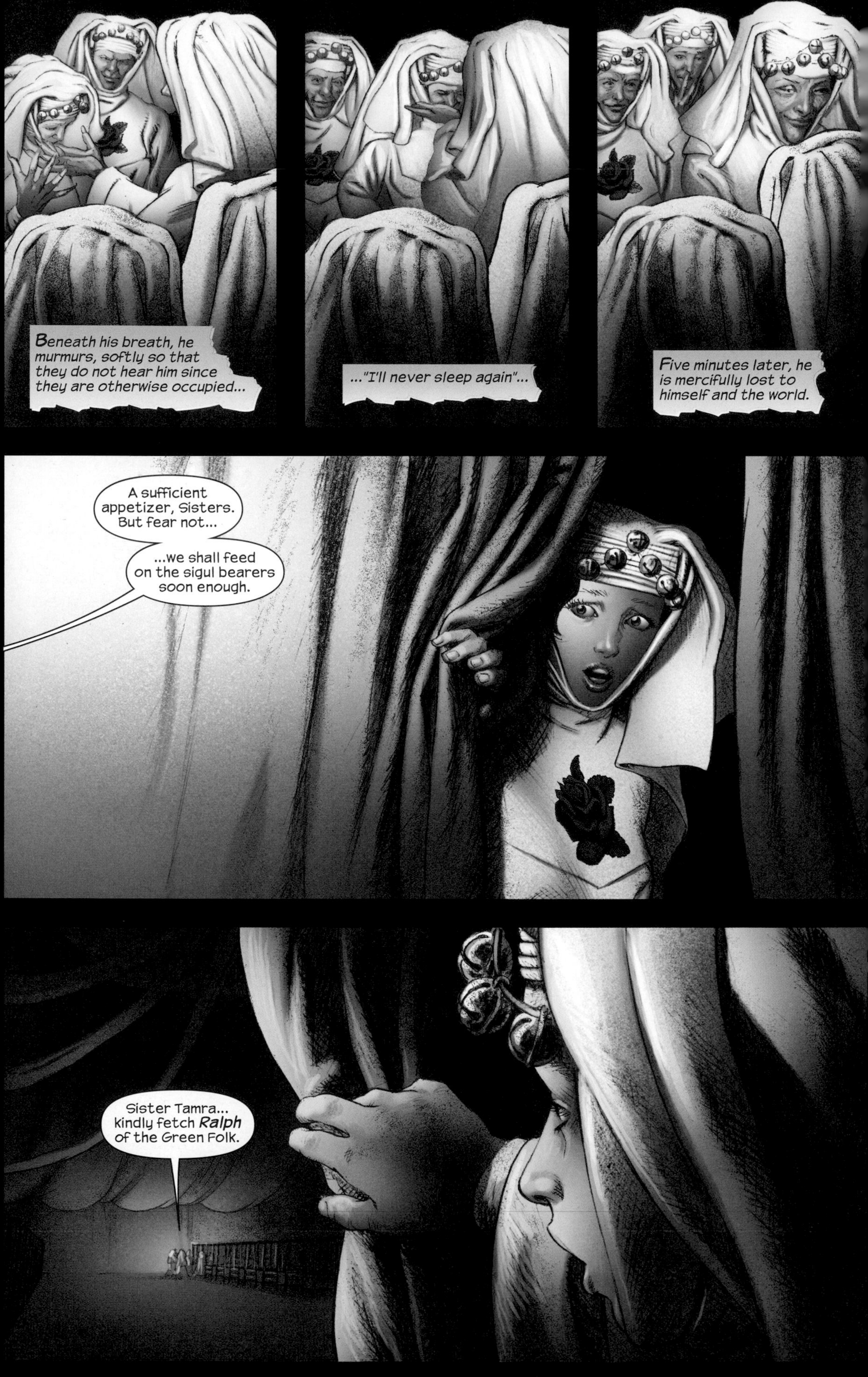
Beneath his breath, he murmurs, softly so that they do not hear him since they are otherwise occupied...
..."I'll never sleep again"...
Five minutes later, he is mercifully lost to himself and the world.
A sufficient appetizer, Sisters. But fear not...
...we shall feed on the sigul bearers soon enough.
Sister Tamra... kindly fetch *Ralph* of the Green Folk.

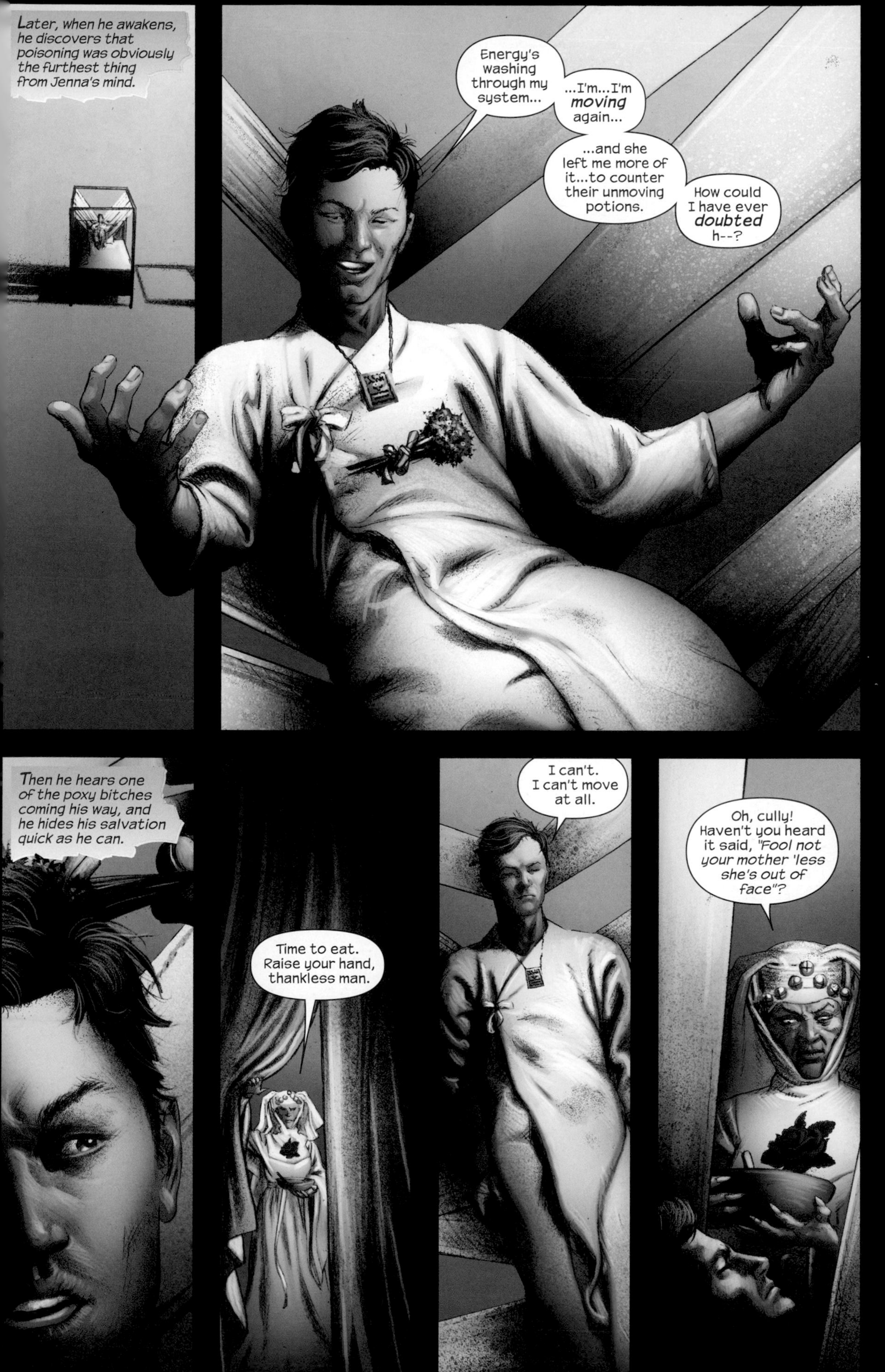
Later, when he awakens, he discovers that poisoning was obviously the furthest thing from Jenna's mind.
Energy's washing through my system...
...I'm...I'm moving again...
...and she left me more of it...to counter their unmoving potions.
How could I have ever doubted h--?
Then he hears one of the poxy bitches coming his way, and he hides his salvation quick as he can.
Time to eat. Raise your hand, thankless man.
I can't. I can't move at all.
Oh, cully! Haven't you heard it said, "Fool not your mother 'less she's out of face"?

I know pretty well what ye can and can't do. Now raise your hand...

...unless you'd like me to *whip* your cooperation out of Sister Jenna's hide.

Ah. There we go.

Touch her...

...and I'll kill you.

Speak not to us of killing, cully, lest we speak of it to you.

He can feel the Sister's foul soup working its numbness through his bones...

...but still finds enough strength to grab Jenna's note...

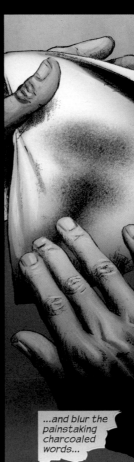

...and blur the painstaking charcoaled words...

...for **nothing** is more important than her not being caught.

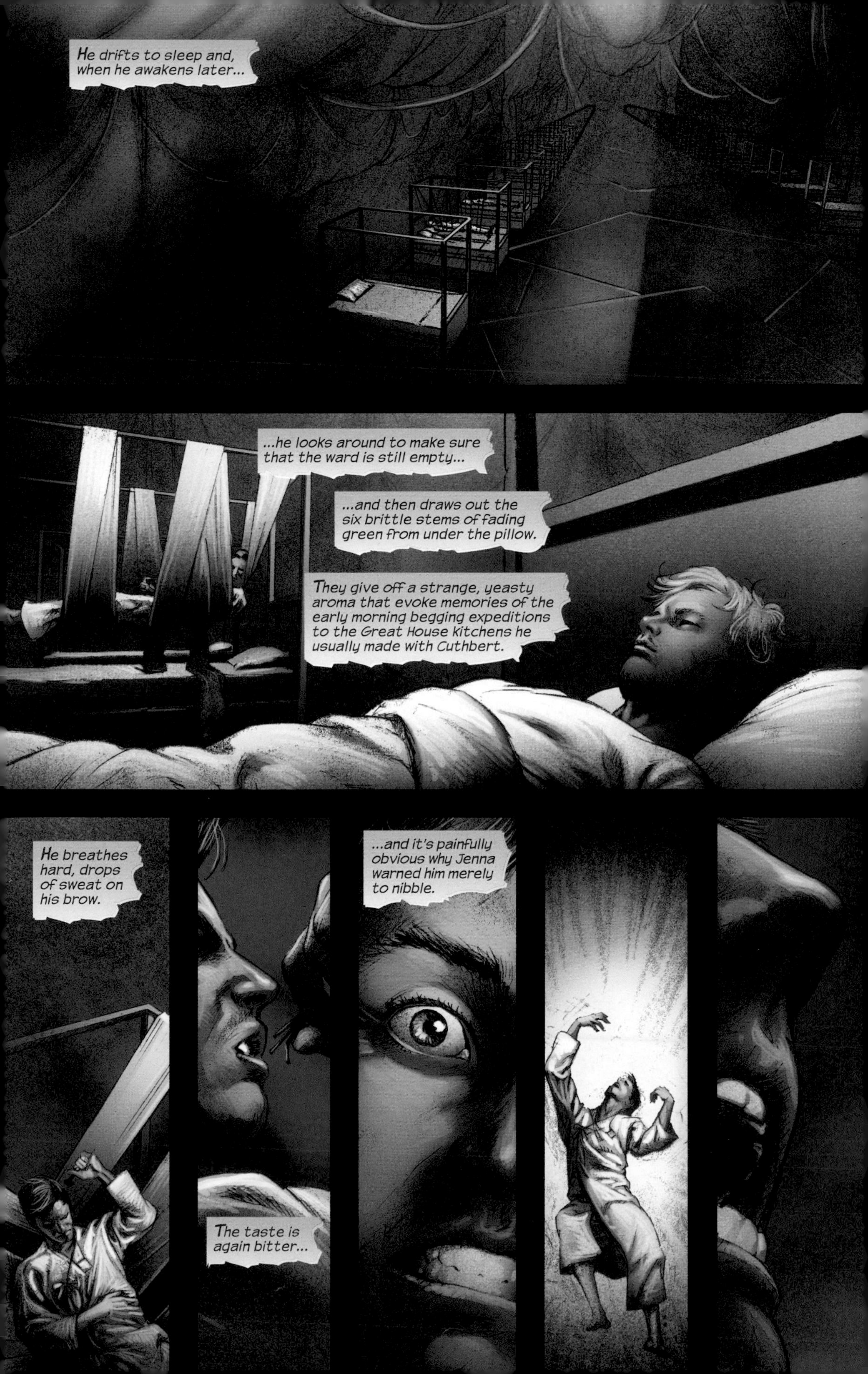
He drifts to sleep and, when he awakens later...
...he looks around to make sure that the ward is still empty...
...and then draws out the six brittle stems of fading green from under the pillow.
They give off a strange, yeasty aroma that evoke memories of the early morning begging expeditions to the Great House kitchens he usually made with Cuthbert.
He breathes hard, drops of sweat on his brow.
The taste is again bitter...
...and it's painfully obvious why Jenna warned him merely to nibble.

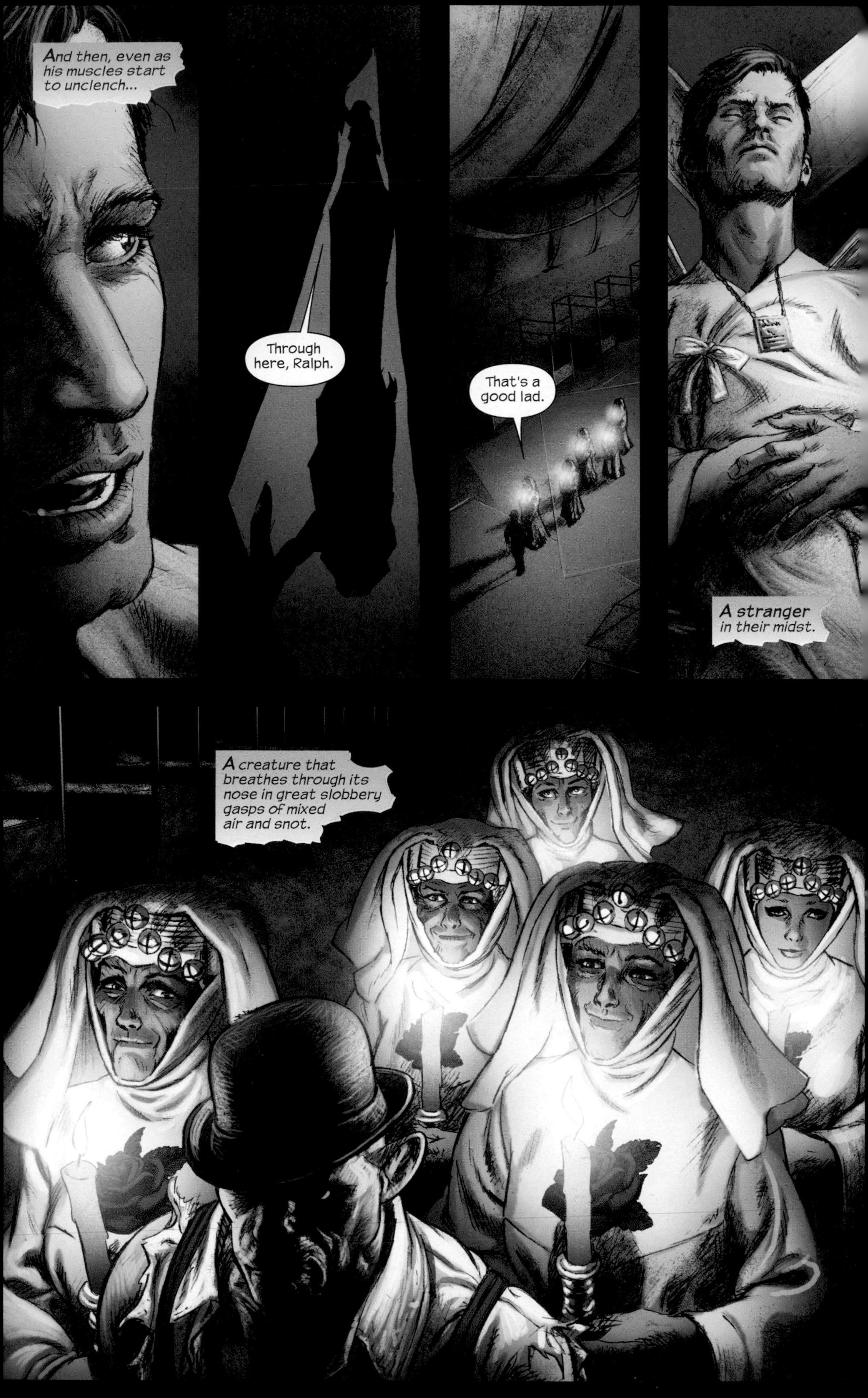
And then, even as his muscles start to unclench...
Through here, Ralph.
That's a good lad.
A stranger in their midst.
A creature that breathes through its nose in great slobbery gasps of mixed air and snot.

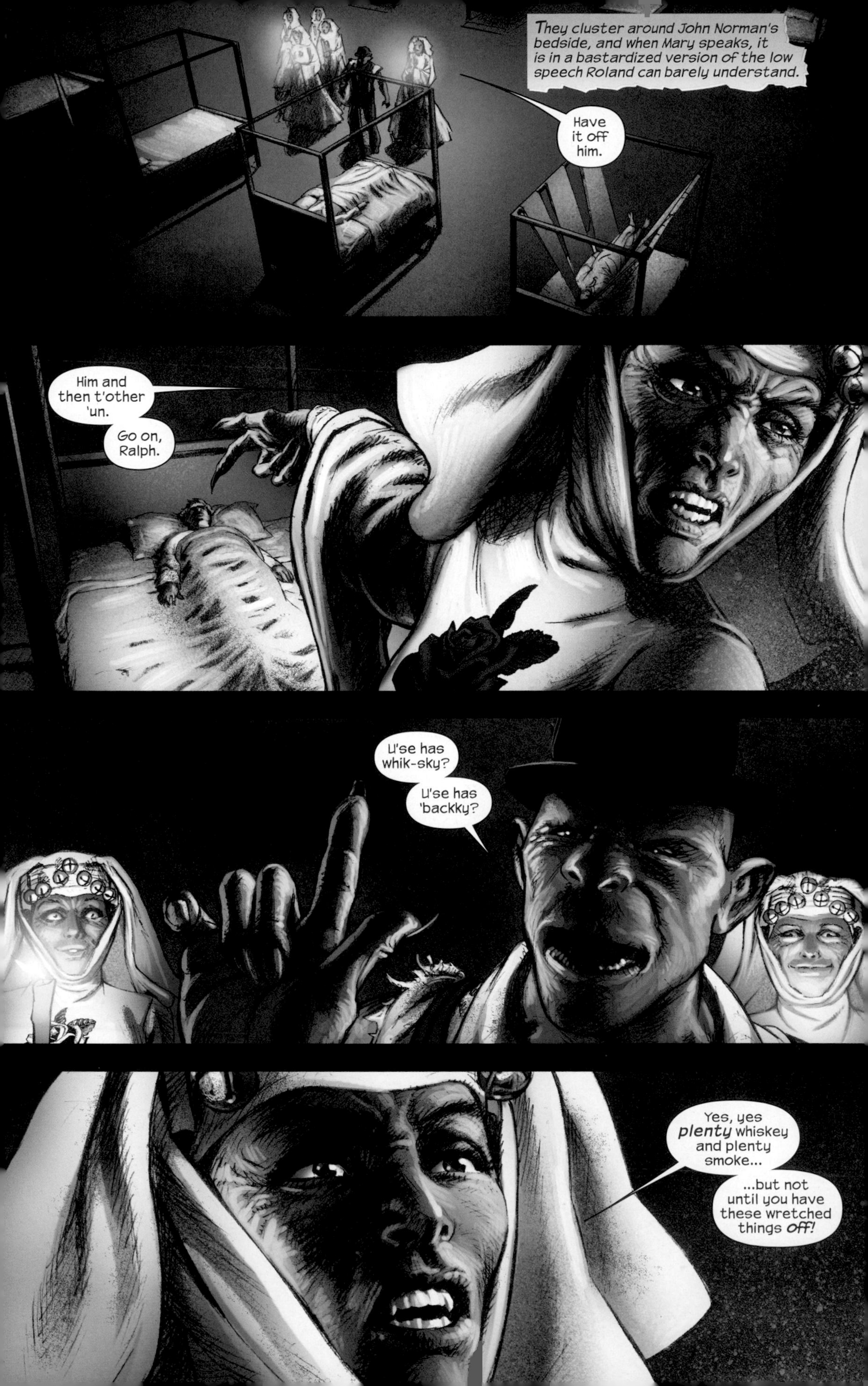

They cluster around John Norman's bedside, and when Mary speaks, it is in a bastardized version of the low speech Roland can barely understand.
Have it off him.
Him and then t'other 'un.
Go on, Ralph.
U'se has whik-sky?
U'se has 'backky?
Yes, yes *plenty* whiskey and plenty smoke...
...but not until you have these wretched things *off!*

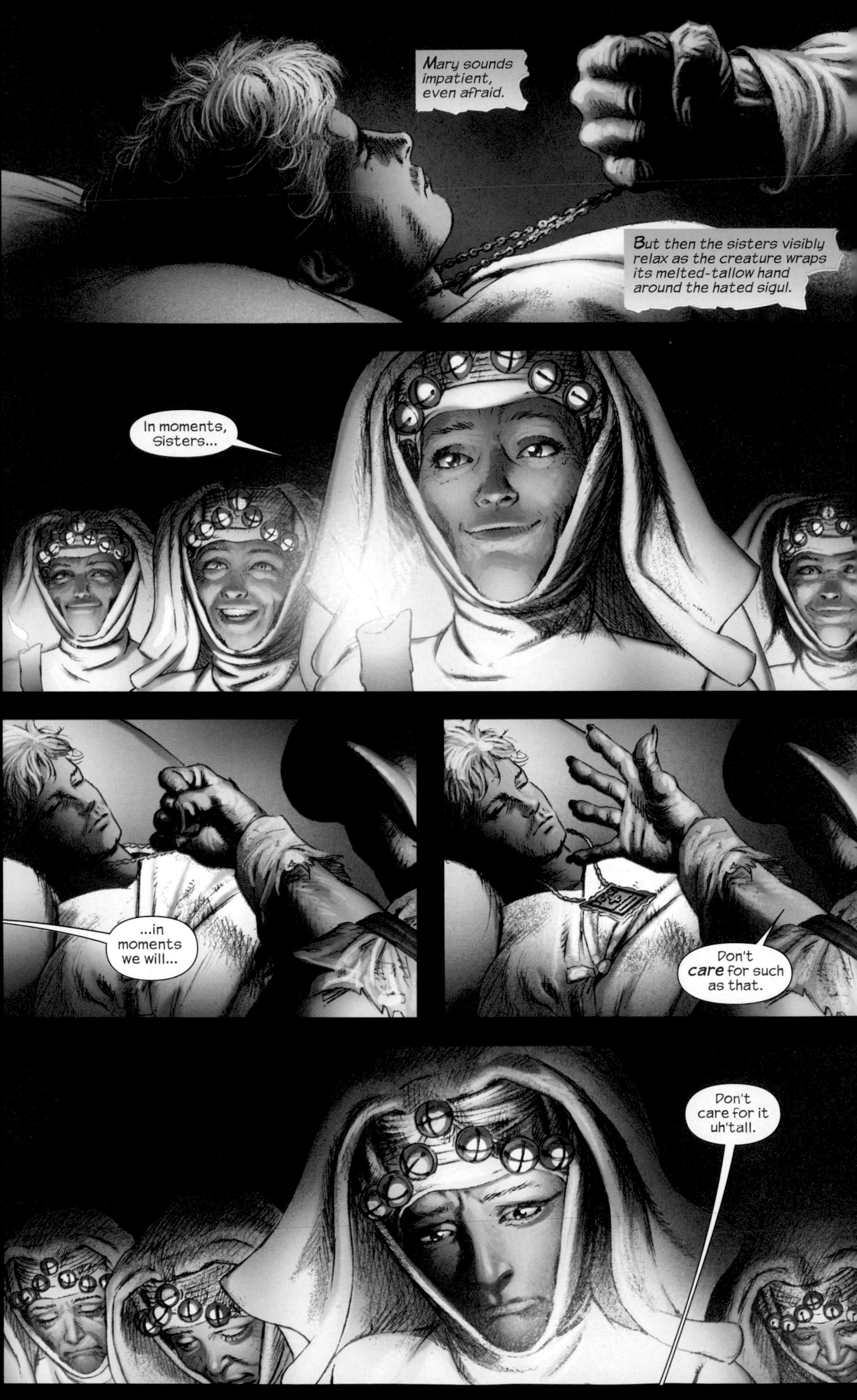

Mary sounds impatient, even afraid.
But then the sisters visibly relax as the creature wraps its melted-tallow hand around the hated sigul.
In moments, Sisters...
...in moments we will...
Don't care for such as that.
Don't care for it uh'tall.

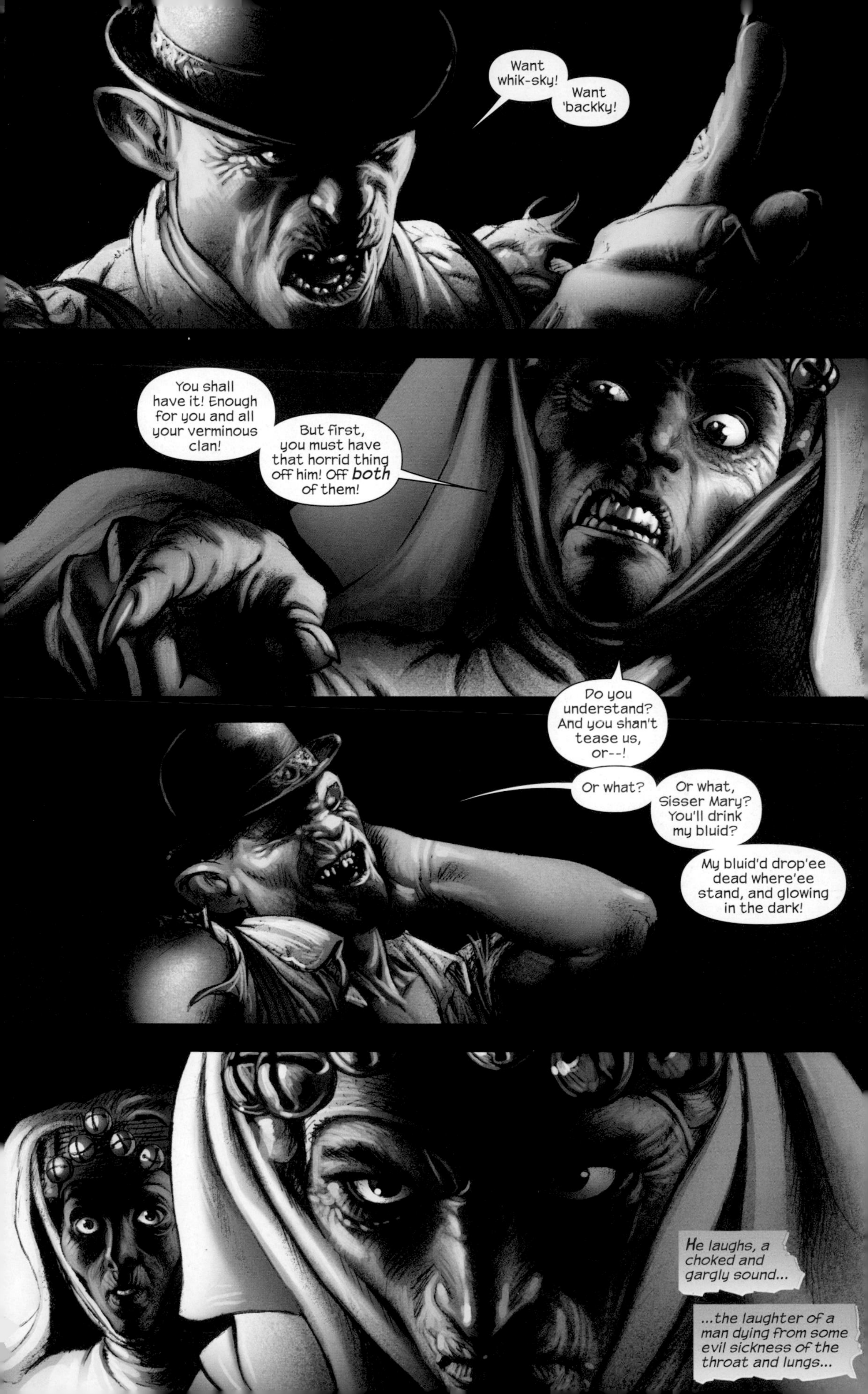
Want whik-sky!
Want 'backky!
You shall have it! Enough for you and all your verminous clan!
But first, you must have that horrid thing off him! Off *both* of them!
Do you understand? And you shan't tease us, or--!
Or what?
Or what, Sisser Mary? You'll drink my bluid?
My bluid'd drop'ee dead where'ee stand, and glowing in the dark!
He laughs, a choked and gargly sound...
...the laughter of a man dying from some evil sickness of the throat and lungs...

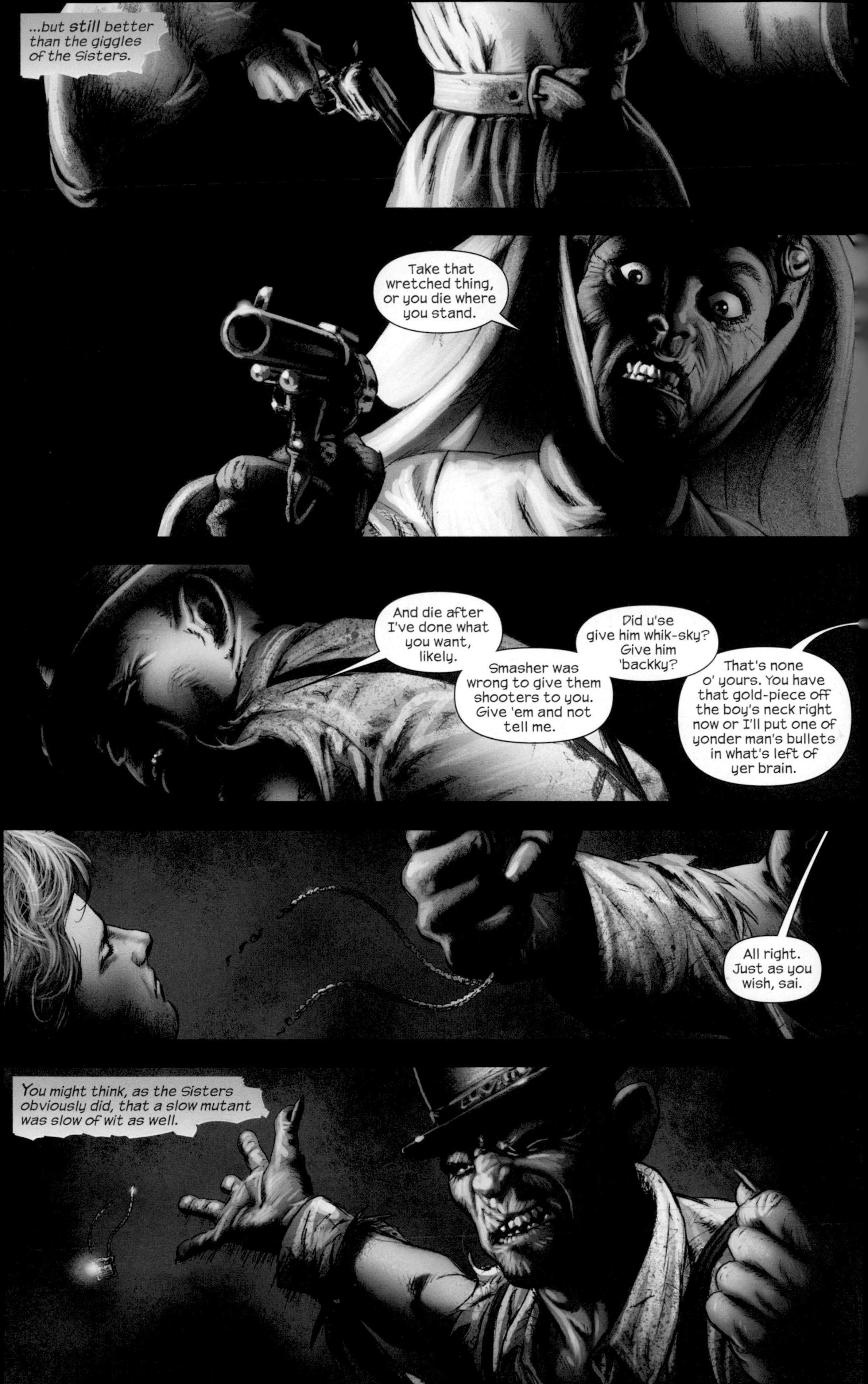
...but still better than the giggles of the Sisters.
Take that wretched thing, or you die where you stand.
And die after I've done what you want, likely.
Smasher was wrong to give them shooters to you. Give 'em and not tell me.
Did u'se give him whik-sky? Give him 'backky?
That's none o' yours. You have that gold-piece off the boy's neck right now or I'll put one of yonder man's bullets in what's left of yer brain.
All right. Just as you wish, sai.
You might think, as the Sisters obviously did, that a slow mutant was slow of wit as well.

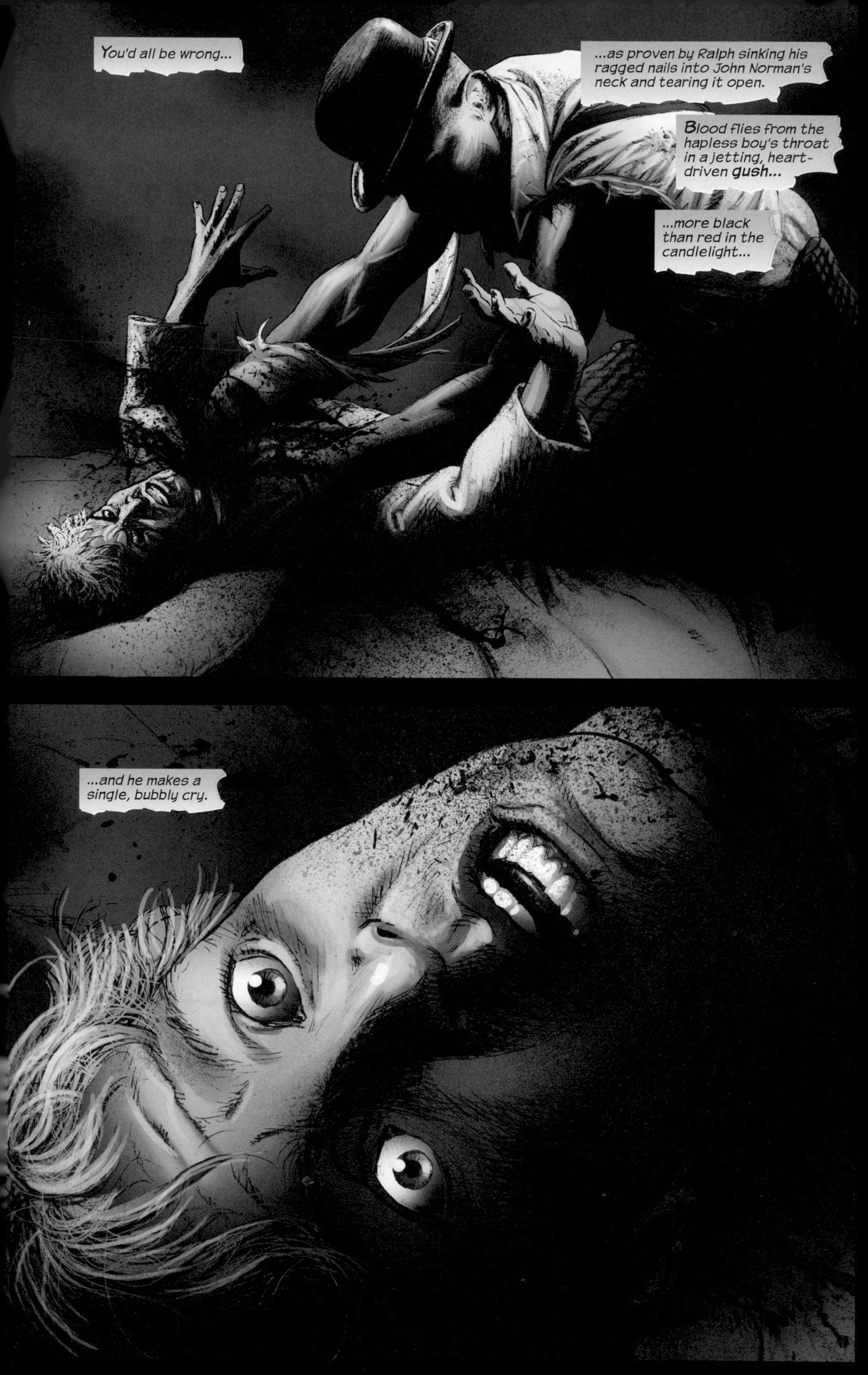
You'd all be wrong...
...as proven by Ralph sinking his ragged nails into John Norman's neck and tearing it open.
Blood flies from the hapless boy's throat in a jetting, heart-driven gush...
...more black than red in the candlelight...
...and he makes a single, bubbly cry.

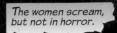

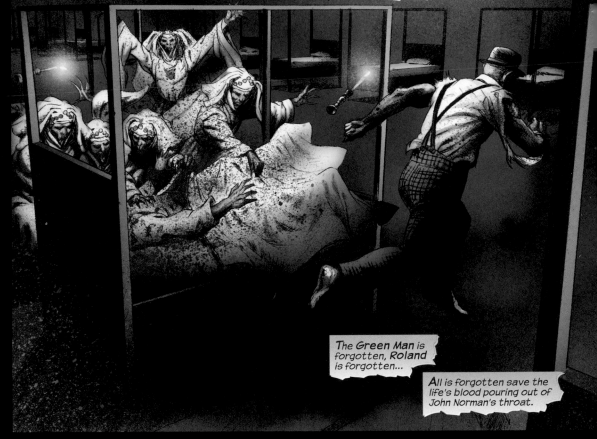

The women scream, but not in horror.

They scream as women do in a frenzy of excitement.

The *Green Man* is forgotten, *Roland* is forgotten...

All is forgotten save the life's blood pouring out of John Norman's throat.

Ralph, he must figure that whiskey and tobacco best be saved for another time, as he concentrates now on saving his own life...

...while the Sisters bend forward to catch as much of the flow as they can before it dries up.

And all Roland can do is lie there in the dark, muscles shivering, heart pounding...

...listening to the harpies as they feed on the boy who he pretended was his brother.

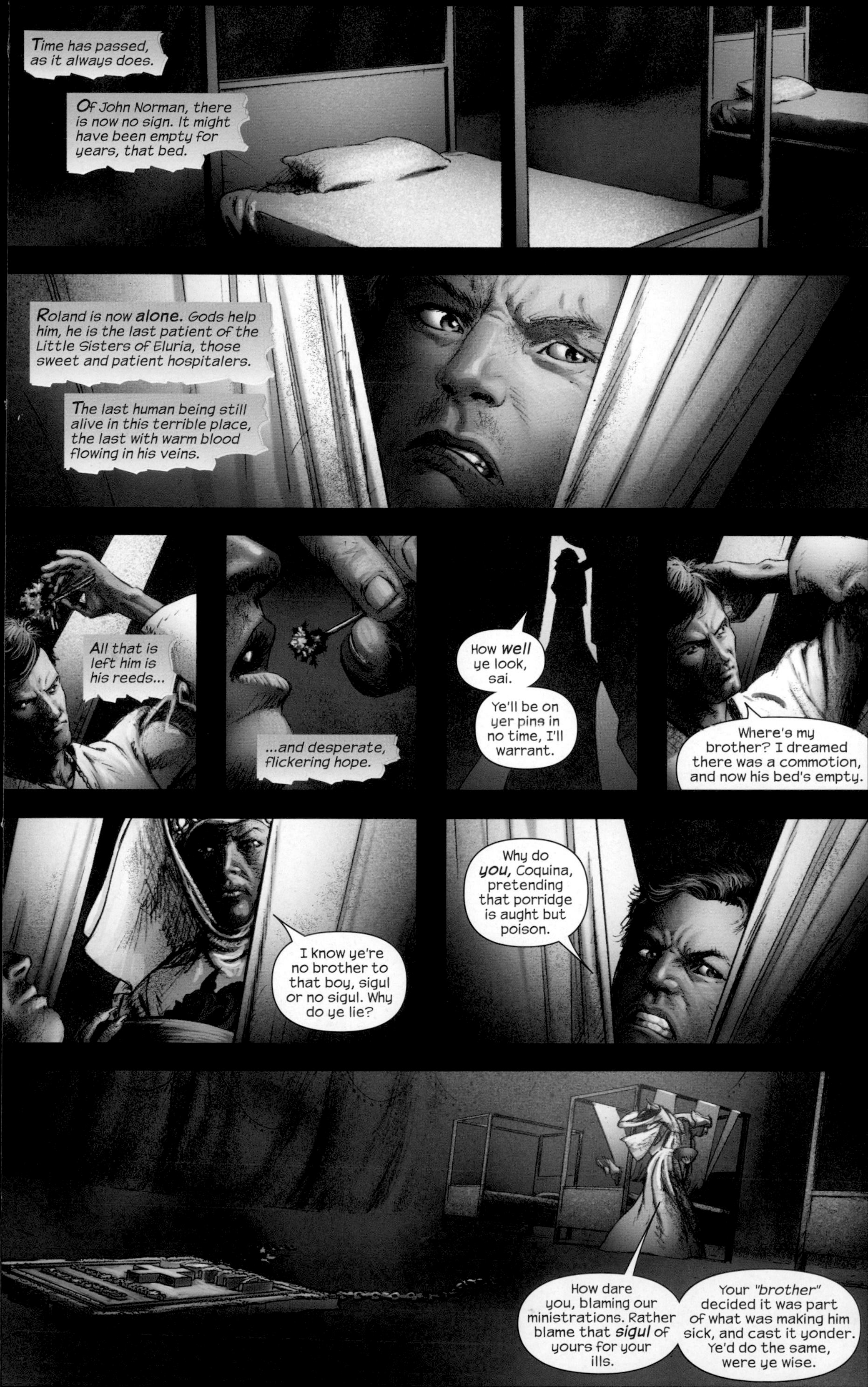
Time has passed, as it always does.
Of John Norman, there is now no sign. It might have been empty for years, that bed.
Roland is now alone. Gods help him, he is the last patient of the Little Sisters of Eluria, those sweet and patient hospitalers.
The last human being still alive in this terrible place, the last with warm blood flowing in his veins.
All that is left him is his reeds...
...and desperate, flickering hope.
How well ye look, sai.
Ye'll be on yer pins in no time, I'll warrant.
Where's my brother? I dreamed there was a commotion, and now his bed's empty.
I know ye're no brother to that boy, sigul or no sigul. Why do ye lie?
Why do you, Coquina, pretending that porridge is aught but poison.
How dare you, blaming our ministrations. Rather blame that sigul of yours for your ills.
Your "brother" decided it was part of what was making him sick, and cast it yonder. Ye'd do the same, were ye wise.

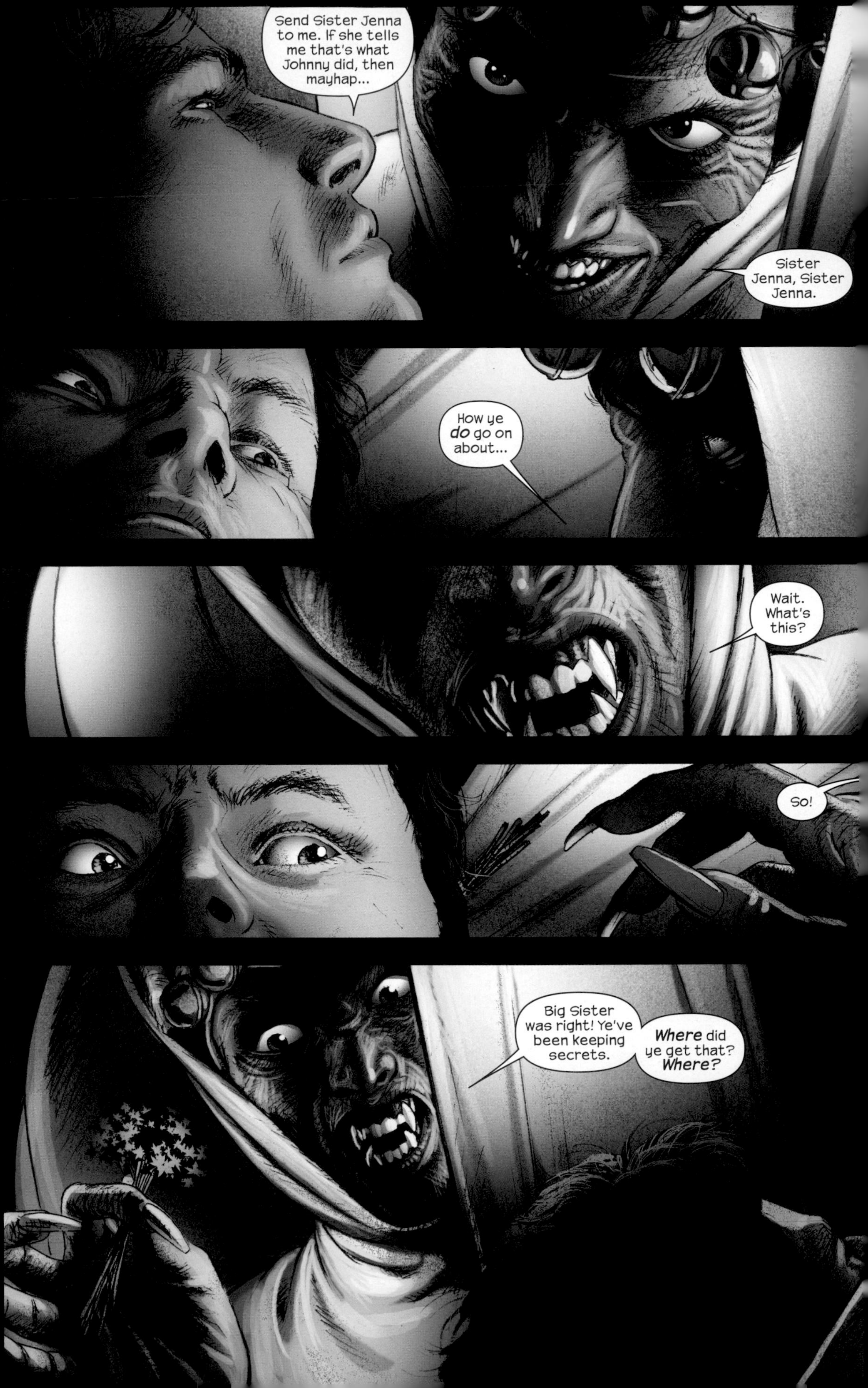

Send Sister Jenna to me. If she tells me that's what Johnny did, then mayhap...
Sister Jenna, Sister Jenna.
How ye *do* go on about...
Wait. What's this?
So!
Big Sister was right! Ye've been keeping secrets.
*Where* did ye get that? *Where?*

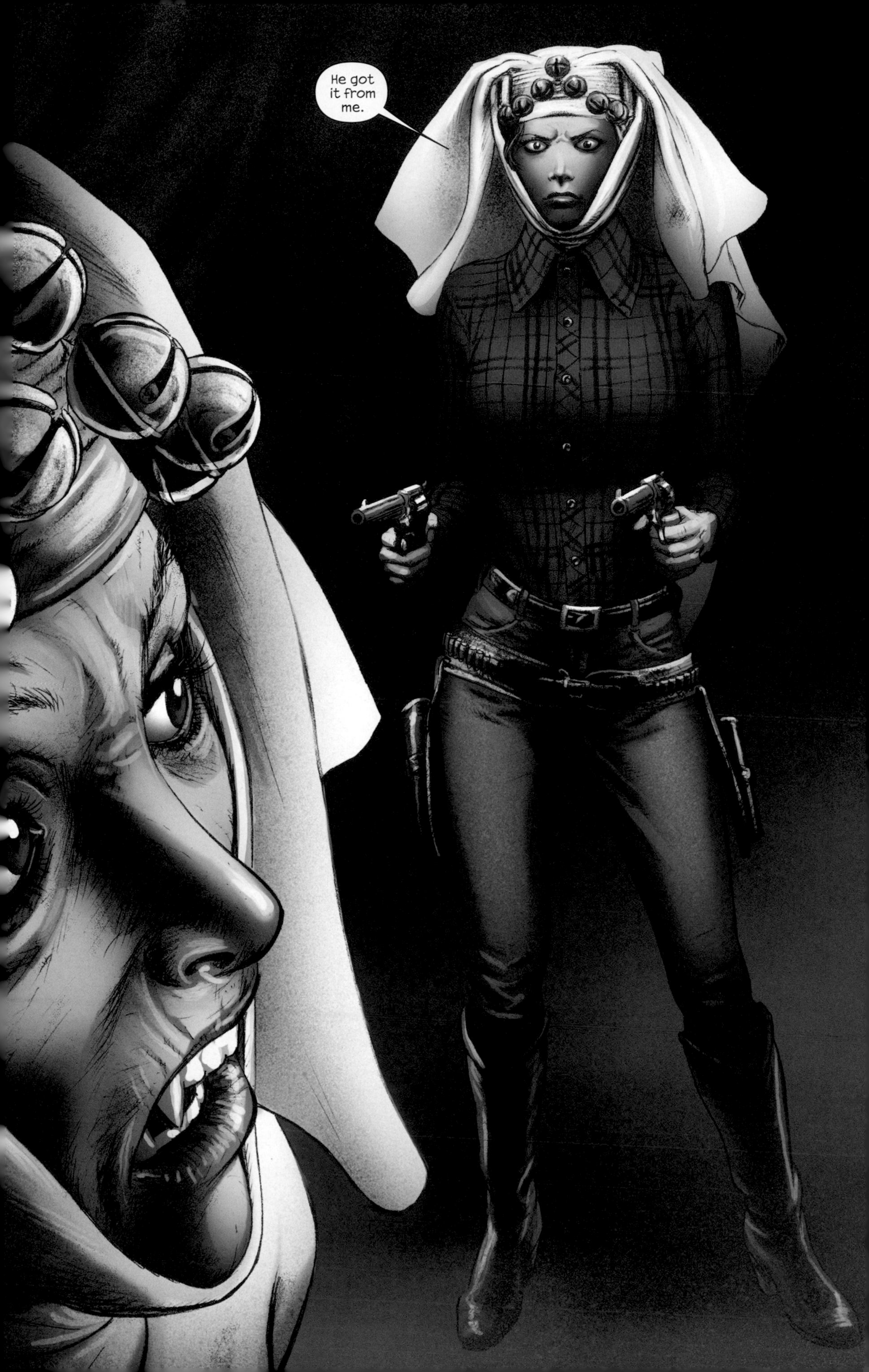
He got it from me.

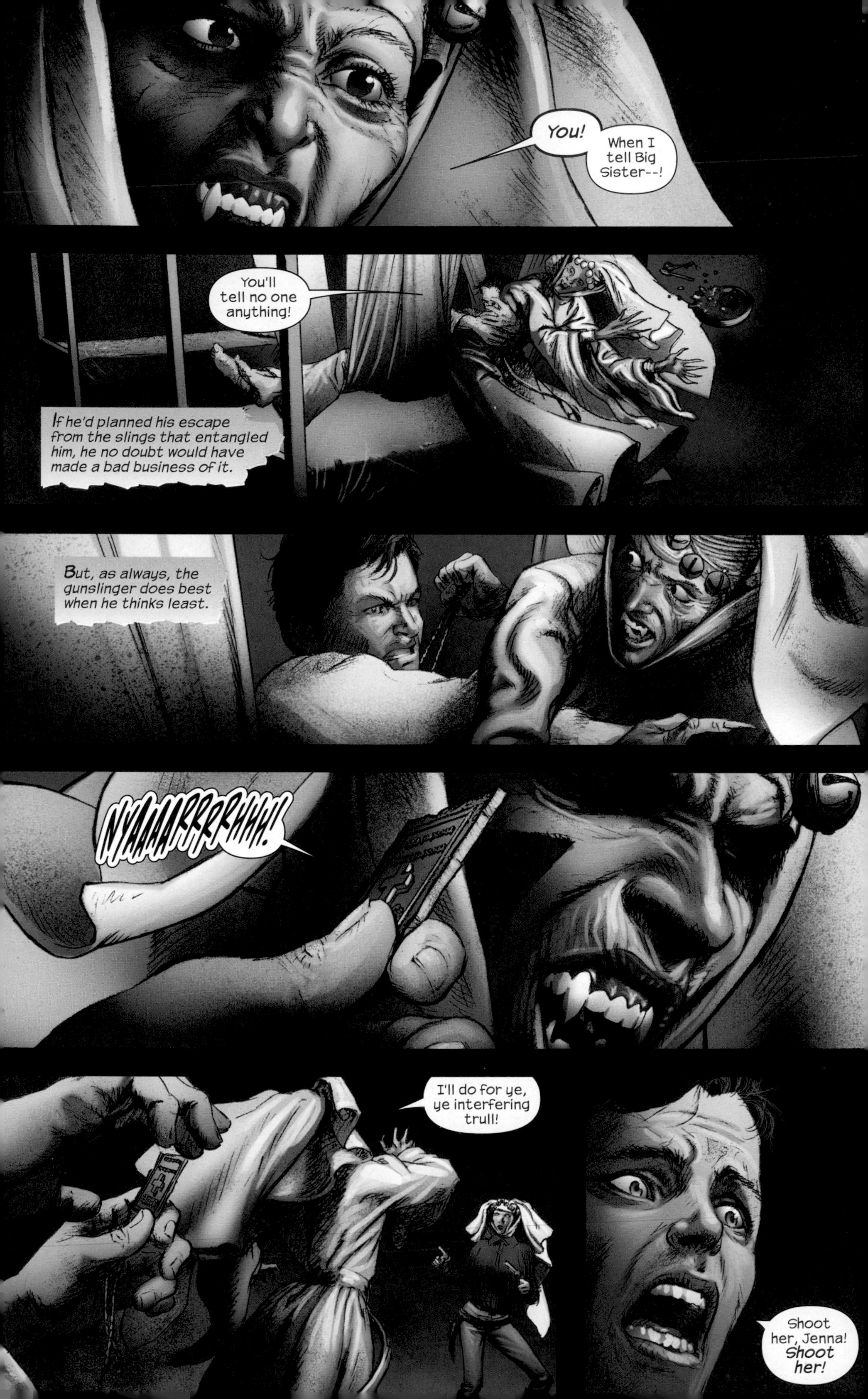
YOU!
When I tell Big Sister--!
You'll tell no one anything!
If he'd planned his escape from the slings that entangled him, he no doubt would have made a bad business of it.
But, as always, the gunslinger does best when he thinks least.
NYAAAARRRRHHH!
I'll do for ye, ye interfering trull!
Shoot her, Jenna! Shoot her!

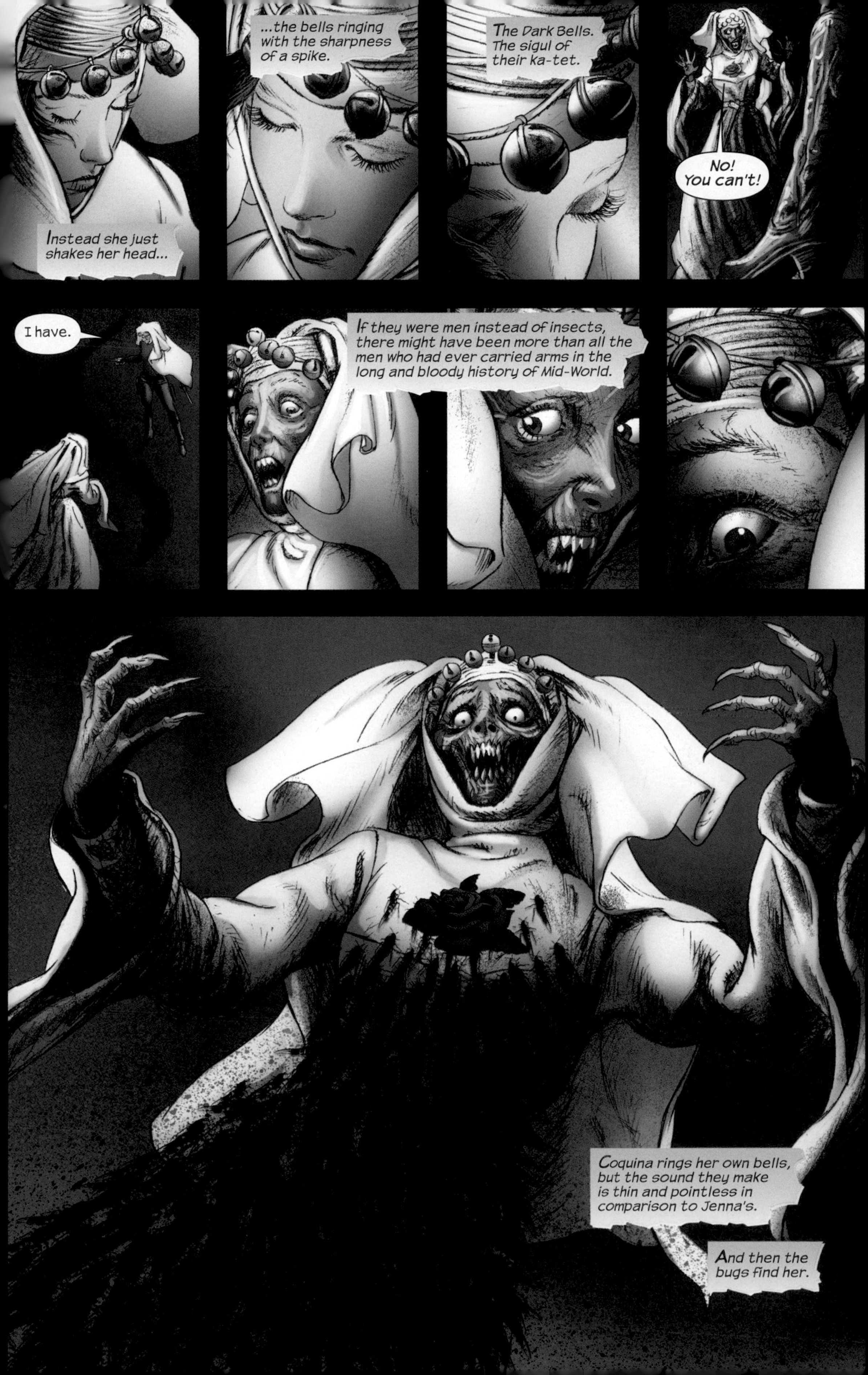
Instead she just shakes her head...
...the bells ringing with the sharpness of a spike.
The Dark Bells. The sigul of their ka-tet.
No! You can't!
I have.
If they were men instead of insects, there might have been more than all the men who had ever carried arms in the long and bloody history of Mid-World.
Coquina rings her own bells, but the sound they make is thin and pointless in comparison to Jenna's.
And then the bugs find her.

STEPHEN KING

# THE DARK TOWER

## ~THE GUNSLINGER~

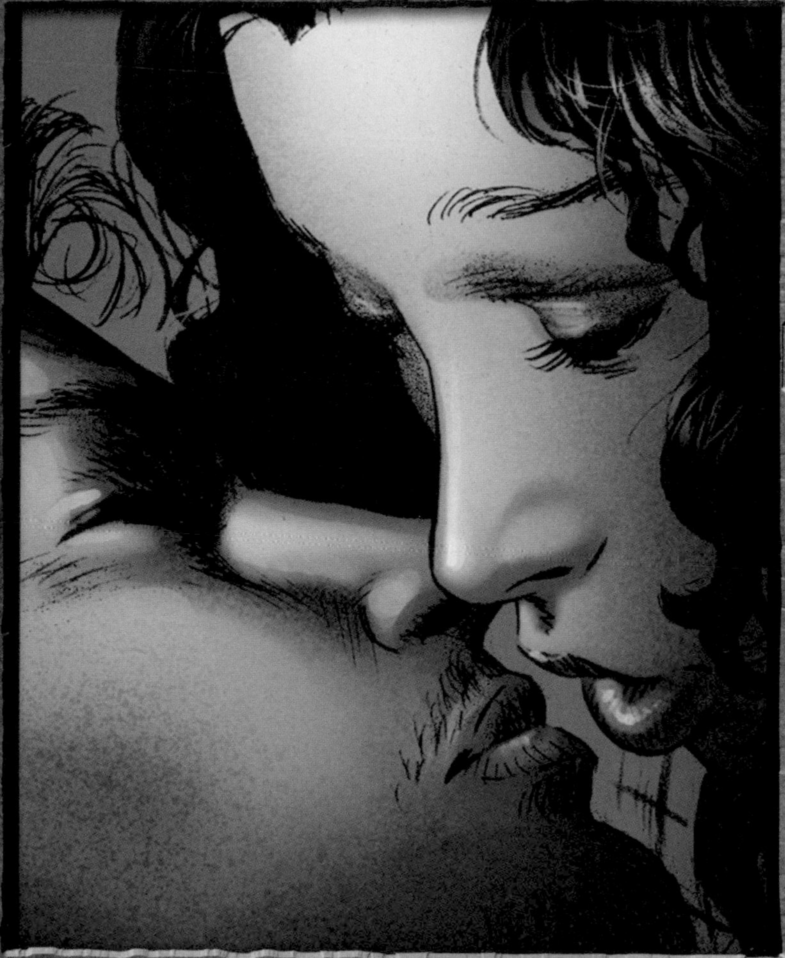

# THE LITTLE SISTERS OF ELURIA

## CHAPTER FIVE

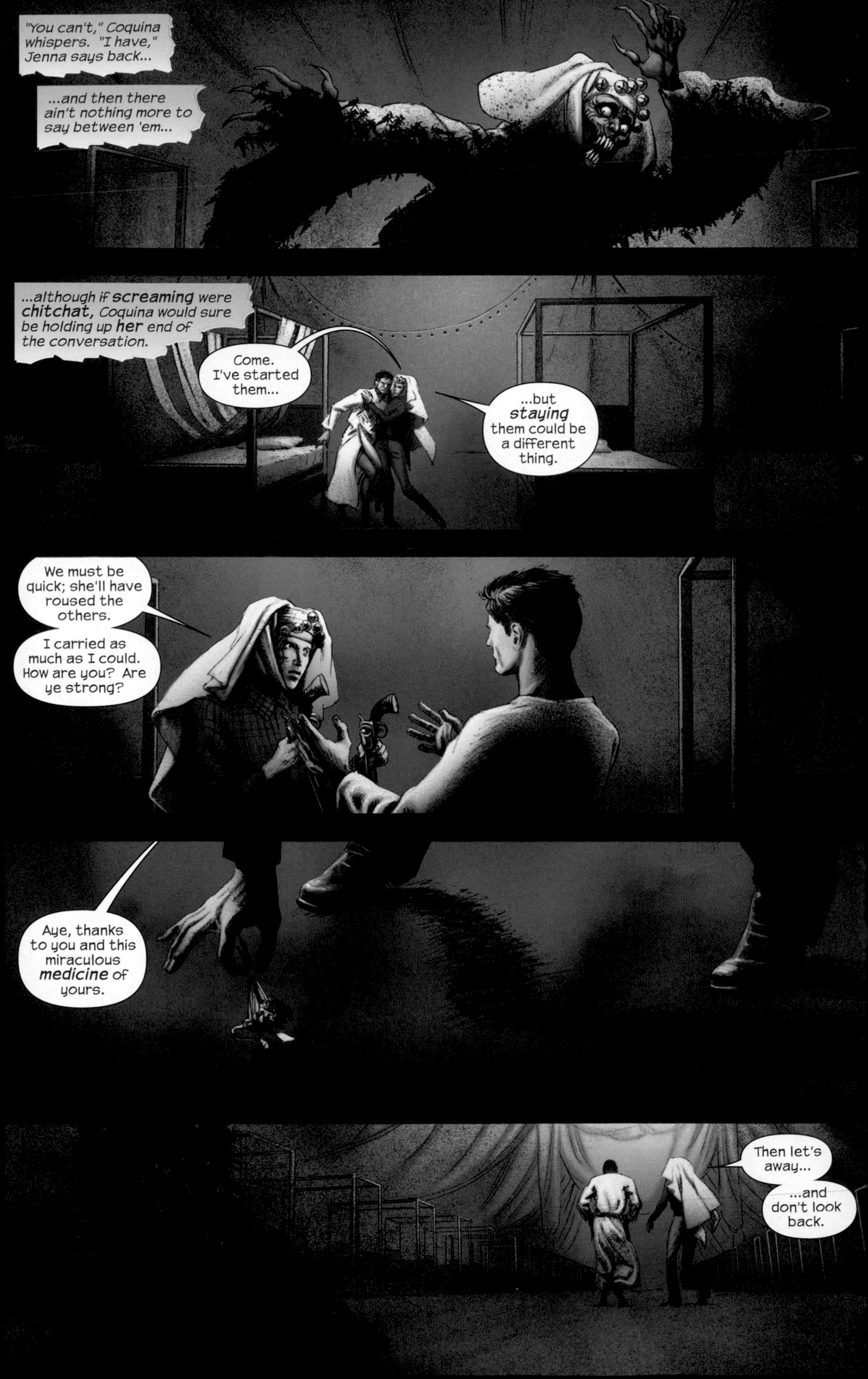
"You can't," Coquina whispers. "I have," Jenna says back...
...and then there ain't nothing more to say between 'em...
...although if screaming were chitchat, Coquina would sure be holding up her end of the conversation.
Come. I've started them...
...but staying them could be a different thing.
We must be quick; she'll have roused the others.
I carried as much as I could. How are you? Are ye strong?
Aye, thanks to you and this miraculous medicine of yours.
Then let's away...
...and don't look back.

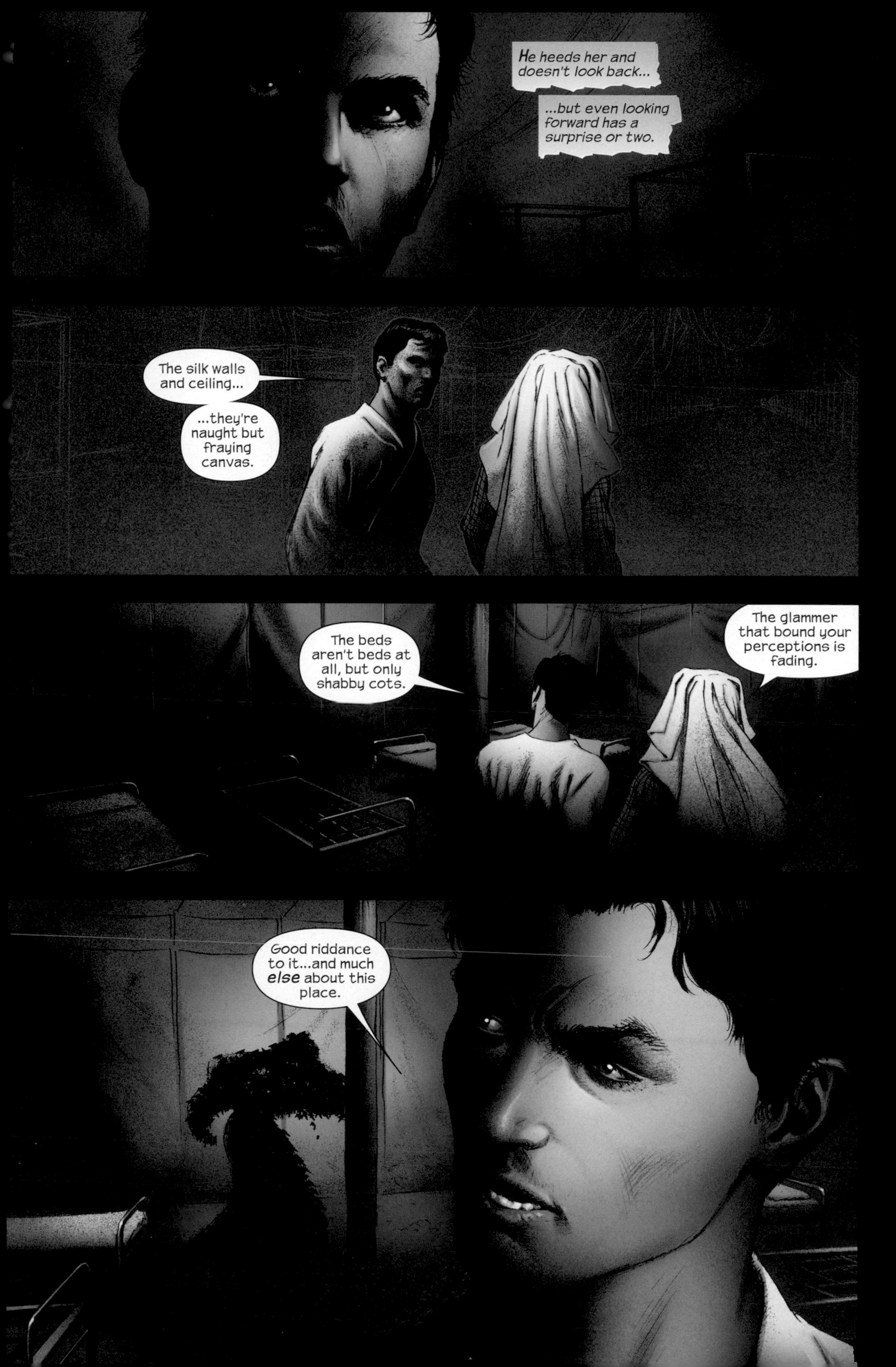
He heeds her and doesn't look back...
...but even looking forward has a surprise or two.
The silk walls and ceiling...
...they're naught but fraying canvas.
The beds aren't beds at all, but only shabby cots.
The glammer that bound your perceptions is fading.
Good riddance to it...and much *else* about this place.

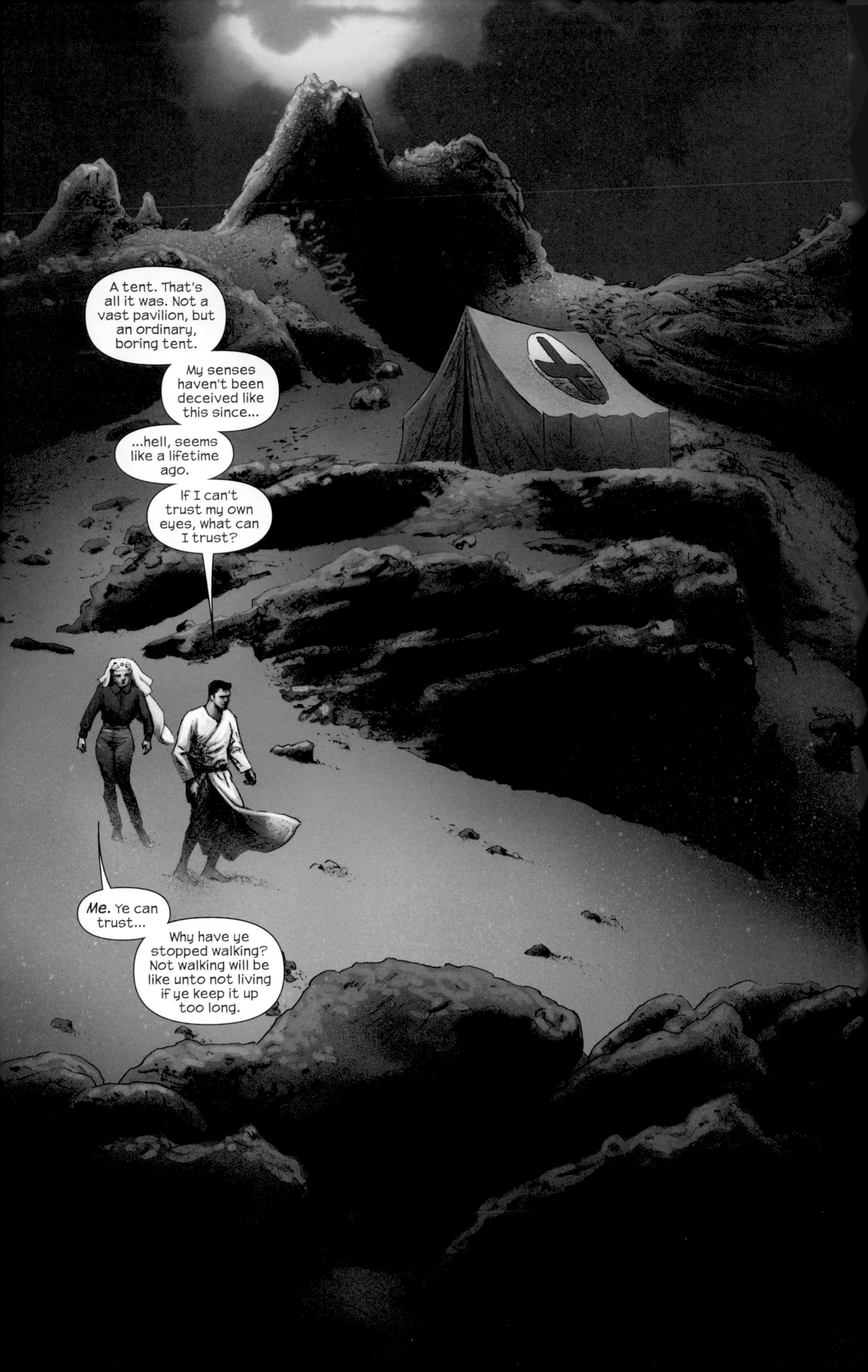

A tent. That's all it was. Not a vast pavilion, but an ordinary, boring tent.
My senses haven't been deceived like this since...
...hell, seems like a lifetime ago.
If I can't trust my own eyes, what can I trust?
*Me.* Ye can trust...
Why have ye stopped walking? Not walking will be like unto not living if ye keep it up too long.

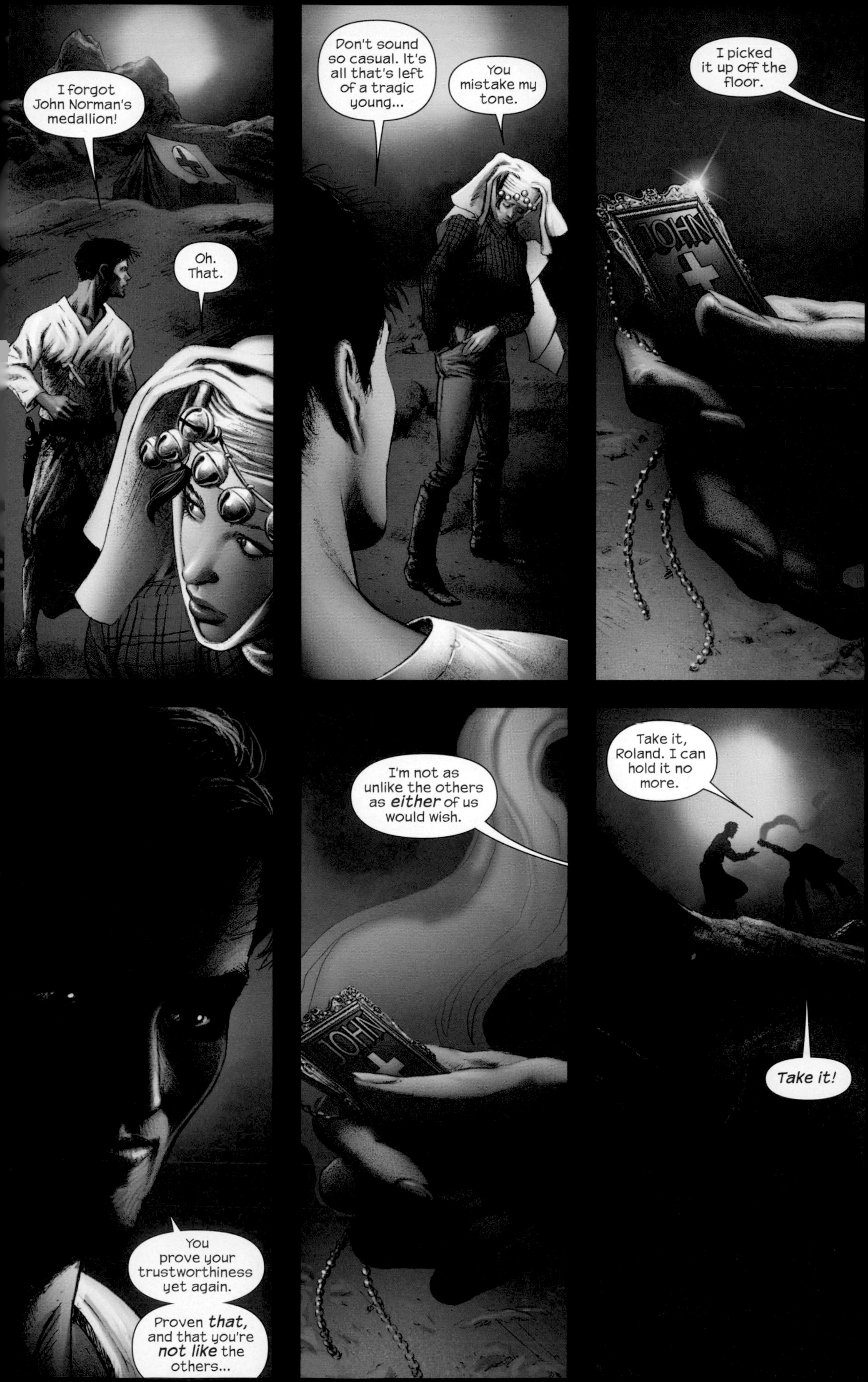
I forgot John Norman's medallion!
Oh. That.
Don't sound so casual. It's all that's left of a tragic young...
You mistake my tone.
I picked it up off the floor.
JOHN
You prove your trustworthiness yet again.
Proven *that,* and that you're *not like* the others...
I'm not as unlike the others as *either* of us would wish.
JOHN
Take it, Roland. I can hold it no more.
*Take it!*

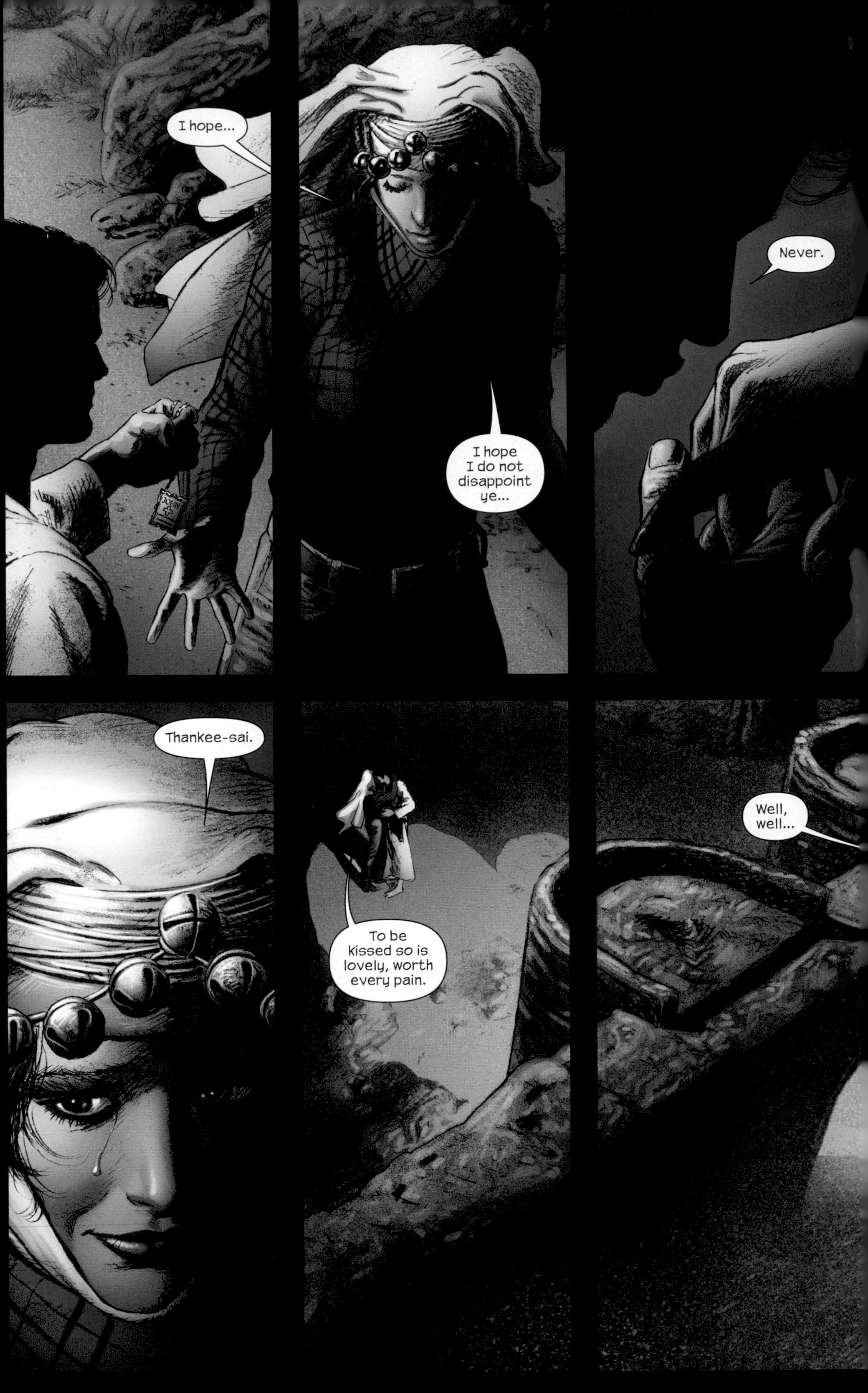
I hope...
I hope I do not disappoint ye...
Never.
Thankee-sai.
To be kissed so is lovely, worth every pain.
Well, well...

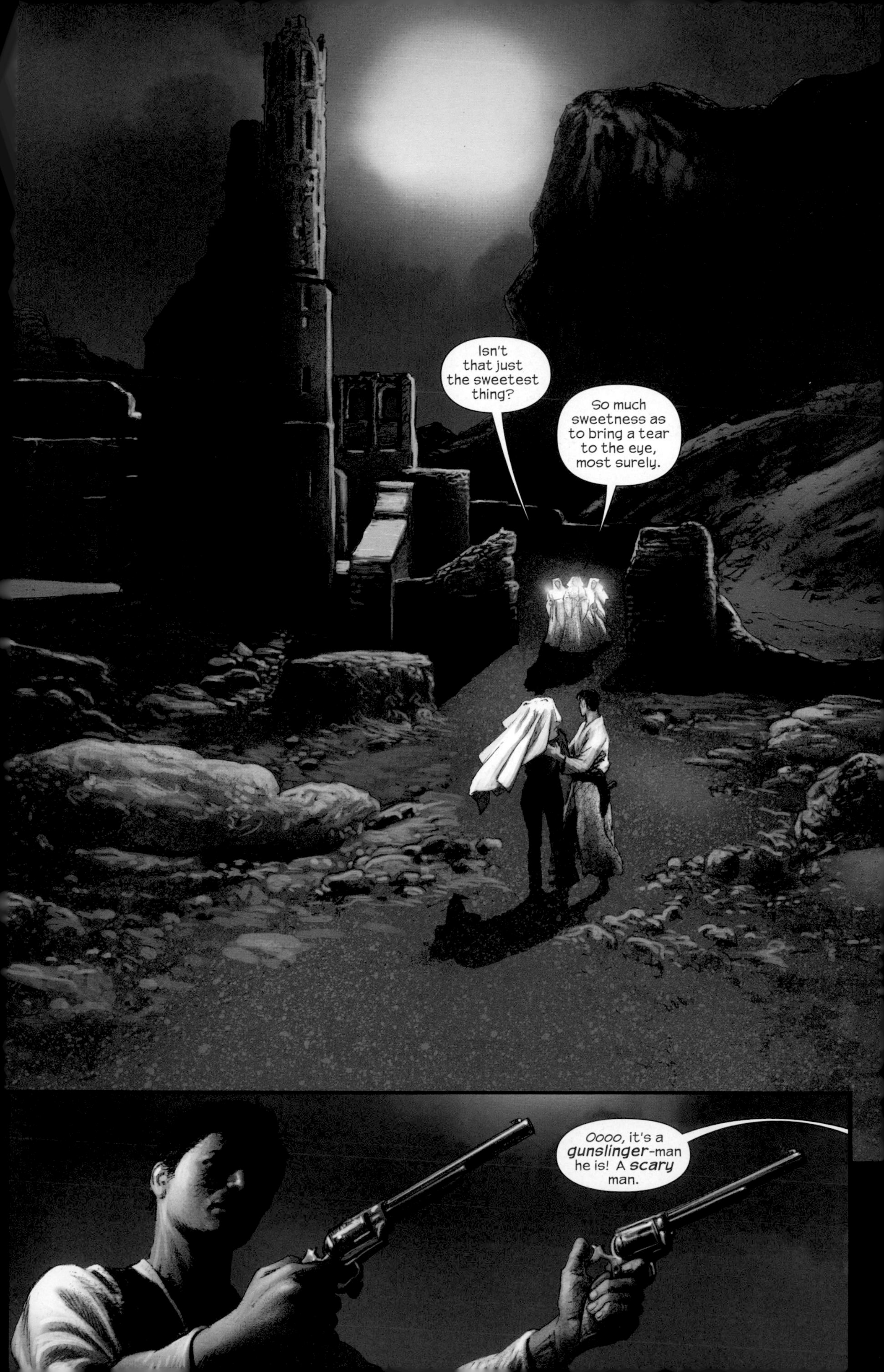
Isn't that just the sweetest thing?
So much sweetness as to bring a tear to the eye, most surely.
*Oooo*, it's a ***gunslinger***-man he is! A ***scary*** man.

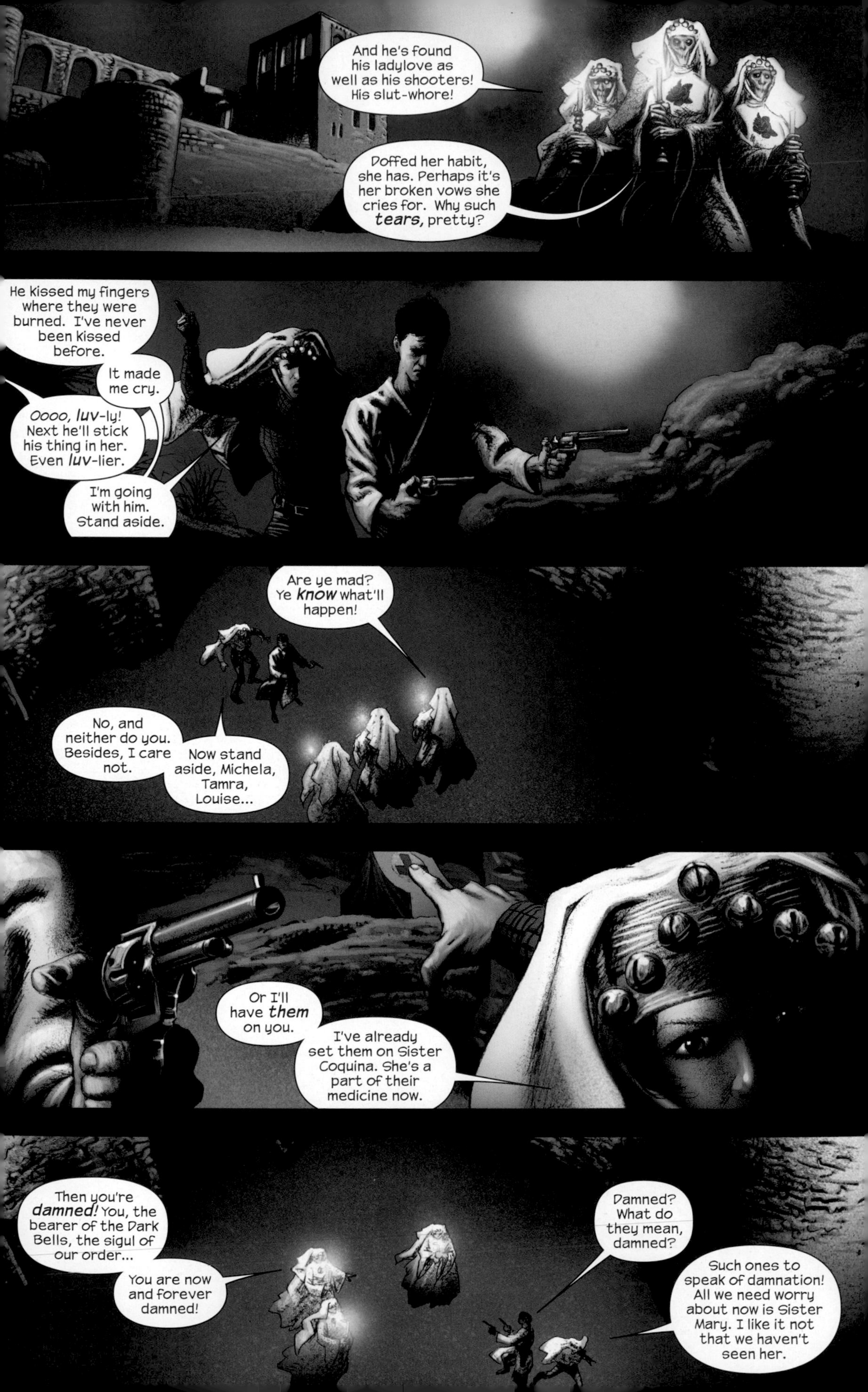
And he's found his ladylove as well as his shooters! His slut-whore!
Doffed her habit, she has. Perhaps it's her broken vows she cries for. Why such tears, pretty?
He kissed my fingers where they were burned. I've never been kissed before.
It made me cry.
Oooo, luv-ly! Next he'll stick his thing in her. Even luv-lier.
I'm going with him. Stand aside.
Are ye mad? Ye know what'll happen!
No, and neither do you. Besides, I care not.
Now stand aside, Michela, Tamra, Louise...
Or I'll have them on you.
I've already set them on Sister Coquina. She's a part of their medicine now.
Then you're damned! You, the bearer of the Dark Bells, the sigul of our order...
You are now and forever damned!
Damned? What do they mean, damned?
Such ones to speak of damnation! All we need worry about now is Sister Mary. I like it not that we haven't seen her.

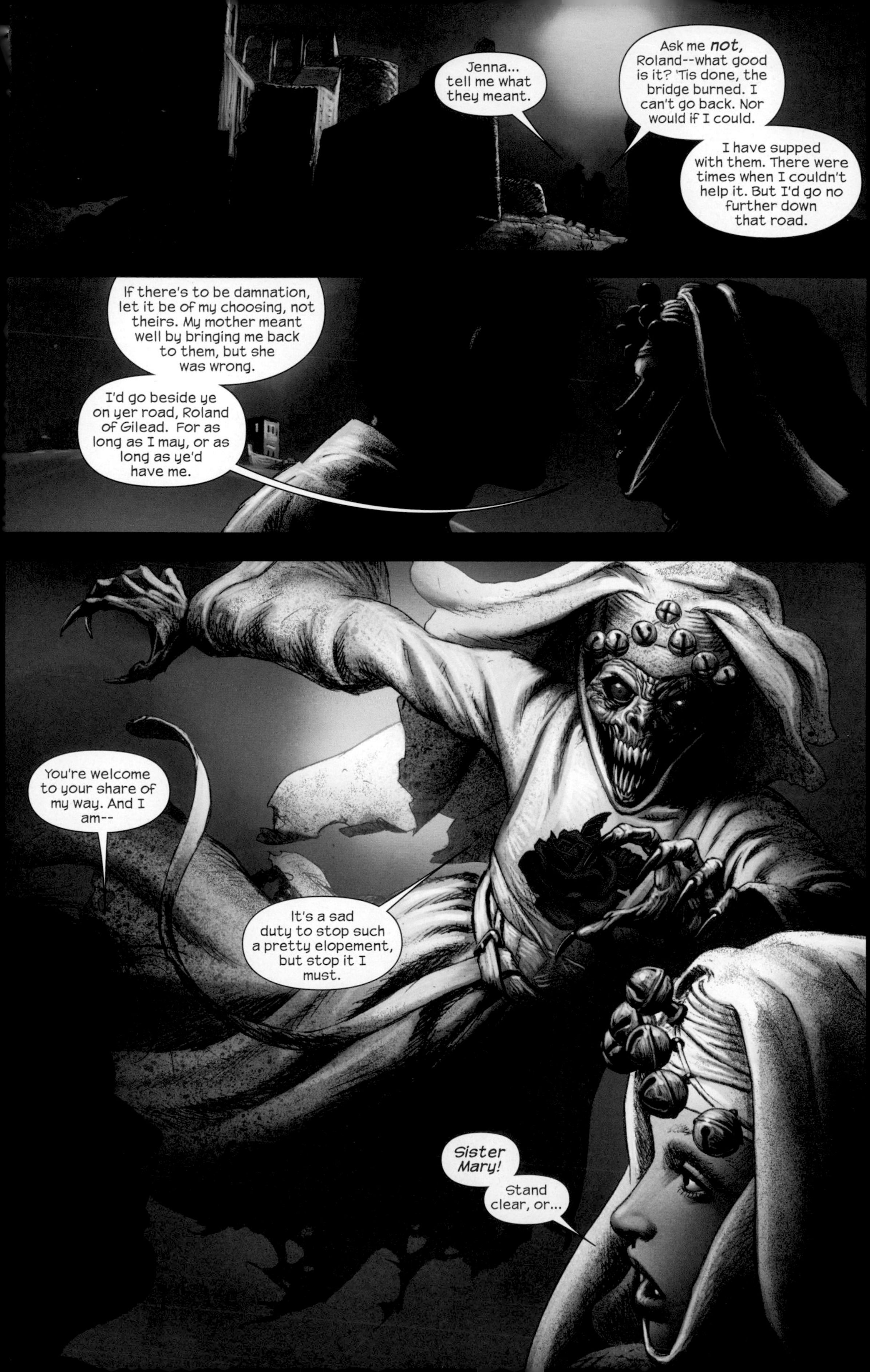
Jenna... tell me what they meant.
Ask me *not,* Roland--what good is it? 'Tis done, the bridge burned. I can't go back. Nor would if I could.
I have supped with them. There were times when I couldn't help it. But I'd go no further down that road.
If there's to be damnation, let it be of my choosing, not theirs. My mother meant well by bringing me back to them, but she was wrong.
I'd go beside ye on yer road, Roland of Gilead. For as long as I may, or as long as ye'd have me.
You're welcome to your share of my way. And I am--
It's a sad duty to stop such a pretty elopement, but stop it I must.
*Sister Mary!*
Stand clear, or...

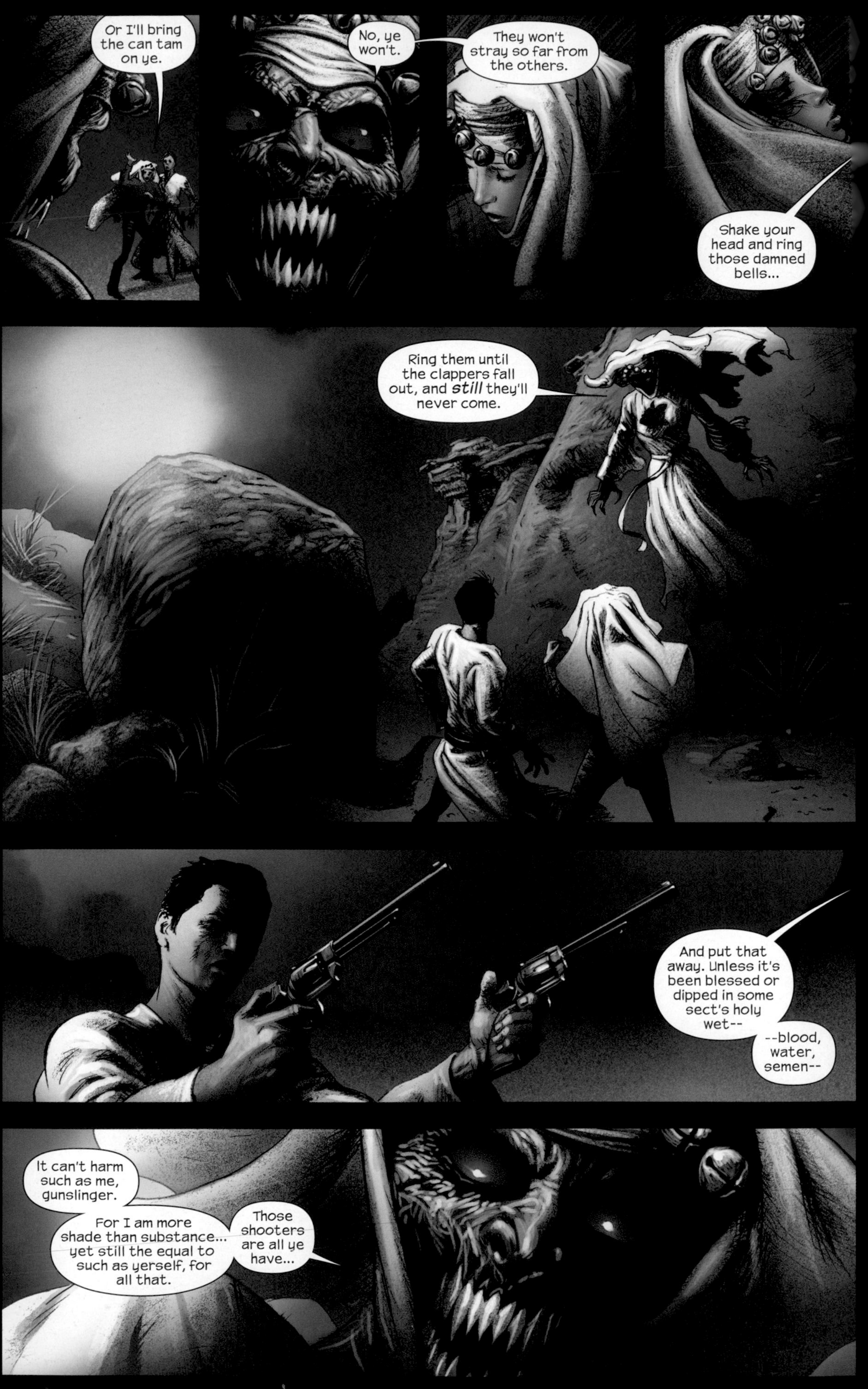
Or I'll bring the can tam on ye.
No, ye won't.
They won't stray so far from the others.
Shake your head and ring those damned bells...
Ring them until the clappers fall out, and *still* they'll never come.
And put that away. Unless it's been blessed or dipped in some sect's holy wet--
--blood, water, semen--
It can't harm such as me, gunslinger.
For I am more shade than substance... yet still the equal to such as yerself, for all that.
Those shooters are all ye have...

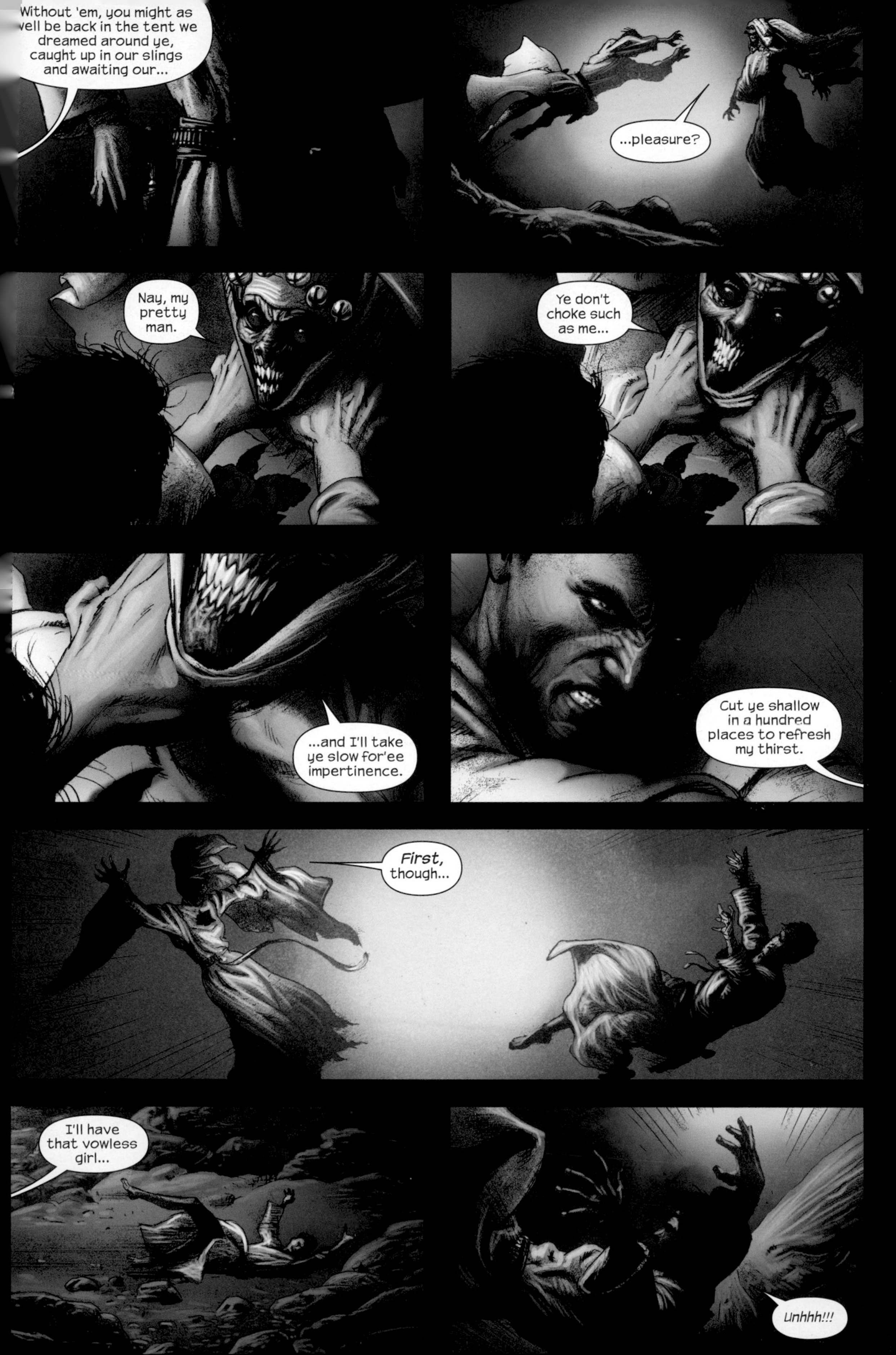
Without 'em, you might as well be back in the tent we dreamed around ye, caught up in our slings and awaiting our...
...pleasure?
Nay, my pretty man.
Ye don't choke such as me...
...and I'll take ye slow for'ee impertinence.
Cut ye shallow in a hundred places to refresh my thirst.
First, though...
I'll have that vowless girl...
Unhhh!!!

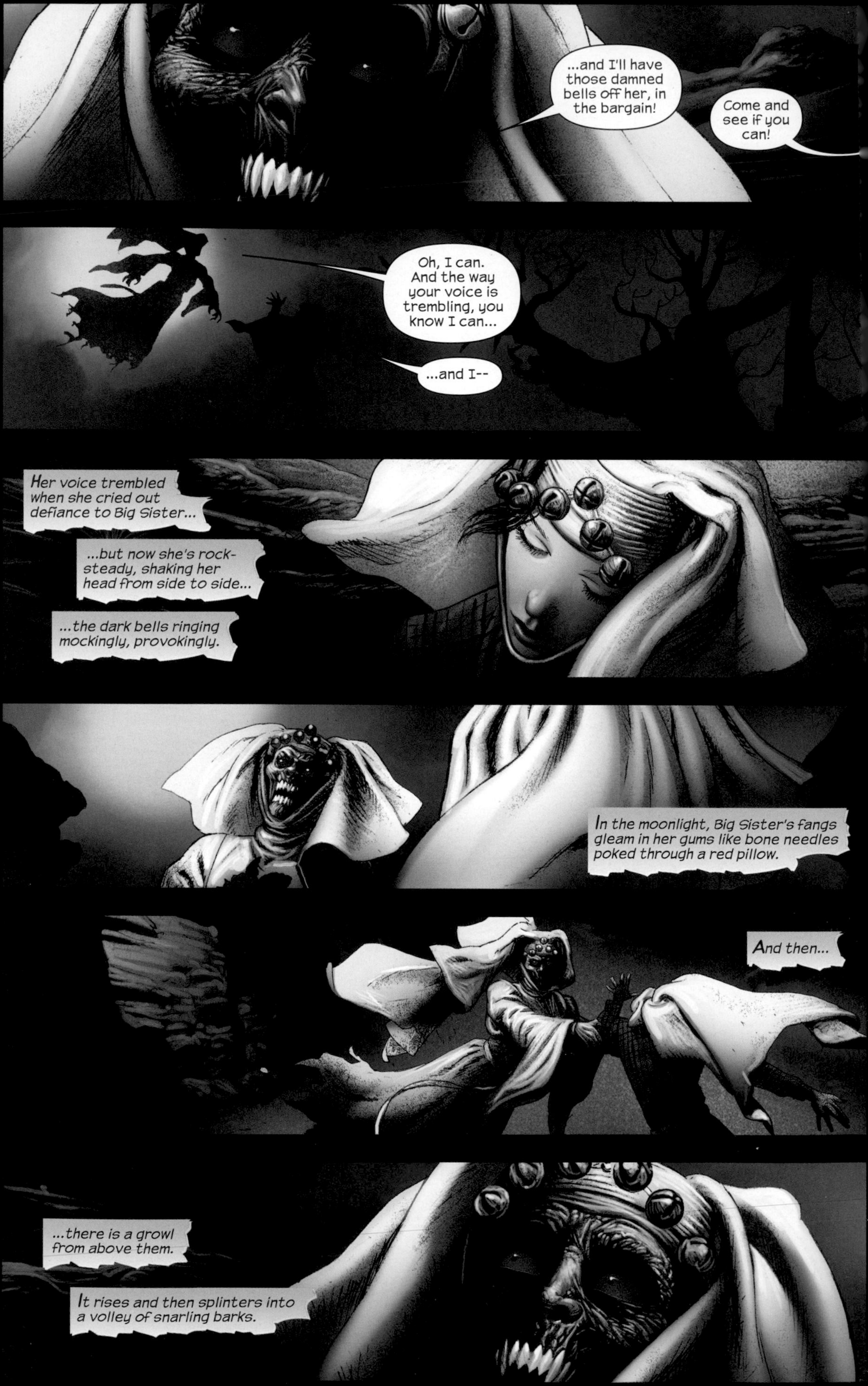
...and I'll have those damned bells off her, in the bargain!
Come and see if you can!
Oh, I can. And the way your voice is trembling, you know I can...
...and I--
Her voice trembled when she cried out defiance to Big Sister...
...but now she's rock-steady, shaking her head from side to side...
...the dark bells ringing mockingly, provokingly.
In the moonlight, Big Sister's fangs gleam in her gums like bone needles poked through a red pillow.
And then...
...there is a growl from above them.
It rises and then splinters into a volley of snarling barks.

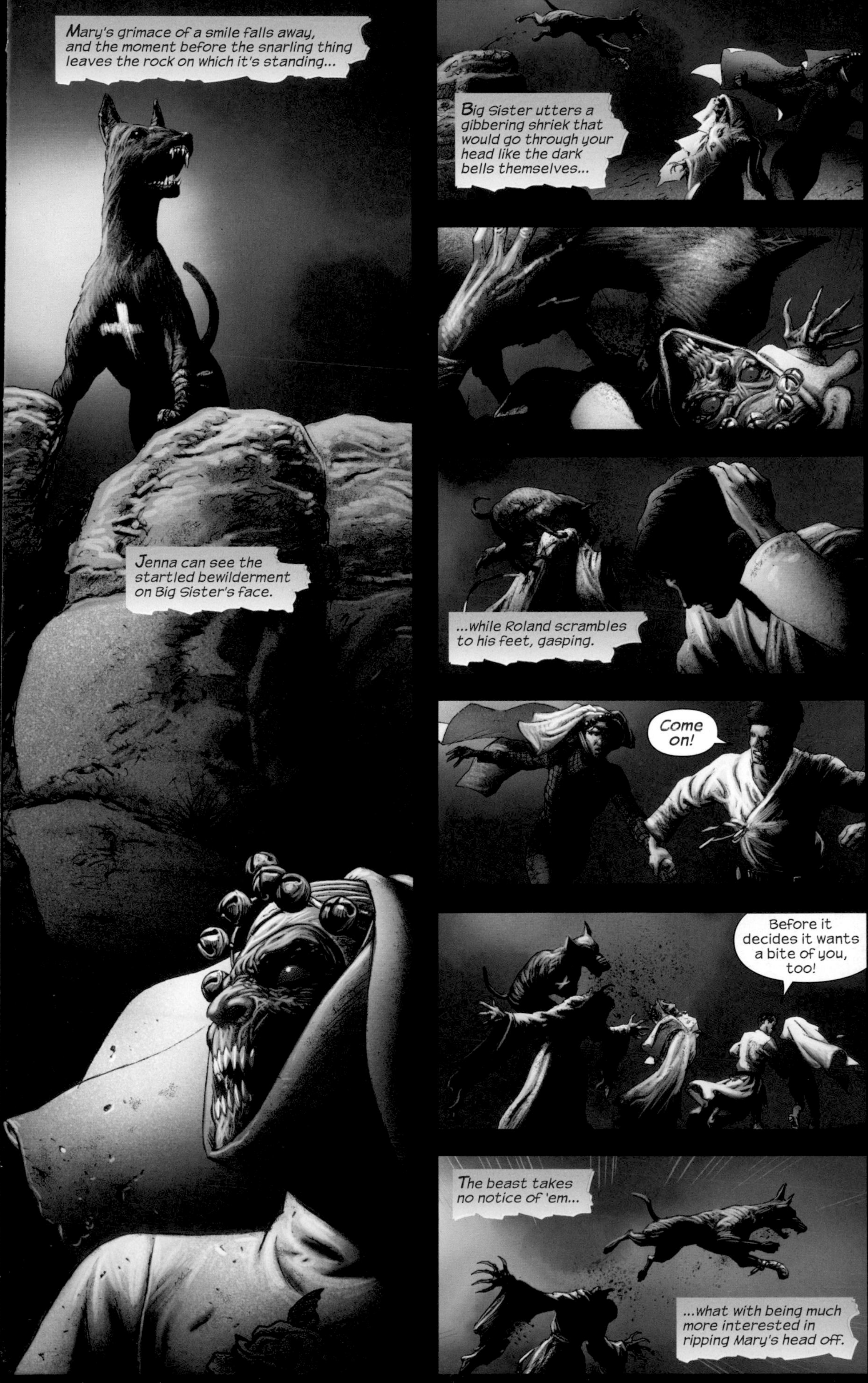
Mary's grimace of a smile falls away, and the moment before the snarling thing leaves the rock on which it's standing...
Jenna can see the startled bewilderment on Big Sister's face.
Big Sister utters a gibbering shriek that would go through your head like the dark bells themselves...
...while Roland scrambles to his feet, gasping.
Come on!
Before it decides it wants a bite of you, too!
The beast takes no notice of 'em...
...what with being much more interested in ripping Mary's head off.

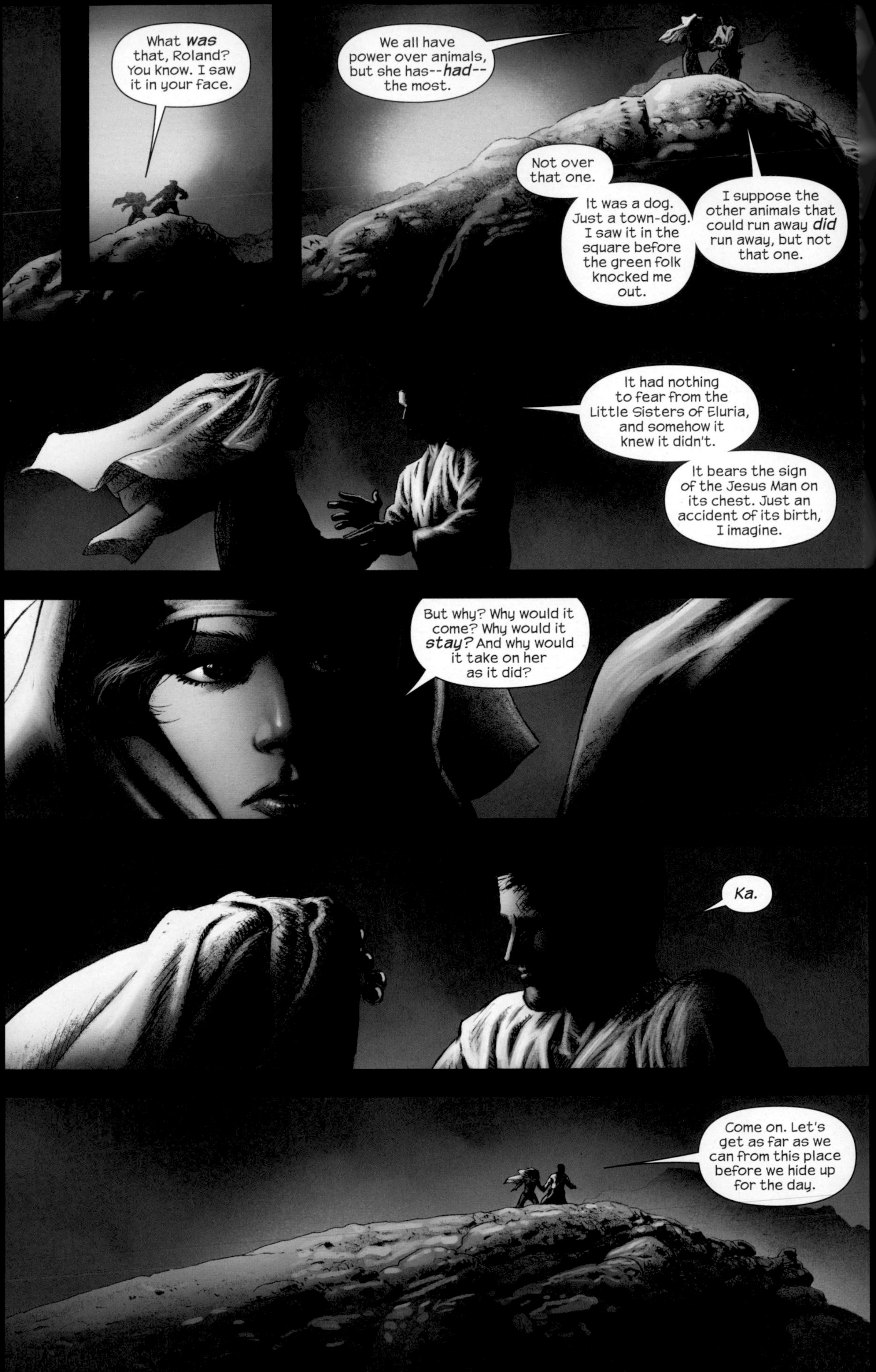
What *was* that, Roland? You know. I saw it in your face.
We all have power over animals, but she has--*had*-- the most.
Not over that one.
It was a dog. Just a town-dog. I saw it in the square before the green folk knocked me out.
I suppose the other animals that could run away *did* run away, but not that one.
It had nothing to fear from the Little Sisters of Eluria, and somehow it knew it didn't.
It bears the sign of the Jesus Man on its chest. Just an accident of its birth, I imagine.
But why? Why would it come? Why would it *stay?* And why would it take on her as it did?
*Ka.*
Come on. Let's get as far as we can from this place before we hide up for the day.

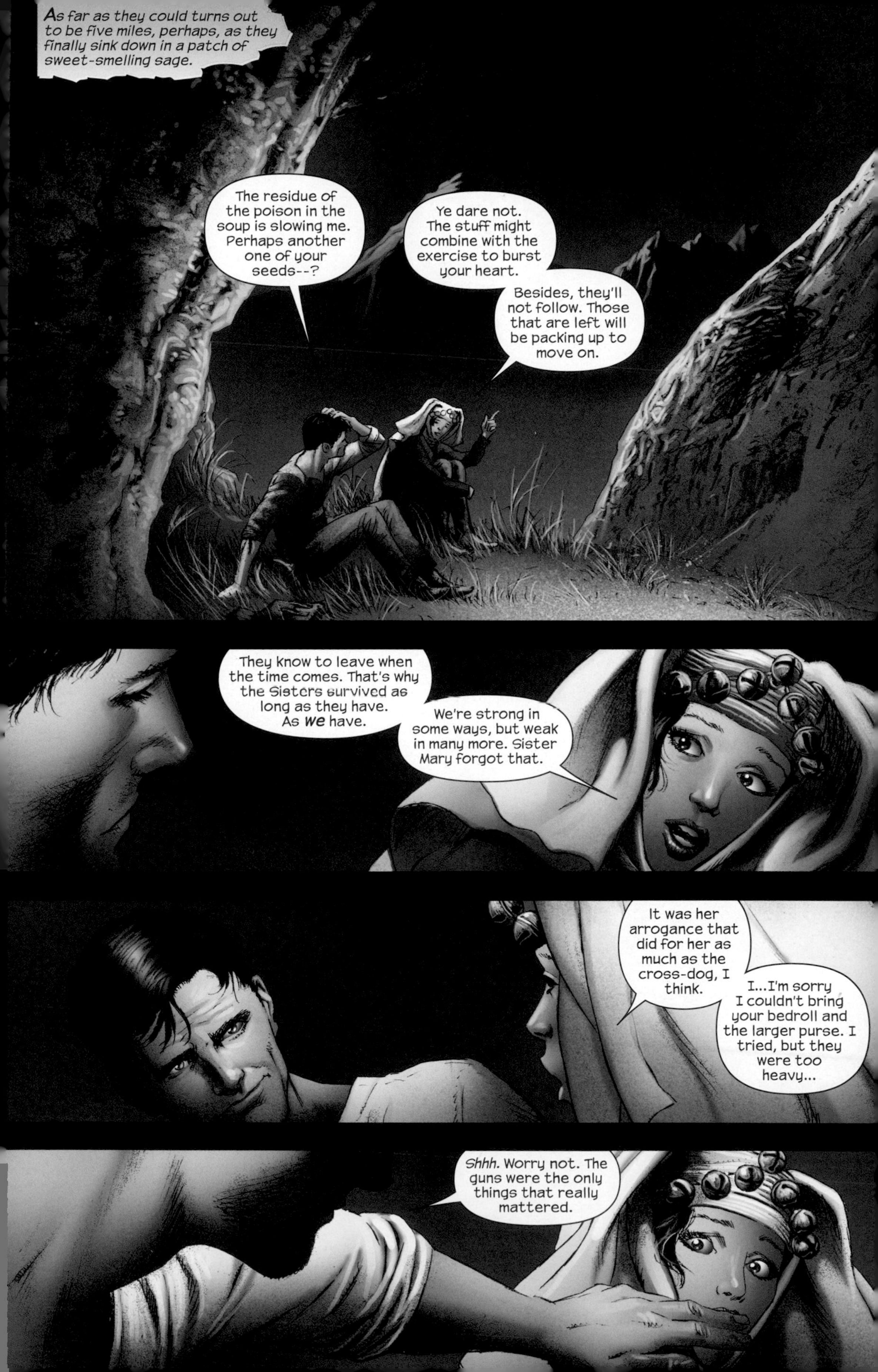
As far as they could turns out to be five miles, perhaps, as they finally sink down in a patch of sweet-smelling sage.
The residue of the poison in the soup is slowing me. Perhaps another one of your seeds--?
Ye dare not. The stuff might combine with the exercise to burst your heart.
Besides, they'll not follow. Those that are left will be packing up to move on.
They know to leave when the time comes. That's why the Sisters survived as long as they have. As *we* have.
We're strong in some ways, but weak in many more. Sister Mary forgot that.
It was her arrogance that did for her as much as the cross-dog, I think.
I...I'm sorry I couldn't bring your bedroll and the larger purse. I tried, but they were too heavy...
*Shhh.* Worry not. The guns were the only things that really mattered.

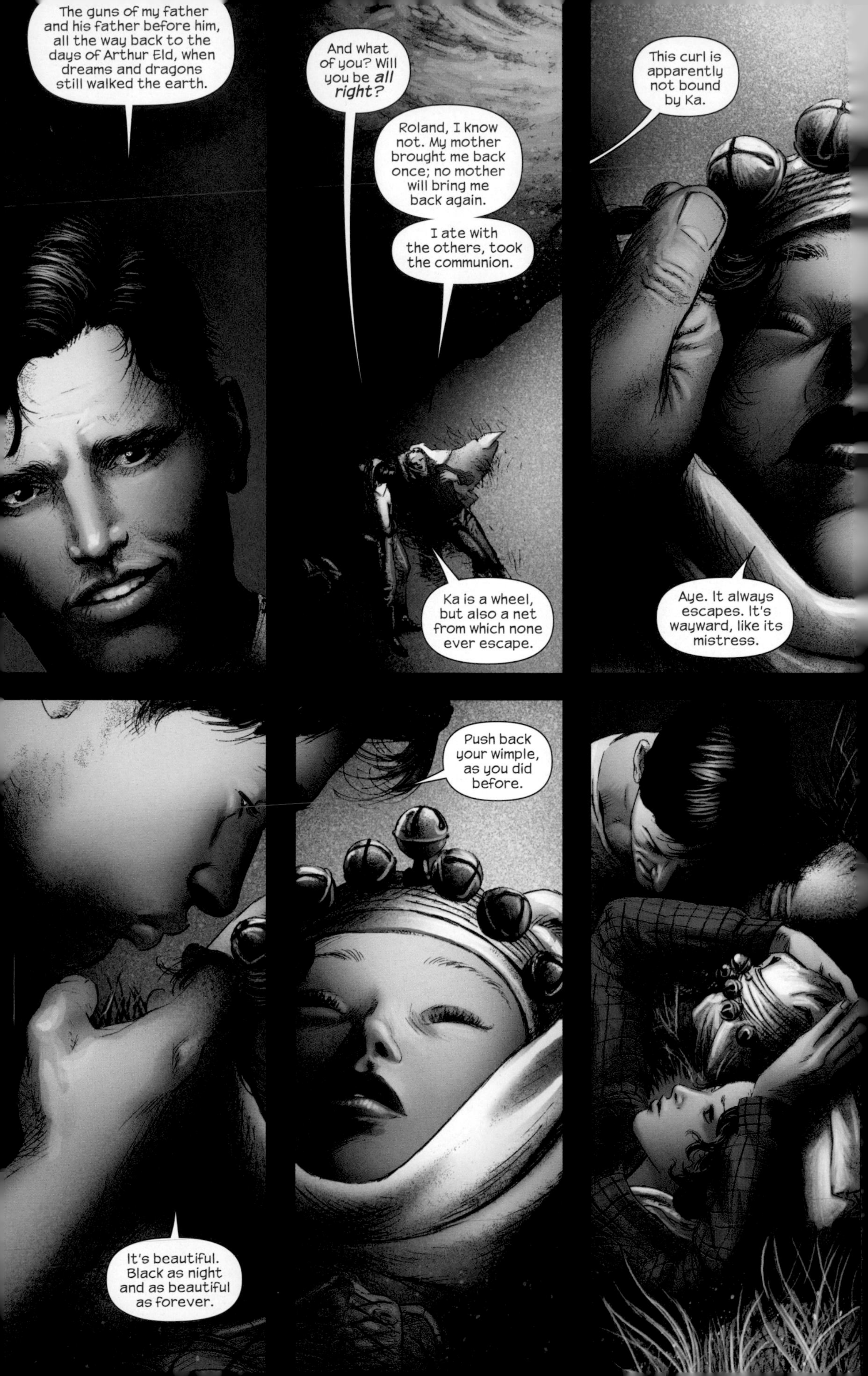
The guns of my father and his father before him, all the way back to the days of Arthur Eld, when dreams and dragons still walked the earth.
And what of you? Will you be *all right?*
Roland, I know not. My mother brought me back once; no mother will bring me back again.
I ate with the others, took the communion.
Ka is a wheel, but also a net from which none ever escape.
This curl is apparently not bound by Ka.
Aye. It always escapes. It's wayward, like its mistress.
It's beautiful. Black as night and as beautiful as forever.
Push back your wimple, as you did before.

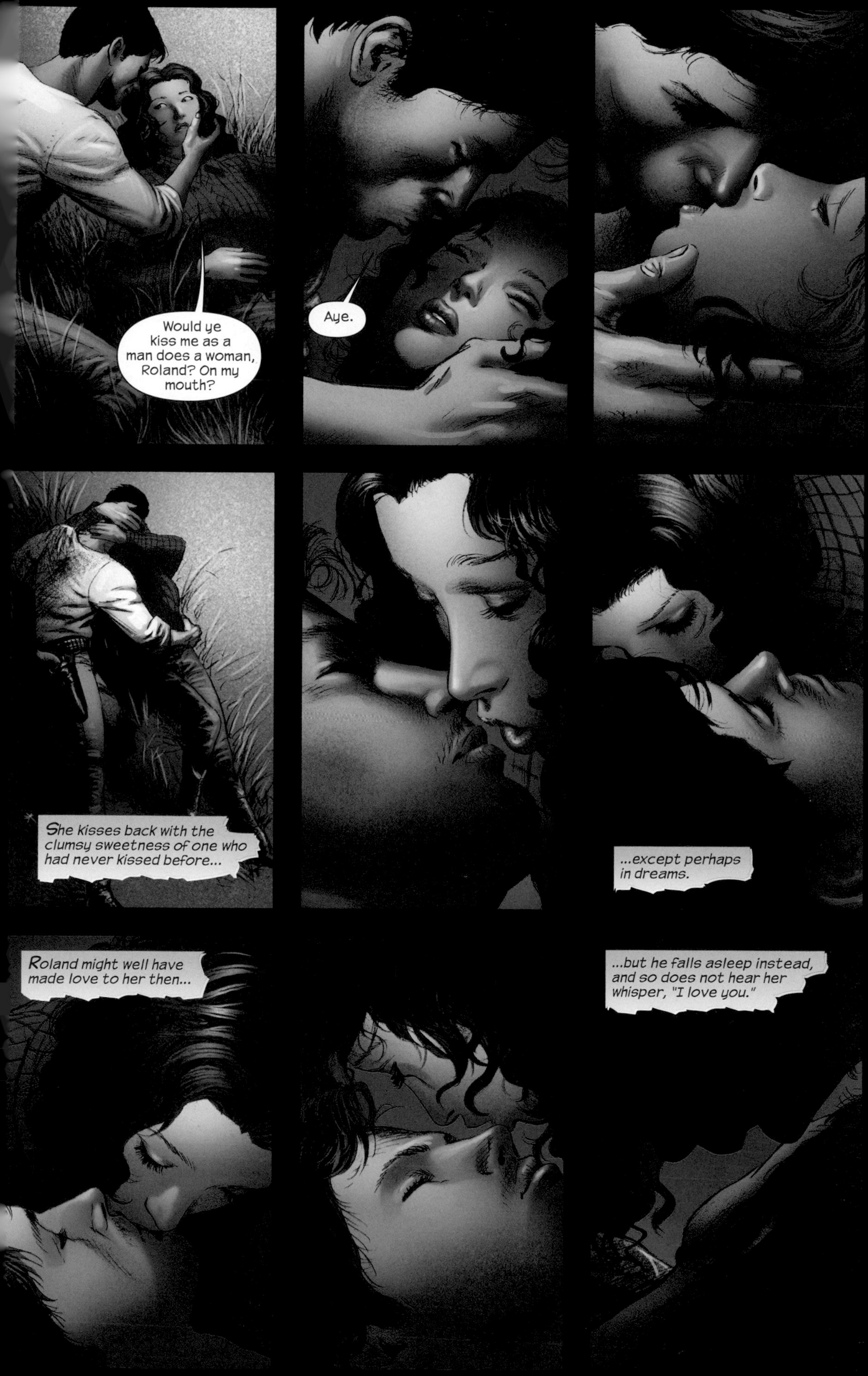
Would ye kiss me as a man does a woman, Roland? On my mouth?
Aye.
She kisses back with the clumsy sweetness of one who had never kissed before...
...except perhaps in dreams.
Roland might well have made love to her then...
...but he falls asleep instead, and so does not hear her whisper, "I love you."

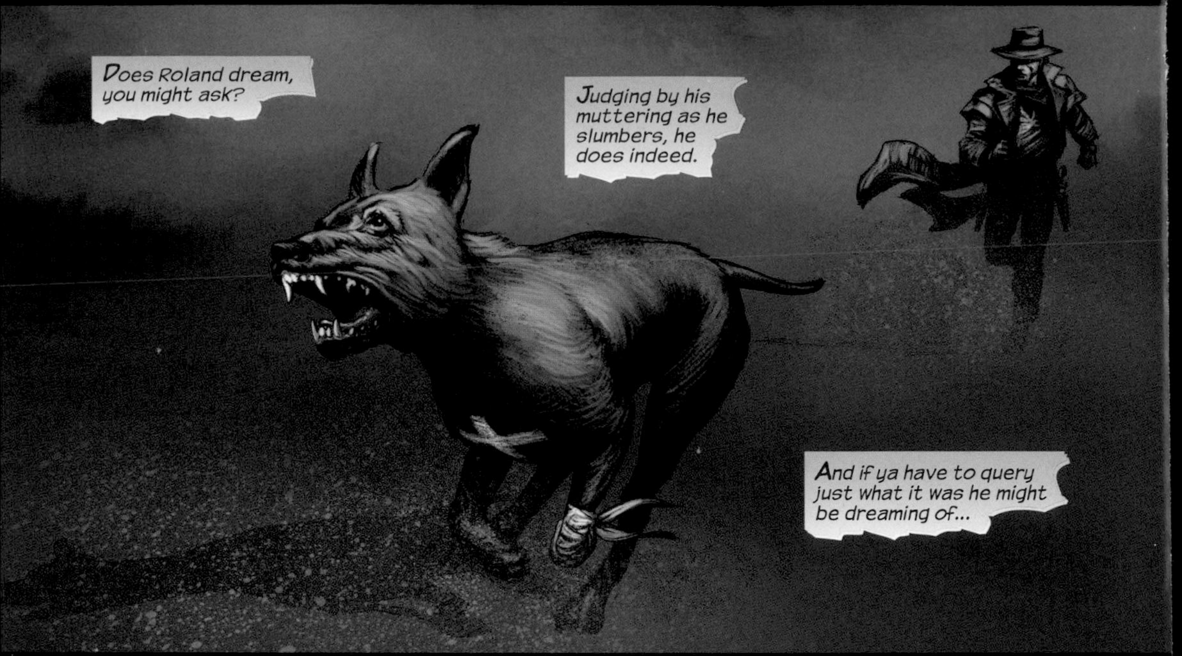
Does Roland dream, you might ask?
Judging by his muttering as he slumbers, he does indeed.
And if ya have to query just what it was he might be dreaming of...

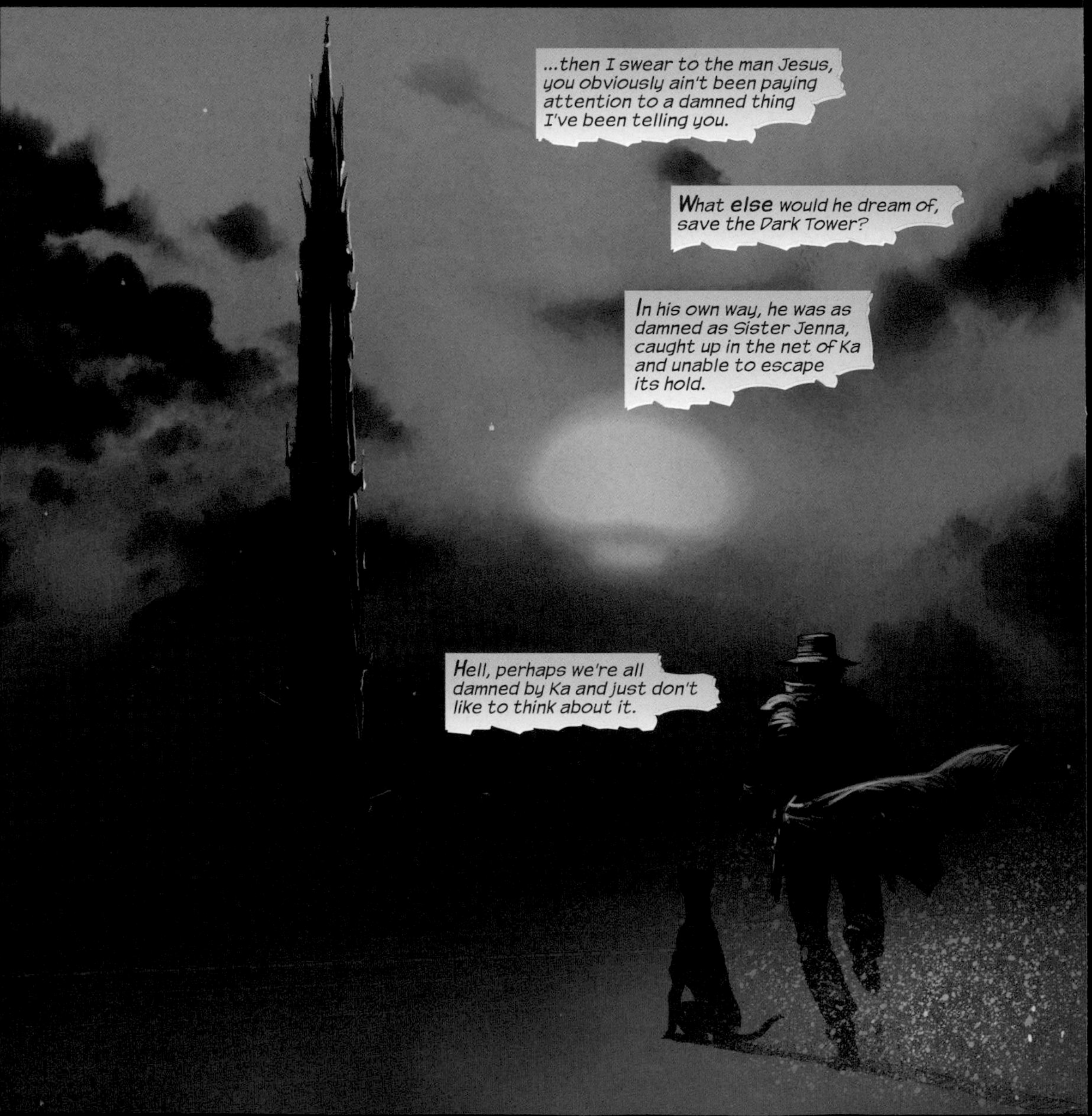
...then I swear to the man Jesus, you obviously ain't been paying attention to a damned thing I've been telling you.
What else would he dream of, save the Dark Tower?
In his own way, he was as damned as Sister Jenna, caught up in the net of Ka and unable to escape its hold.
Hell, perhaps we're all damned by Ka and just don't like to think about it.

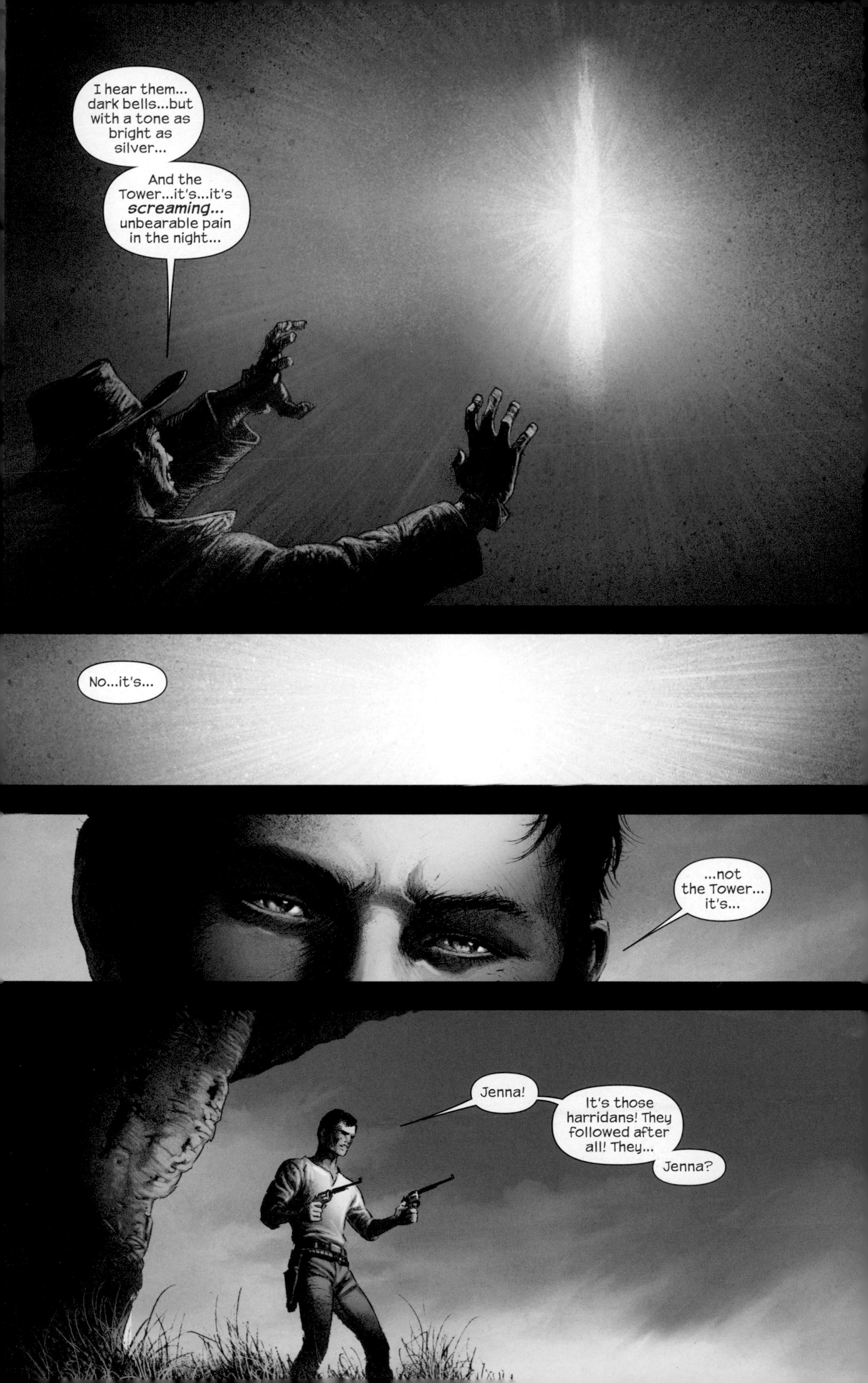
I hear them... dark bells...but with a tone as bright as silver...
And the Tower...it's...it's *screaming...* unbearable pain in the night...
No...it's...
...not the Tower... it's...
Jenna!
It's those harridans! They followed after all! They...
Jenna?

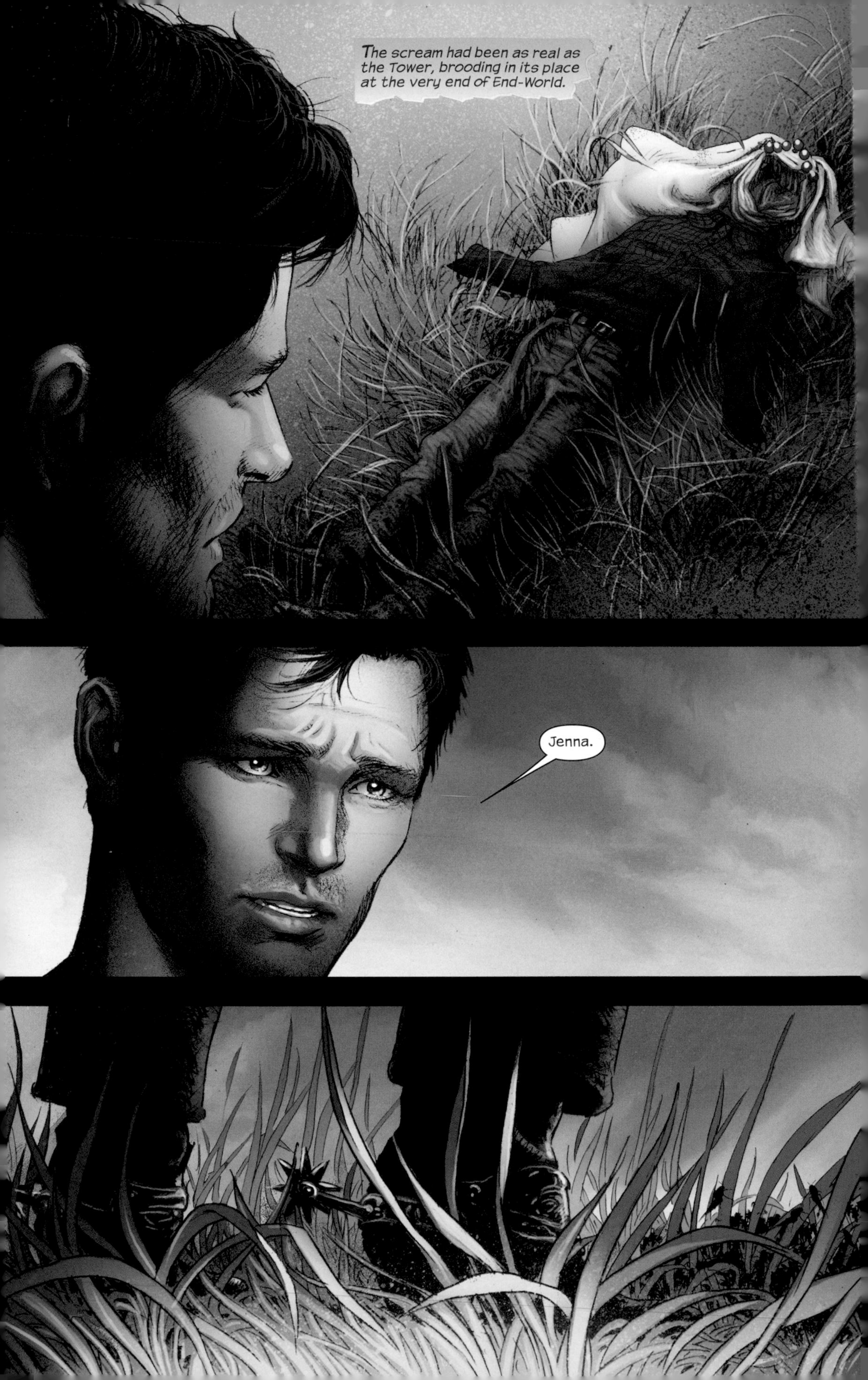
The scream had been as real as the Tower, brooding in its place at the very end of End-World.
Jenna.

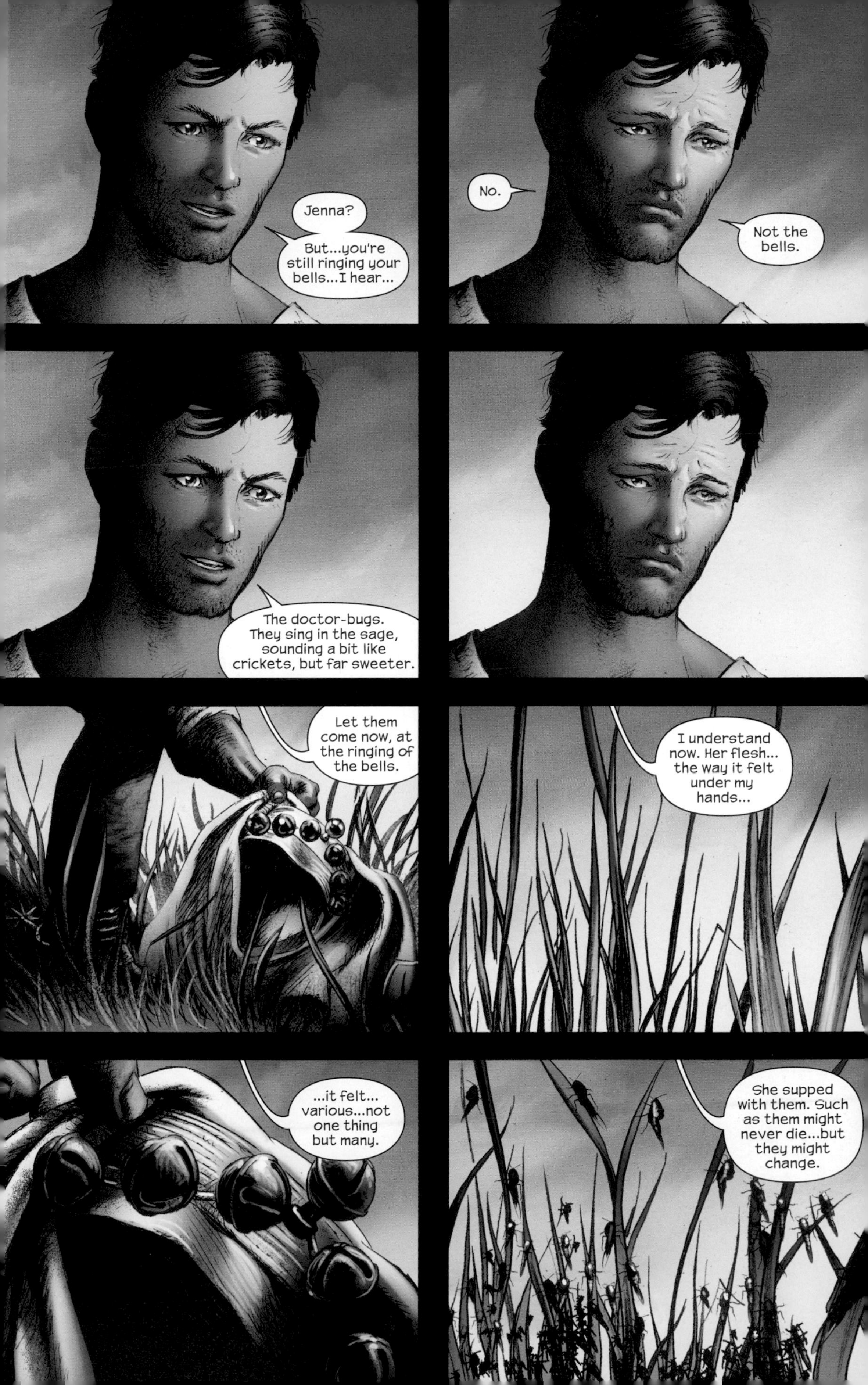
Jenna?
But...you're still ringing your bells...I hear...
No.
Not the bells.
The doctor-bugs. They sing in the sage, sounding a bit like crickets, but far sweeter.
Let them come now, at the ringing of the bells.
I understand now. Her flesh... the way it felt under my hands...
...it felt... various...not one thing but many.
She supped with them. Such as them might never die...but they might change.

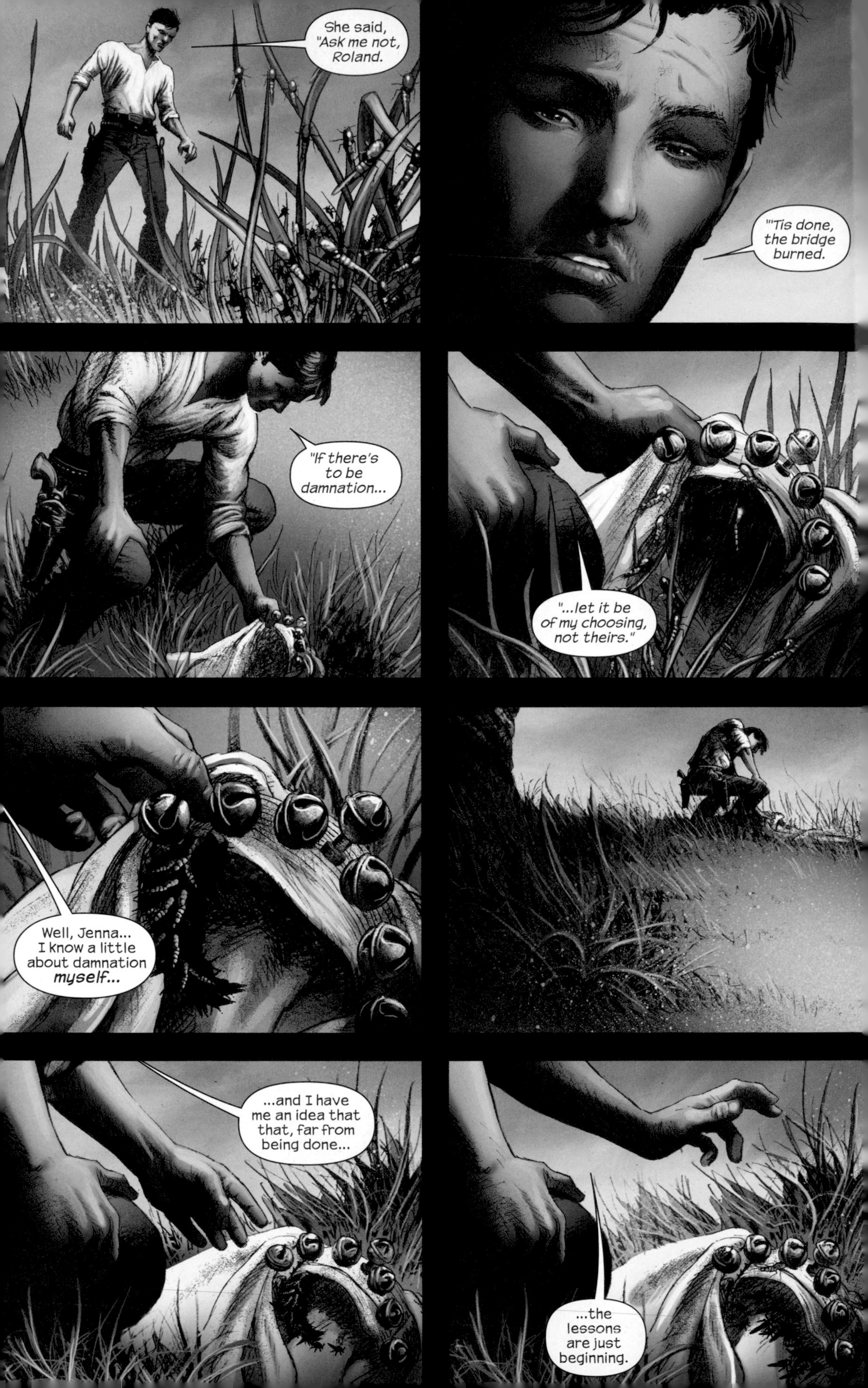
She said, "Ask me not, Roland.
"'Tis done, the bridge burned.
"If there's to be damnation...
"...let it be of my choosing, not theirs."
Well, Jenna... I know a little about damnation *myself*...
...and I have me an idea that that, far from being done...
...the lessons are just beginning.

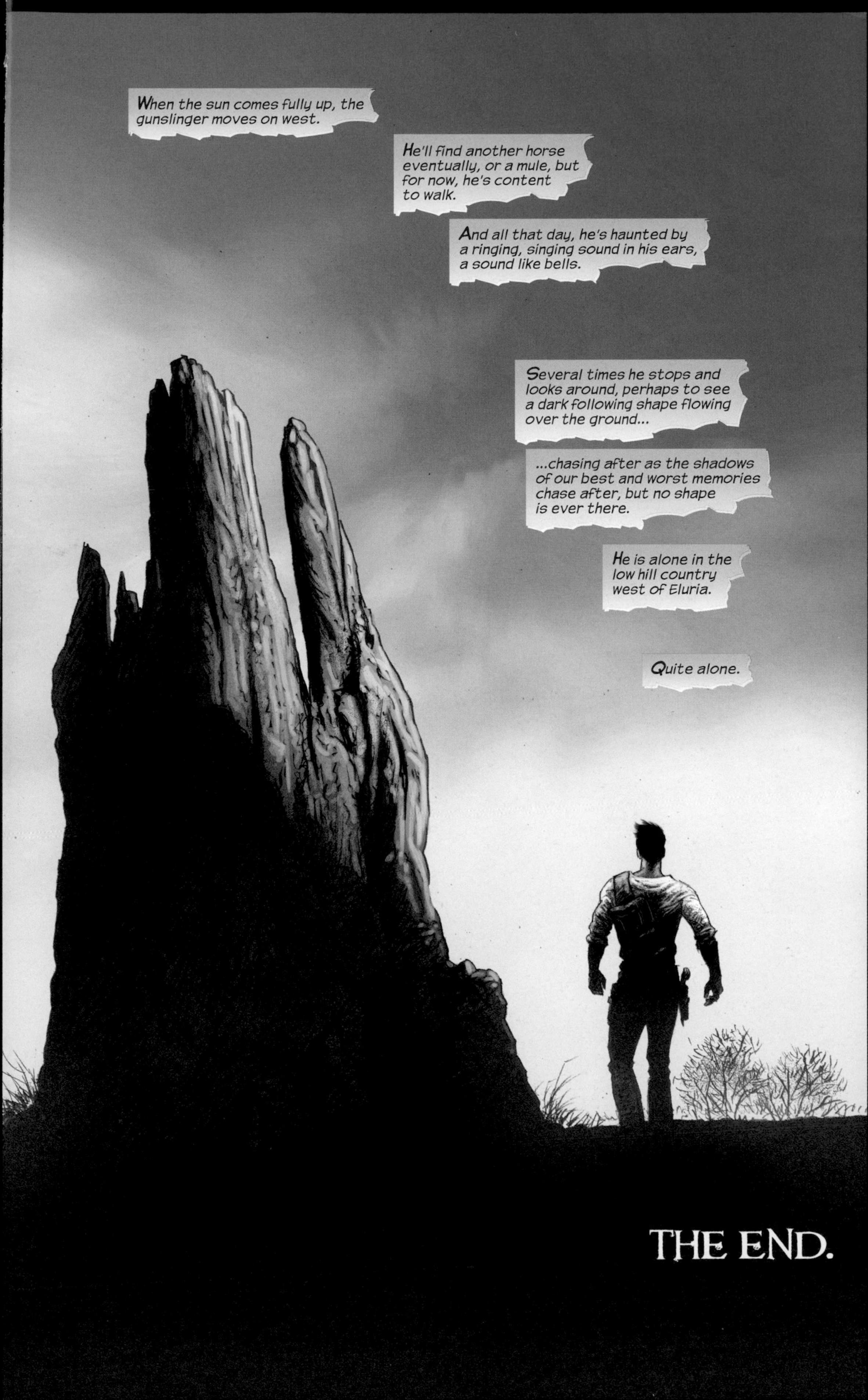
When the sun comes fully up, the gunslinger moves on west.
He'll find another horse eventually, or a mule, but for now, he's content to walk.
And all that day, he's haunted by a ringing, singing sound in his ears, a sound like bells.
Several times he stops and looks around, perhaps to see a dark following shape flowing over the ground...
...chasing after as the shadows of our best and worst memories chase after, but no shape is ever there.
He is alone in the low hill country west of Eluria.
Quite alone.
THE END.

*The story continues in Dark Tower: The Gunslinger — The Battle of Tull*

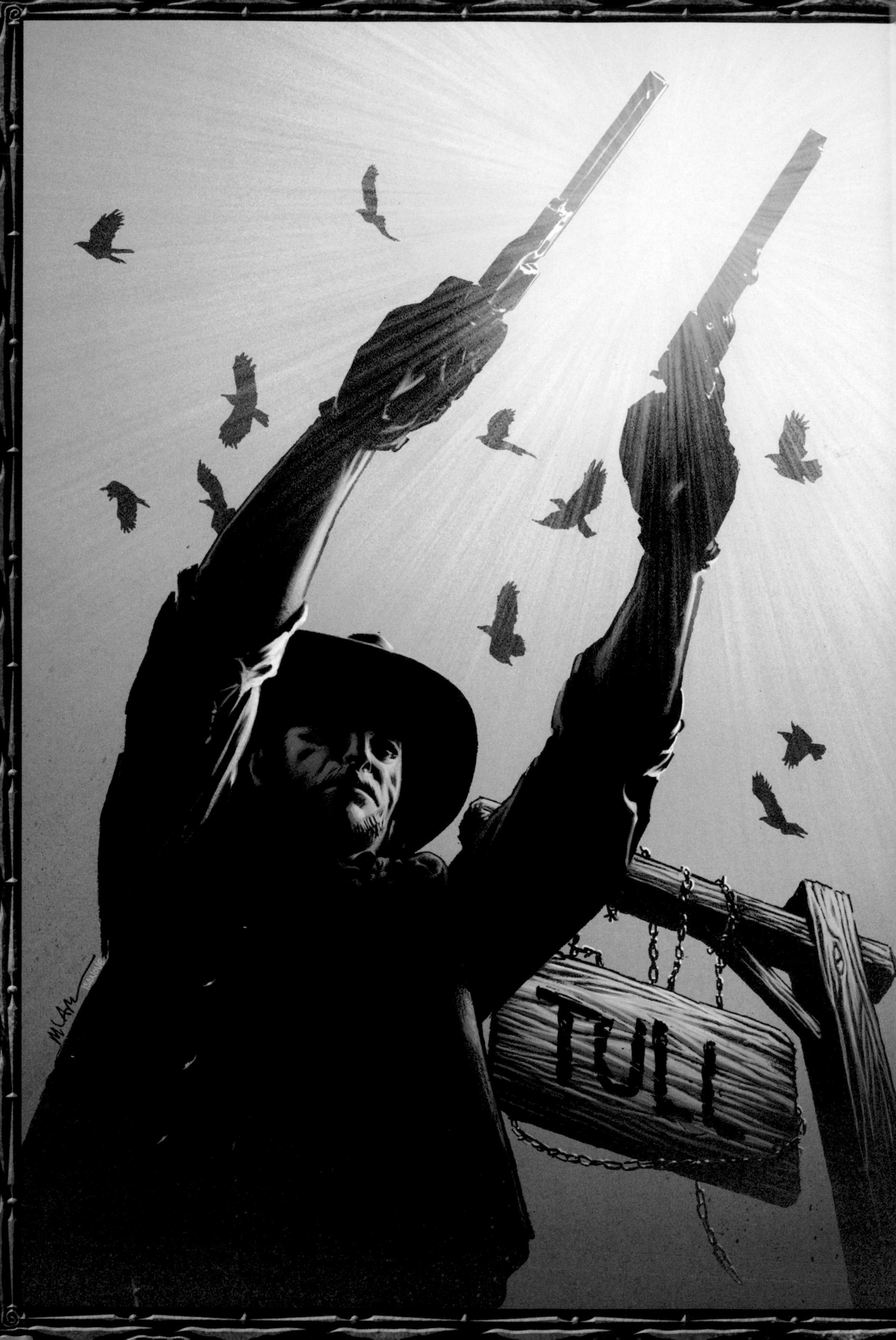
TULL

# THE DARK TOWER READING CHRONOLOGY

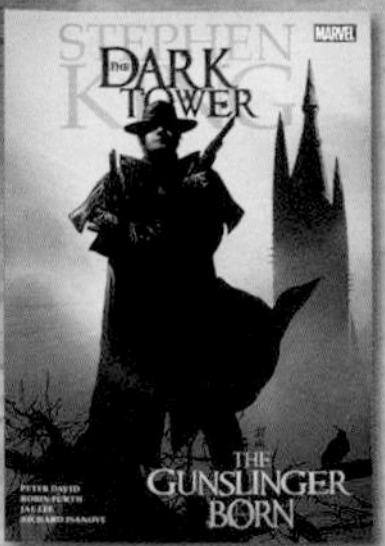
STEPHEN KING
DARK TOWER
MARVEL
THE GUNSLINGER BORN

## THE DARK TOWER THE GUNSLINGER BORN — BOOK 1

ISBN: 978 0 7851 2144 2

A man's quest begins with a boy's test. The world of Roland Deschain — the world of the Dark Tower — has been a thirty-year obsession for Stephen King. And now, King carries his masterwork of fantasy to Marvel, bringing stunning new textures to his epic story! *The Gunslinger Born* seamlessly integrates the wonder of Mid-World and the story of its hard-bitten cast of characters into the finest Marvel Comics storytelling tradition.

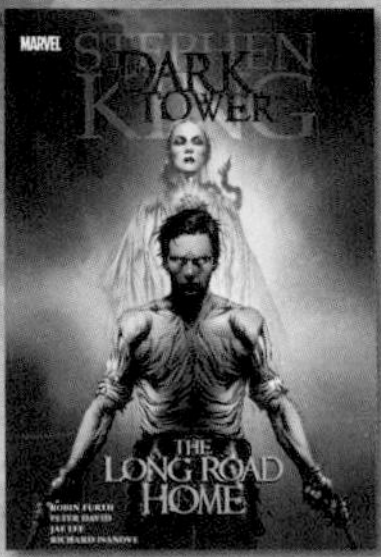
MARVEL
STEPHEN KING
DARK TOWER
THE LONG ROAD HOME

## THE DARK TOWER THE LONG ROAD HOME — BOOK 2

ISBN: 978 0 7851 2709 3

The gunslinger is born into a harsh world of mystery and violence. Susan Delgado is dead. Clay Reynolds and the vestiges of the Big Coffin Hunters are in pursuit. The ka-tet fragments as evil abounds. It will be a long road home. With Roland seemingly lost inside the haunted world of Maerlyn's Grapefruit, and the dark forces therein tugging at his soul, it will take all the courage of his ka-tet to get him out of Hambry and back home. But as the Dogan stirs, portending an evil of which Roland and his ka-tet have no ken, it may very well be that the gunslinger born walks a long road home to death.

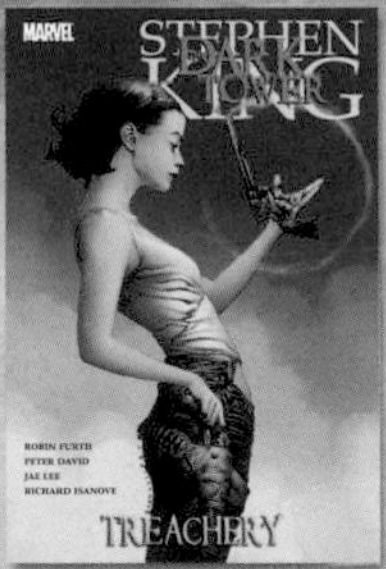
MARVEL
STEPHEN KING
TREACHERY

## THE DARK TOWER TREACHERY — BOOK 3

ISBN: 978 0 7851 3574 6

From the creative team that brought Roland's early adventures to life in *Dark Tower: The Gunslinger Born* and *Dark Tower: The Long Road Home* comes the third chapter of this dark saga of friendship, betrayal and a cosmic quest as conceived by master storyteller Stephen King.

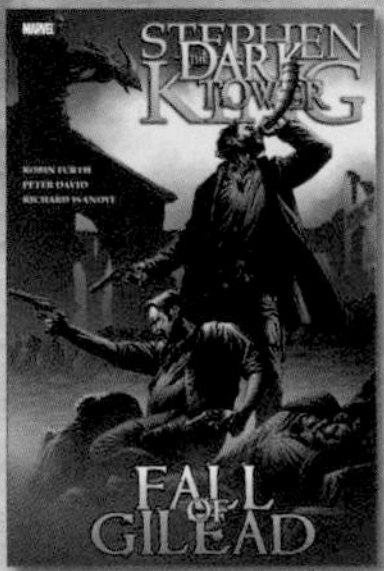
MARVEL
STEPHEN KING
DARK TOWER
FALL OF GILEAD

## THE DARK TOWER FALL OF GILEAD — BOOK 4

ISBN: 978 0 7851 2951 6

How could you have done it, Roland? How could you have killed your own mother? That's what everyone in Gilead's asking — even your grieving father. But you know the answer: Marten Broadcloak and one of them evil grapefruits. That's how. And while you rot in jail, the plot your matricide was only one small part of is wrapping its bloody and black tendrils around Gilead. Your town — the home of the Gunslingers — is the prize possession of the great enemy of the land, John Farson. And he means to have it. Gilead will fall, it will. And it will fall to the death of a thousand cuts. It started with your mother, yes, but it won't end there.

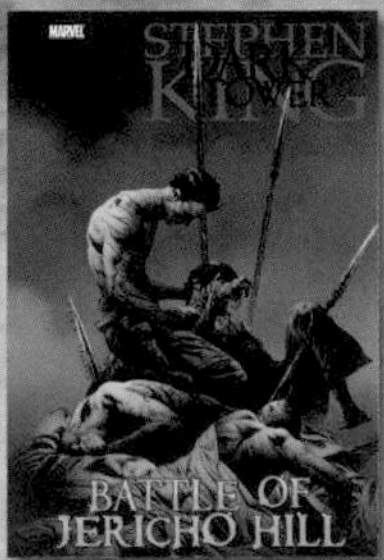
MARVEL
STEPHEN KING
DARK TOWER
BATTLE OF JERICHO HILL

## THE DARK TOWER BATTLE OF JERICHO HILL — BOOK 5

ISBN: 978 0 7851 2953 0

A brand-new story featuring Roland Deschain and his beleaguered ka-tet as they go on the run following the complete destruction of their beloved city of Gilead! And when such as Gilead falls, the pillars of reality itself — the six beams holding all of existence together — begins to crumble. The satanic plan of the Crimson King to return all of existence to the primal state of chaos is nigh.

*The Dark Tower: The Gunslinger — The Little Sisters of Eluria #1* **Cover by Luke Ross & Richard Isanove**

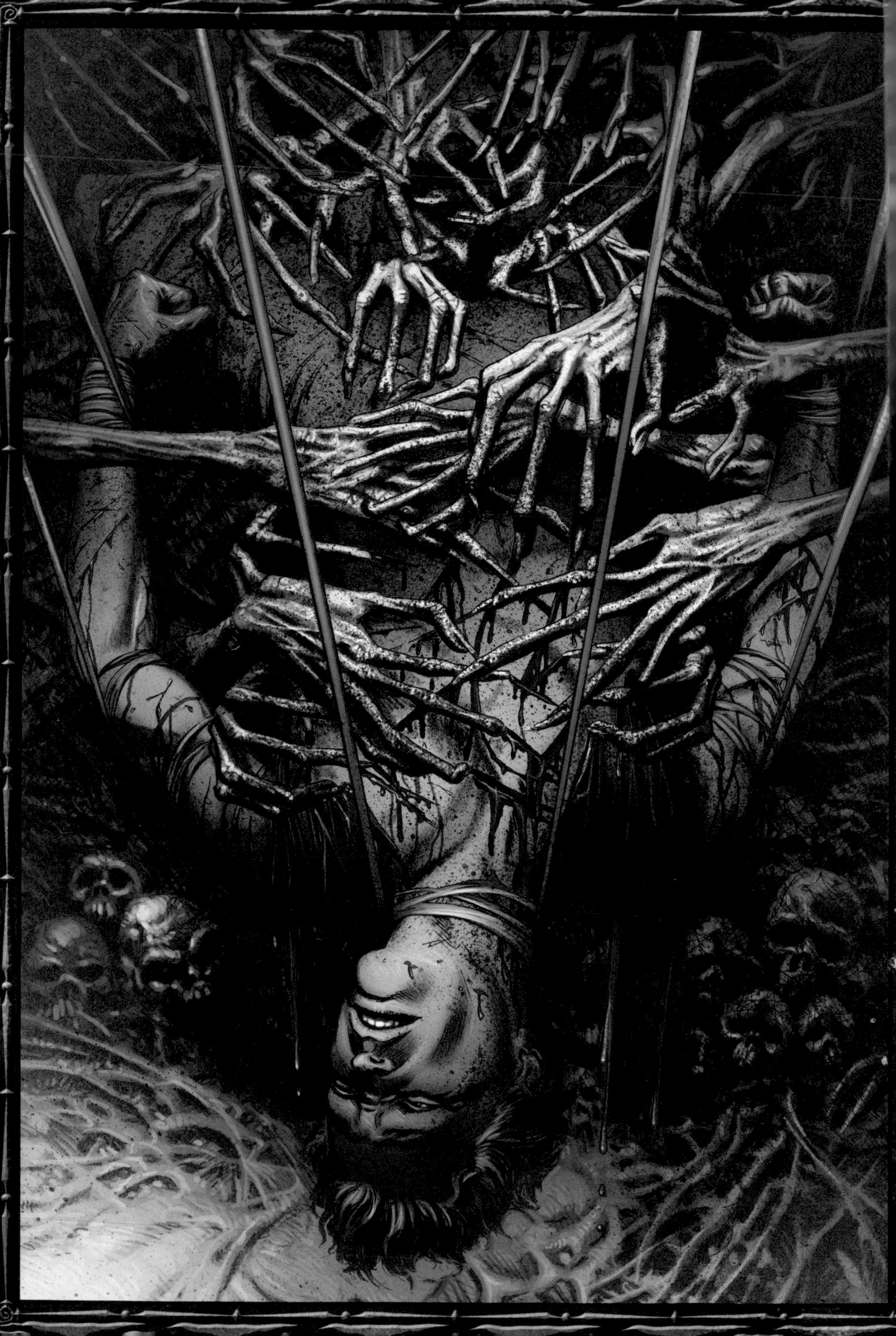

*The Dark Tower: The Gunslinger — The Little Sisters of Eluria* #2 **Cover by Luke Ross & Richard Isanove**

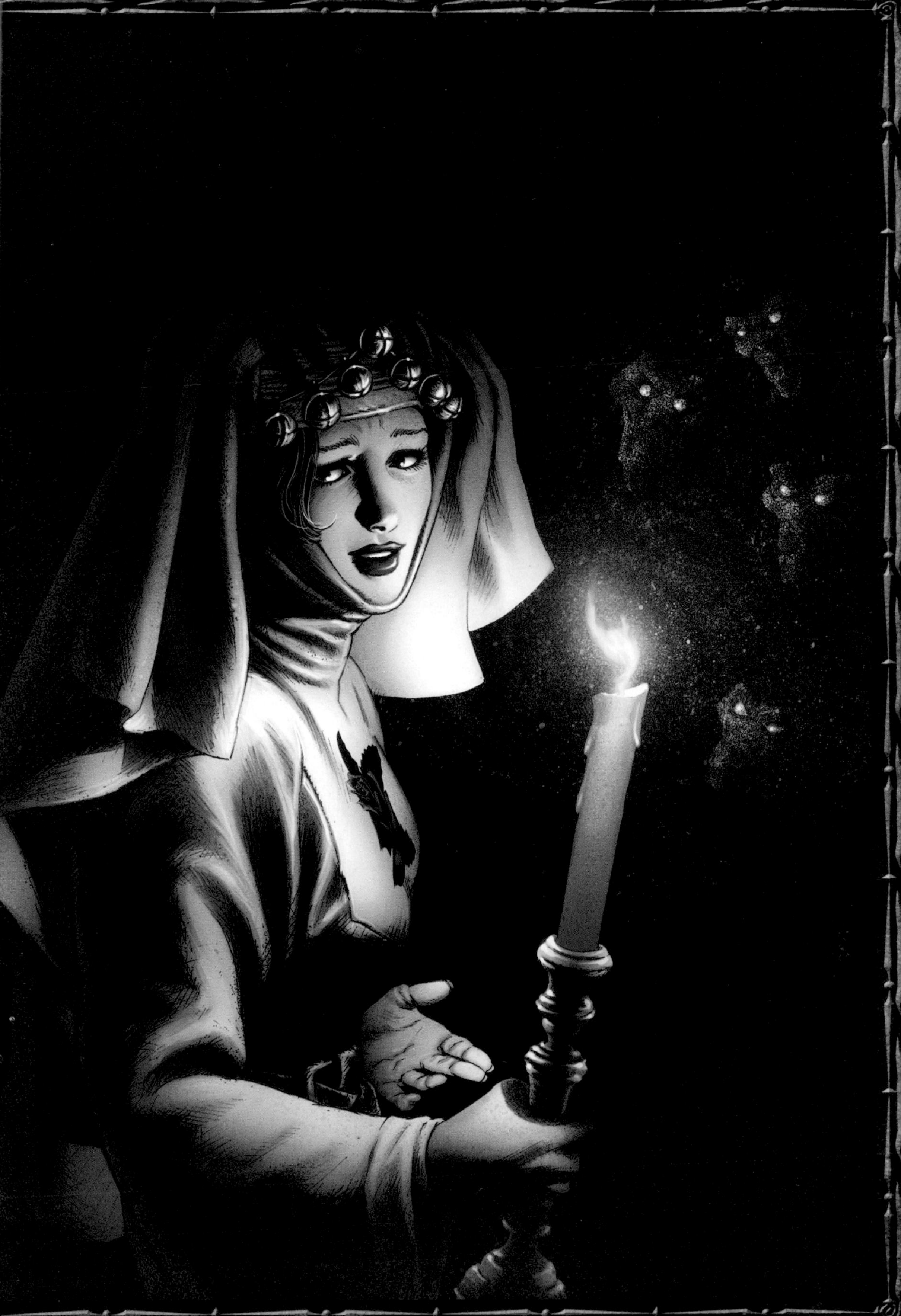

*The Dark Tower: The Gunslinger — The Little Sisters of Eluria* #3 **Cover by Luke Ross & Richard Isanove**

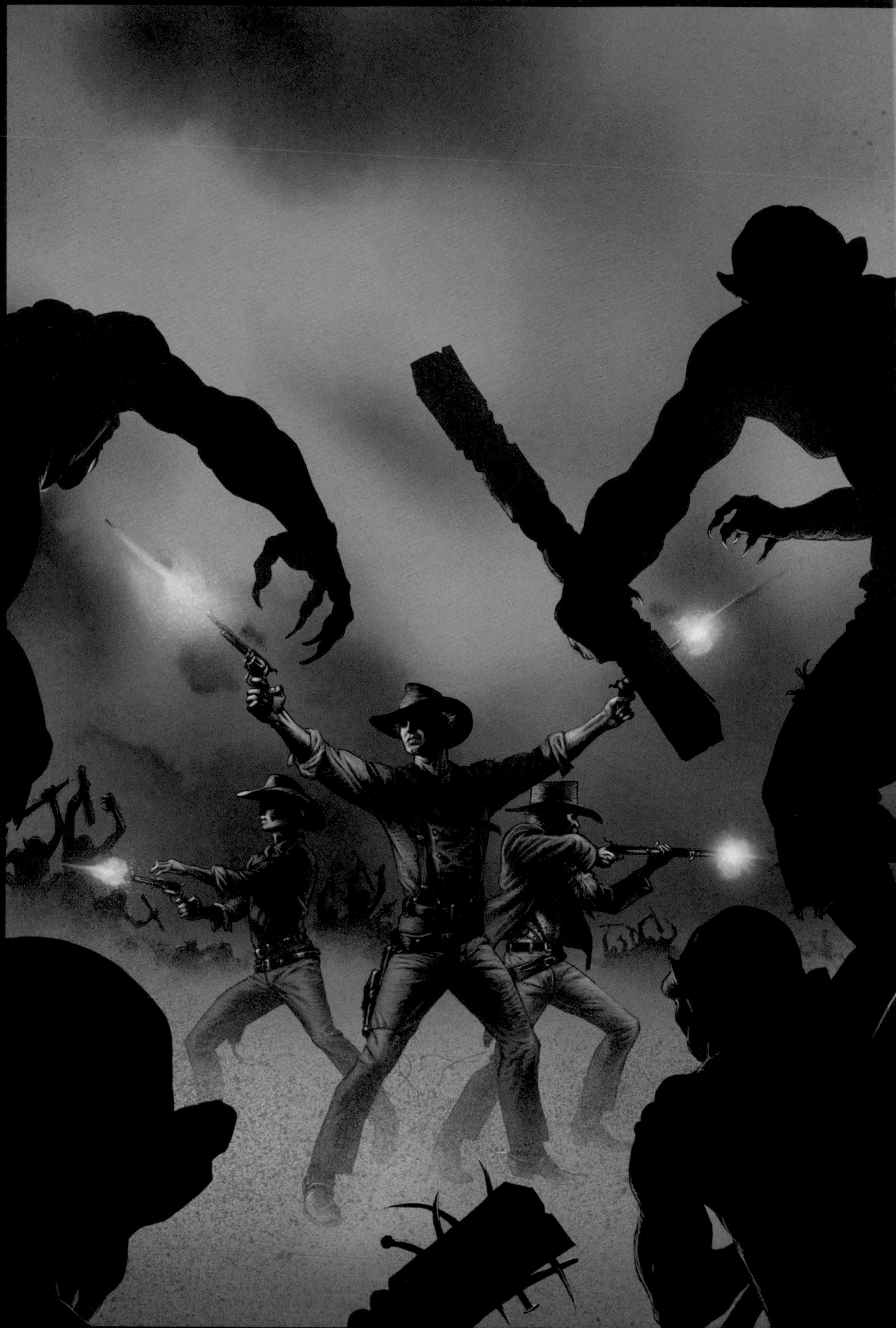

*The Dark Tower: The Gunslinger — The Little Sisters of Eluria* **#4 Cover by Luke Ross & Richard Isanove**

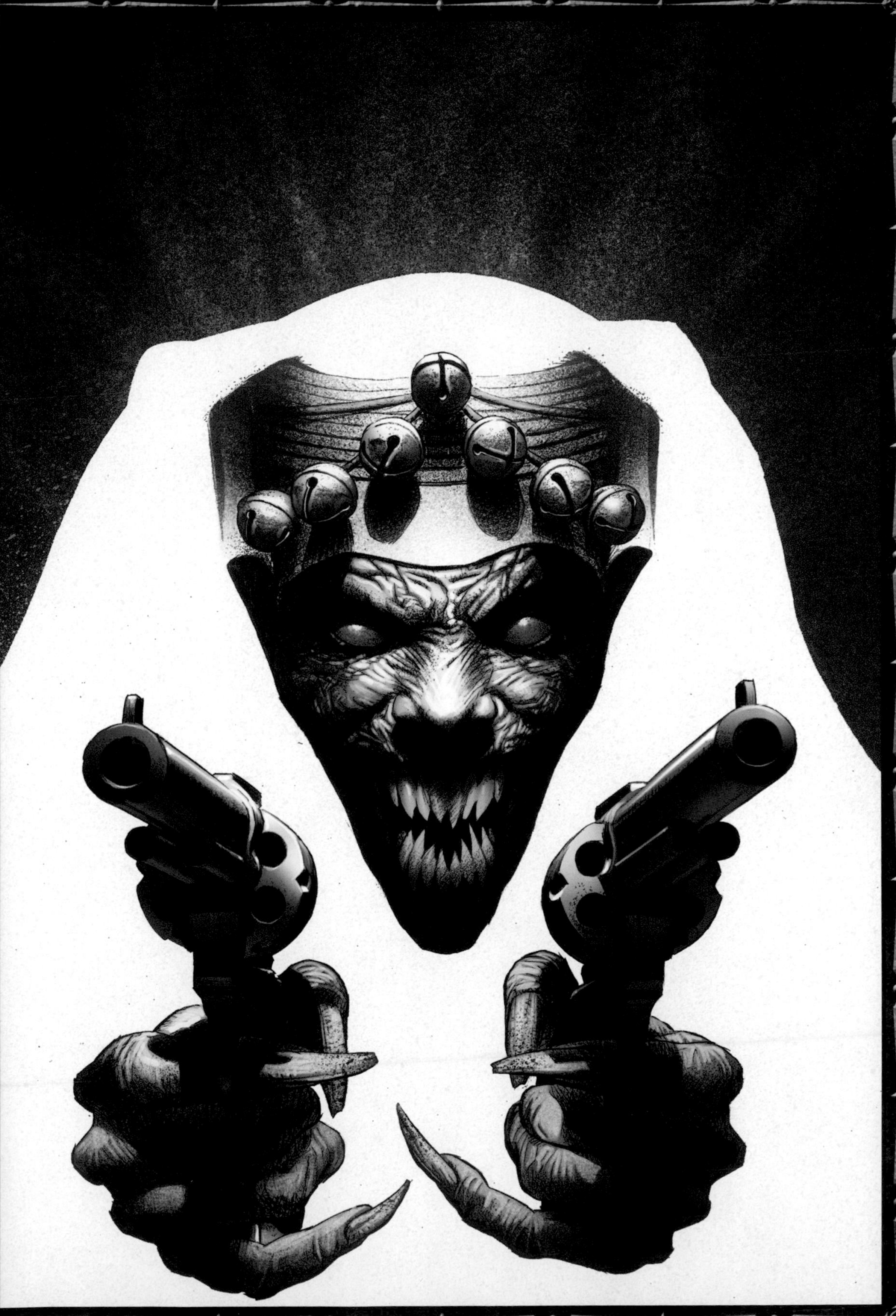

*The Dark Tower: The Gunslinger — The Little Sisters of Eluria #5* **Cover by Luke Ross & Richard Isanove**

*The Dark Tower: The Gunslinger — The Little Sisters of Eluria* #1 **Pencils by Luke Ross**

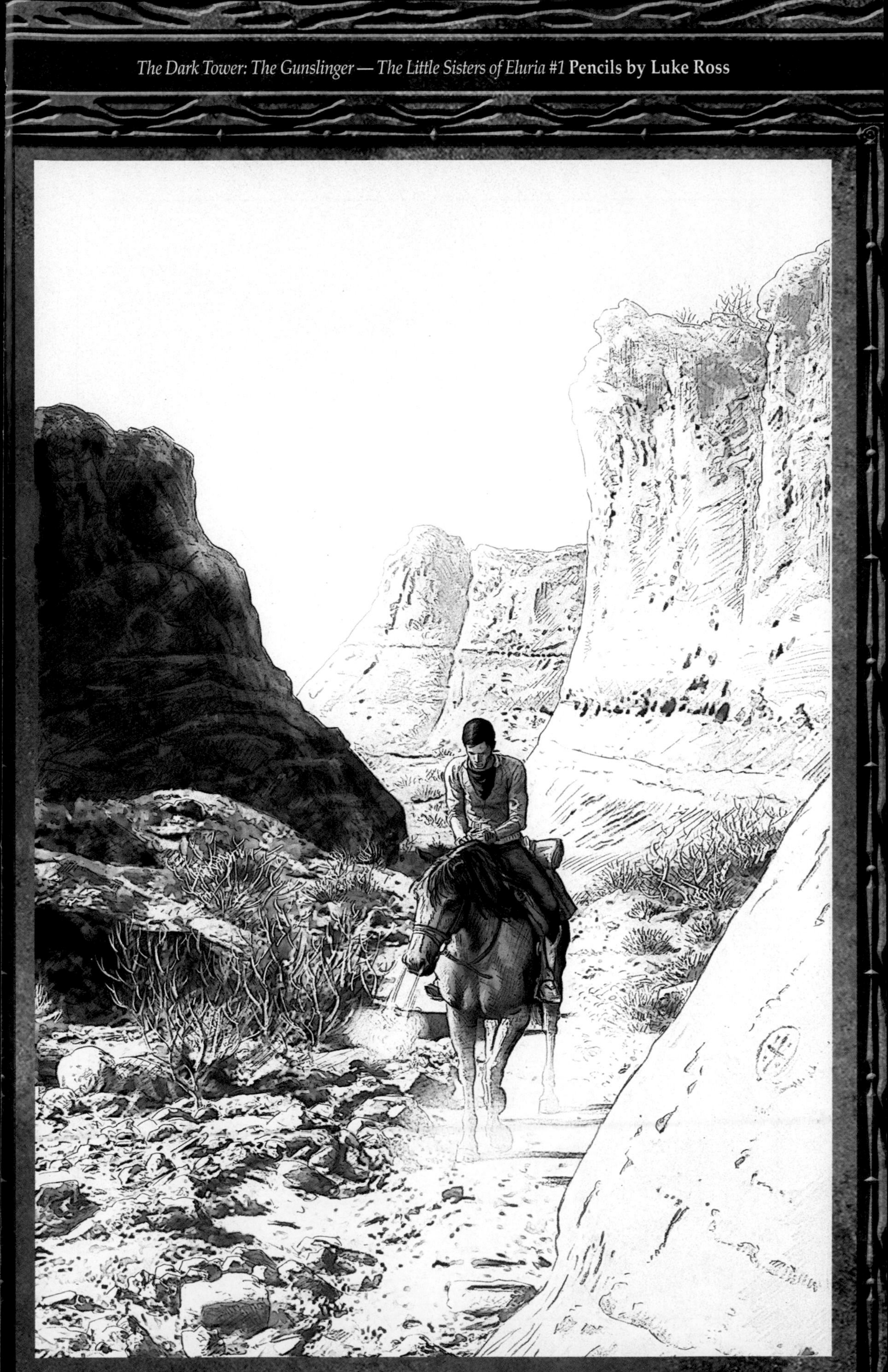

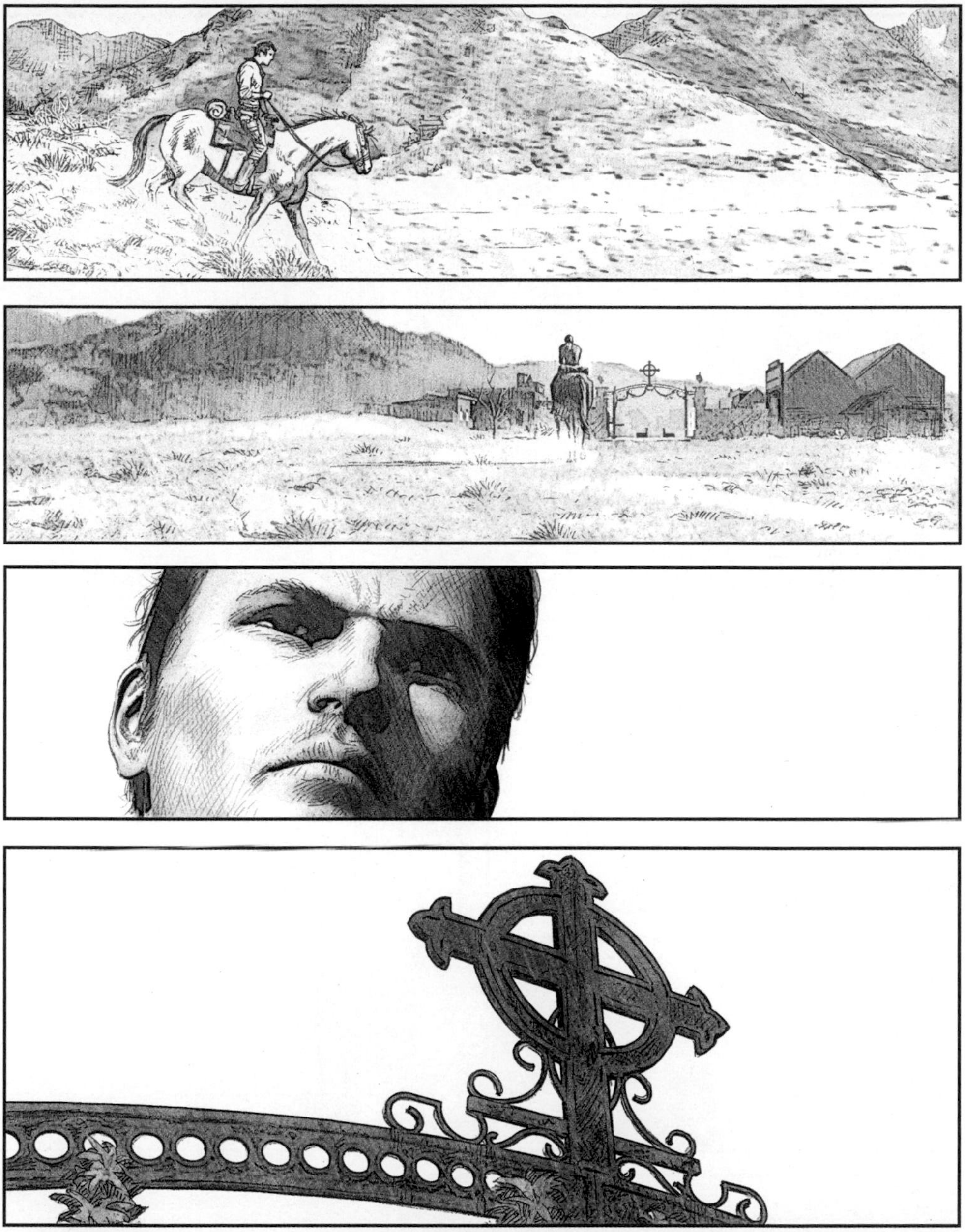

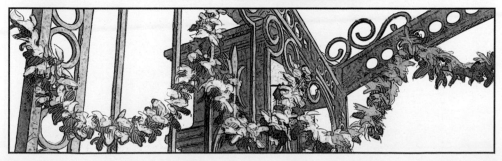

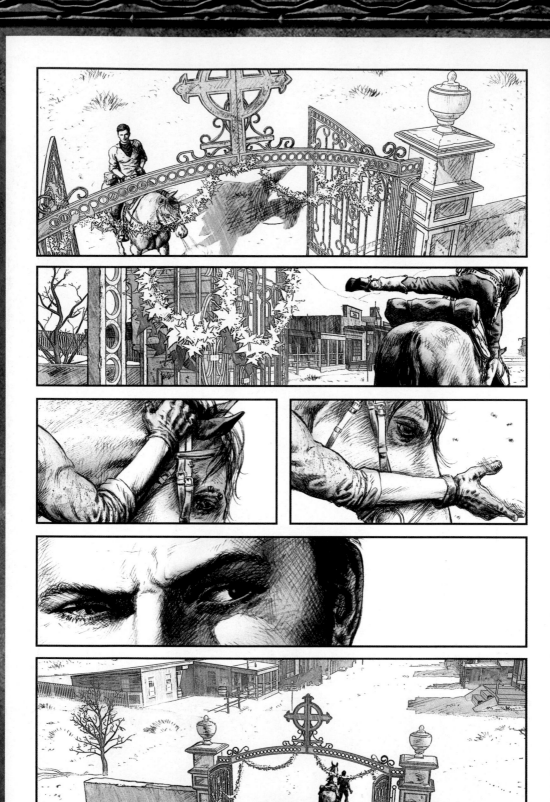